Dark Trees to the Wind

A Cycle of York State Years

Books by CARL CARMER

DEEP SOUTH

STARS FELL ON ALABAMA

LISTEN FOR A LONESOME DRUM

THE HURRICANE'S CHILDREN

THE HUDSON

GENESEE FEVER

DARK TREES
to the WIND

A Cycle of York State Years

by

Carl Carmer

Decorations by
JOHN O'HARA COSGRAVE II

William Sloane Associates
Publishers   New York

The author wishes to thank *Tomorrow* for permission to reprint "Hometown Revisited," Copyright 1949; *The Atlantic Monthly* for "Hanging Day," Copyright 1948; *Woman's Day* for "The White Woman of the Genesee," which originally appeared under the title "Mary Jemison," Copyright 1948; *Town and Country* for "The Whooper Swan of Olivebridge," Copyright 1949, by Hearst Magazines, Inc. The articles, "The Fowlers, Practical Phrenologists" (page 127), and "The Famous Female Somniloquist" (page 243), Copyright 1937, and the poem, "Apple Pickers" (page 303), Copyright 1941, originally appeared in *The New Yorker* and were copyrighted by the F-R Publishing Corporation.

First Printing

Typography and format designed by
LEONARD W. BLIZARD

Published simultaneously in Canada by George J. McLeod, Ltd.
Manufactured in the United States of America

For Elizabeth

"It's always seemed to me that legends and yarns and folk-tales are as much a part of the real history of a country as proclamations and provisos and constitutional amendments. The legends and yarns get down to the roots of the people—they tell a good deal about what people admire and want—about what sort of people they are."

Stephen Vincent Benét

. . . in history, to preserve things of "little importance" may be more valuable—as it is more difficult and more the business of a writer—than to champion a winner.

From *In The American Grain*
by William Carlos Williams

Art begins in the irresponsible imaginations of the people, like a spring in a mountain waste; the spring rises amid rocks, trickles and forms a rivulet, swells into a stream, and after many wanderings, perhaps after a brief sojourn in artificial ponds and basins, it returns to the earth whence it came.

From *Avowals*
by George Moore

Contents

Part One

"It Lies Nice to the Morning Sun" 1

Contents

Part Two

Part Three

Contents

· xiii ·

Contents

Decorations

"It Lies Nice to the Morning Sun"

I said, "You've got quite a farm here."
"It's good land," he said. "It lies nice to the morning sun."

1

York State
Is a Country

I HAVE SPENT MOST OF MY LIFE COMING TO KNOW and trying to understand the people of the region where I was born and raised, the living and dead who have made York State what it is—and while this book is not a history, it is intended as a part of the world of history.

People are both a region and a way of life. Landscape becomes a part of them and they become a part of each other. Generations and institutions enter into this developing pattern but the pattern, present or past, is always people.

The study of my fellow beings whose lives are influenced by the joys, sorrows, and hardships which are theirs by virtue of York State climate and landscape is not an easy one nor is it always aided by the attainment of a knowledge of the writings of formal historians. History is always in the process of being rewritten in the light of new attitudes created by discoveries of new and general truths in many subjects—psychology, commerce, medicine, philosophy. The event recorded as important by the nineteenth-century historian may seem to today's interpreter of the identical period as less revealing of the truth about the people on whose life he is commenting than an incident previously omitted or relegated to a footnote. Who is to measure importance? Selection obviously must rest with the writer. In the quotation from William Carlos Williams that precedes these words of my own the poet has expressed a thoughtful contradiction when he suggests that things generally looked upon in history as of "little importance" may be "more valuable" than those considered by the majority of our ancestors to be most significant.

Those observers who have studied the variegated fabrics of life as it is lived in our separate states know that there are certain generally held qualities, some obvious, some indefinable or nearly so, that differentiate the citizens of one state-country from another. It is these distinctions that I have attempted to recognize in my fellow Yorkers, to understand and to describe in the chapters that follow. I have spent, I hope, the least quantity of my words on the obvious, often omitting or briefly summarizing the things that most Americans know about Yorkers or that Yorkers know about themselves.

As for the more nebulous and indescribable, I have in some cases suggested conclusions and in others simply told a narrative, leaving the assessment of its significance to other minds. I would only say that I considered it important to an understanding of Yorkers or I would not have written it.

This book begins with the western sector of York State and it moves east to its eastern borders. In time it moves in a U curve from the present to the middle of the seventeenth century and returns. Through it all there is, I hope, recognition of the feeling that all sensitive mystic writers who have described this country have tried to put into words. When the pioneers first moved north along its first highways, its flowing waters, into its interior they were so struck by the darkness of its great evergreens, the depths of the shadows under its shade trees, that they spoke of the region as "The Dark Country." After the clearing of many forests the poets, the artists, the musicians of our land still respond to the shadowy blackness of its wild woods, the feeling of the Spirit of Place that lurks in the shade of hemlock and fir, and that as D. H. Lawrence has said, must be atoned for; the doom that he says "seems to whisper in the very dark trees."

York State is a country. Though the bundle of states east of it is called New England, it has more similarities to the largest of the British Isles than any other American area. It is almost the same size—lacking only an inconsequential seven hundred forty-one square miles. Its largest river, the Hudson, is for much of its course a navigable tidal estuary serving as its main port New York City, a metropolis of about eight million people, just as the tidal estuary of the Thames serves the slightly larger city of London. In north central York State is a region of blue waters which, because they lie in long narrow valleys, is called the Finger Lake Country, counterpart of England's famous Lake District.

But Yorkers know that the scales are tilted in their favor.

The average number of acres in a York State farm is something over a hundred and fifteen, in England more than thirty less. In addition to its Londoners, England has nearly thirty-five million people to feed, but exclusive of its biggest city, York State has only about six millions.

For these reasons and others, the knowing Yorker assumes that he is as distinctive as an Englishman and somewhat more important. His country, he feels, is as separate, as decisively bordered, as any island in the sea. No one, he is sure, has for generations mistaken a Yorker for a Yankee. Vowels were meant to be given some value and a Yorker does more with them than do the economy-minded folk across Lake Champlain. After a Yankee has lived in York State for a while the country opens his mouth for him and the sounds that come out, if not the sentiments, are more generous.

Water separates York State from Canada and, though in some cases it is a forty-mile-wide inland sea and in others it is only a river, you could never mistake a Canadian for a Yorker or (fantastic idea!) vice versa.

As for Pennsylvania, Yorker motorists swear they can feel the difference when they cross the boundary. Pennsylvania has its own kind of land, its special gray fieldstone for its farmhouses, its unreasonable German neatness. Nice people live there. It is a fine state. But once you are back in the York State hills after a visit there—you know it.

Hills. Perhaps they are the especial asset that makes this country what it is, for they cover nearly all the state. The Hudson begins among high and ancient rocks that lie at the roots of the dark tree-covered Adirondacks. Travelers beside its waters see, before reaching its mouth, the low boulder-dotted upland meadows of the Helderbergs, the steeper, rougher Taghkanicks, the high blue ridges of the Catskills, the rounded tops of the Highlands (the Matteawan Mountains), the pine-striped summits of the Ramapos.

West from the Hudson that old highway, the Cherry Valley Pike, curves on roller-coaster ups and downs—some a mile long, and more—until lakes lie between the ridges and north of them stand the separate mounds of drumlins, south of them the foothills of the Alleghenies. Only on Lake Ontario's coastal plain, stretching along the state's northwestern border, does the land flatten out among the sandy apple orchards and the vineyards not far from Ohio.

This is the uneven and rolling land that was the American idea-frontier of the nineteenth century when outraged New Englanders (once rebels dreaming of freedom) pushed their newer visionaries westward to a less hostile environment. In other volumes are narratives of the mystics who settled the York State valleys, feeling strange inspiration from not knowing what lay above and beyond the close, hill-printed horizons. Their minds were outward and upward bound to find truths that transcended their practical earthly experiences—for Yorkers have carried two purses through life, one for the hard coin of common sense and the other for pennies that throw back the light of the moon. To pay their way on journeys above and beyond the hills that have shut them into a world where they must make a living they have dipped into their pokes o' moonshine. Obeying voices speaking from no visible mouths, they have sought salvation, like the Shakers and the Jemimakins (disciples of the "Publick Universal Friend"), by not marrying enough, or like the Oneida Perfectionists or the followers of Mormon Joseph Smith, by marrying too much. They have dressed themselves in their white ascension robes and clambered to high places to await the immediate end of the world. They have listened to knockings they recognized as the language of the dead. They have believed in unbelief and in divine messages so direct that they might, while they were hearing them, touch the robes of divinity. So many of them have felt the presence of supernatural beings who thread the mist-hung valleys, stride the hills, that there are those who believe there is a wide belt, a kind of psychic highway, across the state that is enchanted as are few landscapes.

There are other evidences of the area's magic.

Barbara Heynemann, a poor and ignorant Alsatian serving girl whom the Lord had chosen as an instrument to make His will known, traveled to the western border of York State in 1842 with her fellow members of the cult of "True Inspiration." Under the leadership of stern, strong Christian Metz, these pious German people had bought from the Seneca Indians, at ten dollars an acre, five thousand acres of their old reservation near Buffalo and established thereon the community of Eben-Ezer ("Hitherto the Lord hath helped us").

After proving her right to be deemed the Lord's representative, Barbara had so shocked her people by stating that she wished to be married that they had deprived her of her honors and authority until repentance and renunciation had softened their hearts toward her. Her unceasing love of George Landmann proved stronger than her desire to be an interpreter of divine purposes, however, and her marriage to him brought about another rebuke and official disgrace. Nevertheless, the messages of the Lord so possessed her that their authenticity was eventually recognized and Barbara, though married, became second in authority only to Christian Metz.

In and around their various villages known as Upper, Lower, Middle Eben-Ezer, these sincere and honest folk prospered by thrifty and intelligent farming. Like the Shakers, they "shook" when they were inspired by divine messages. Like the Perfectionists, they practiced stern criticisms of their fellows. Foot washing was a part of the ritual of their religious love feast (Liebesmahl). The Lord spoke often to them on the fertile shores of Lake Erie, sometimes through the instrument of Barbara Heynemann, and York State lost more than a thousand worthy citizens when in 1854 He finally directed them to go west to Iowa and build a new home to be called Amana. There Christian Metz died and the twice-reproved Barbara became their accepted leader. Still prosperous and happily serene, they now live under less stringent discipline than she used to exert upon them.

While the Germans at Eben-Ezer were making a garden spot of their land beside Lake Erie a group of Atheistic Communists led by John A. Collins also were making remarkable progress toward riches on the shores of Skaneateles Lake near the center of the state. Amazingly successful in a material way, they were, nevertheless, so riven by internal disagreements that after two years, 1844 through 1846, they sold their property and disbanded. Collins, who had grandly announced the fundamental purpose of his community to be the working out of "a perfect regeneration of the race by bringing man into harmony with the physical, moral, and intellectual laws of his being," finally modified it to "Believe what you may, but act as well as you can" and ended the experiment when he found himself in irreconcilable conflict with an influential member described by a writer of the time as a "long headed, tonguey Syracuse lawyer."

Most recent of the long list of proofs of York State's quality is the story of the ninety followers of L. T. Nichols (the initials representing no actual given names) who for the first two years of the twentieth century wandered the waters of the Mississippi, Ohio, and Cumberland in a big three-deck, double-stack steamboat which had been christened *Megiddo*, a Hebrew word signifying "God is in this place with a band of troops." Their enormous Bible lashed high above the bow, their brass band blaring out the hymns of their faith, they visited the river towns of Kentucky, Indiana, and Tennessee to tell the populace that the true Christmas is March 25 and that Elijah will shortly return to earth to announce the Second Coming of the Christ. These water pilgrims finally found more lasting haven in their neat homes that now cluster about their church—the Megiddo Mission on Thurston Street in Rochester. There they have worshiped for the past forty-seven years. There they still wait, sure of the nearness of the Great Day. Though their leader died in 1912, their membership has grown to nearly three hundred and they live on serenely, expecting all converts to cease from marrying, dancing, drinking alcoholic liquors, and going to the movies.

The story of Koresh, the Great Alchemist at Utica, who was instructed by a supernatural, ethereal, and beautiful woman that man lives on the inside of the earth sphere is a later section of this book.

York State Is a Country

The average Yorker is a hale, humorous fellow, as secure as most Americans because of his being a part of a regional economy that is usually prosperous. He eats well of the food that is produced around him, though he prefers western beef. Upstate cooking is good without being so imaginative as the long tradition of fertile upstate fancy would lead you to believe. Few Yorkers, despite their visits to the special restaurants of New Orleans or Paris, really like the sauces on which these cities pride themselves. Gravies and ketchups are the Yorker's favorite addition to his hearty helping of meat and potatoes. Upstate restaurants have built their reputations for cuisine on quantity as well as quality and the latter is what is usually called in New York "first-rate tea-room cooking." French bistros of the kind that flourish in Manhattan because of one dish which they prepare particularly well and serve sparingly are not likely to be found in upstate towns.

As for dress, the Yorker is also conservative. Upstate ladies are not often tempted by specialty shops into the excesses that Paris recommends and New York copies. Their husbands are likely to "draw the line" on experiments. Generally the Yorker ladies dress neatly and with a proper regard for the occasion. They are always in good taste but tend toward frilly department store uniformity rather than unique distinction through expensive simplicity.

Socially Yorkers are free and democratic. For the most

part they gravitate toward friends of similar interests. High Society is a game played more by the newspapers to gain circulation by putting the names of subscribers and possible subscribers in the paper than by the people who bear those names. It would be false to intimate that there are no snobs, no "climbers," but the general atmosphere among people of the middle and high income groups who set the tone of a town's society is pleasant, easy, unmarred by assumed superiorities. As the Indian half-breed guide, Free Burley, remarked while attending in his only costume— the worn clothes of his calling—the fashionable wedding of the daughter of one of his employers, "Thems that knows don't care, thems that don't knows, I don't give a damn."

About six millions of the fourteen millions of people who inhabit the state of New York live outside New York City and regard themselves as the only true Yorkers. The city of Greater New York whose capital is City Hall on the separate island of Manhattan is, to their way of thinking, an alien unit fortunately blessed by the wise discipline it receives from Albany, where the state's Assembly and Senate are always strongly influenced, if not dominated, by that wisdom which is the natural consequence of rural environment.

To make sure of the permanence of this salutary condition, the number of city members of the Assembly has been set by law at 67 out of a total of 150, the number of city senators at 25 out of 56.

For this upstate, "father-knows-best" guidance, New York City pays through the nose. It has not been the practice at Albany to allow the big town a proportion of the benefits derived from state taxes that would represent the percentage paid from the pocketbooks of citizens of the city of Greater New York. John Gunther succinctly points out in his *Inside U.S.A.*: "New York City has something over 55 per cent of the population of the state and it contributes 74 per cent of all state taxes. Yet from the state it gets only 57 per cent of state aid. An area of 365.4 square miles contributes to the state, in other words, nearly three quarters of the revenue of an area of 49,576 square miles. . . . Of every dollar the state receives and spends New York City has contributed 74 cents . . ."

Moreover, the state's governing bodies do not always permit the nation's largest metropolis to solve its own difficulties, preferring to force it to stew in its own juice for its sins—which good cockfighting, applejack-making upstaters believe to be many and unnatural. So strong is this conviction that the upstate Republican majority has rewarded with the governorship two men, Charles W. Whitman and Thomas E. Dewey, who were not even natives of the state for the apparent reason that, while prosecuting attorneys, they tried to put behind prison bars as many residents of New York City as they could.

To infer from these facts that Yorkers have a practical and more than casual interest in politics would, however, be erroneous. The majority of upstaters are good-naturedly indifferent to the machinery of their state government. They know that the salaries of their representatives at Albany are notoriously low and do not attract able men. With an occasional exception, their opinion seems to be that windfall Yorkers, if they elect enough of them, are more than a match for the slick smoothies and the intense laborites, recognizably top-of-the-barrel boys, elected by the

burning Democrats of New York City's teeming districts. They like to boast that the governorship of New York is regarded as a step toward the White House and to scoff at the suggestion made by objective political commentators that the job of being mayor of the city of Greater New York is not only harder than that of governor of the state but is second in difficulty only to the Presidency.

In a few upstate counties the aristocratic tradition in politics, which was established after the American Revolution and began its decline soon after the end of the War of 1812, still persists; in a very few others, competent men who have attained ample means choose to round out their lives in service to the state. But most Yorkers find themselves satisfied to live their reasonably prosperous lives undisturbed by what they regard as minor political responsibilities. They consider well their votes for governor—and woe to their Republican candidate if he does not measure up to the qualifications of such paragons of civic virtue as the Democrats have wisely nominated—Al Smith and Herbert Lehman are still remembered gratefully. But they are debonairly careless in lesser affairs. Though by nature opposed to "machine rule" and frequently articulate in their attacks on it, they look with complacency on their state capital lying at the mercy of Democrat bosses whom even a Republican governor cannot oust and on their own Republican cities ruled by colorless autocrats who have not even the picturesqueness of nineteenth-century political highbinders to recommend them.

The result has been a state capital which, while it takes itself seriously and believes that it is honest and sincere, does not even avoid the appearance of evil by ruling lobbyists off the floors of its legislative chambers, a capital in which there are too few first-rate thinkers, where roaring good humor and the qualities of the "good fellow" are too often mistaken for democratic virtues. From Albany legislators are likely to come ideas that have long been discarded by better minds in the capitals of conservative New England or liberal Midwest. The thesis that teachers should not be allowed tenure—the right to hold their jobs after they have proved themselves capable of them—is advanced by a leading senator, who disregards the dangers of political influence in our public schools by arguing from the silly and false analogy that if he buys coal from one dealer one year he should not be forced to buy from him in succeeding years. A state official subscribes to childish folklore with the thought that an inmate of a prison deserves no credit for having made himself into a skilled artist while incarcerated "because his talents are born in him."

Once in a while stupidities such as these will suddenly shine through the murk that veils Albany doings to reveal themselves to the intelligent minds of the upstate Yorkers. Then there will be howls of rage, as once when an administration that had prided itself on rich surpluses which made it possible to cut income taxes suggested to audiences at the Syracuse State Fair and elsewhere that through local option sales taxes might be adopted to defray the costs of such benefits as better schools. Realizing that the first community to adopt a sales tax would immediately be boycotted by the farmers of the surrounding area (who would at once begin enriching a nearby town with no sales tax), the Yorkers received the idea with boos so loud that even upstate politicians, who almost automatically accept all noises made by their constituents as applause, recognized them as protests.

Mr. Gunther has explained the shortcomings of the up-state "hinterland," as he calls it, by saying that it is often "a peripheral area barren of ideas." However, since many Yorkers west of the Manhattan-to-Albany line have distinguished themselves in national politics and in business enterprises, it seems safe to conclude that their faults so far as state politics are concerned are attributable to a lack of interest and not to brainlessness. Despite the political power at Albany of the west-of-the-Hudson counties, comprising geographically more than three quarters of the state, only about one quarter of the men elected to the governorship have been born west of the Hudson Valley area of influence. Since slightly more than another quarter—thirteen, to be exact—were natives of other states, and of these aliens ten were by birth New England Yankees, two Jersey-ites, and only one a product of a region west of central New York, the preponderance of eastern influence is emphatic and seems to prove that too few able men of the western counties have had the ambition to be governor.

Because the governors have generally been men of remarkably high average of intelligence and integrity and the members of the two chambers have not been comparable with them, a curious situation has developed of which few Yorkers can be proud. Warren Moscow, political reporter for the New York *Times*, calls attention to it in his perhaps justifiably cynical *Politics in the Empire State*, when he reports that in recent administrations the governor of New York State has preferred having the opposing party in the majority in the legislature, so that he may fight for legislation which the electorate recognizes as constructive and which the legislators therefore dare not vote against, rather than find himself embarrassed by the demands of legislators of his own party that he support their inept or stupid recommendations when they are in the saddle. Mr. Moscow names Alfred E. Smith, Franklin D. Roosevelt, and Herbert Lehman as having held this point of view. The inference as to the quality of the legislators of both parties is obvious.

Perhaps this political weakness of Yorkers may best be studied in the light of comments by the most popular of modern theorists in the field of history.

"Still, taking all in all—soil, climate, transport facilities and the rest—" writes Arnold J. Toynbee in his widely accepted A Study of History, "it is impossible to deny that the original colonial home of the New Englanders was the hardest country of all. Thus North American history tells in favor of the proposition: the greater the difficulty, the greater the stimulus." He qualifies this later. Massachusetts he admires: "It would appear that the hardness of the New England environment which stands at its optimum in Massachusetts is accentuated in Maine to a degree at which it brings in diminishing returns of human response."

Since he holds that ease also is inimical to civilization, it seems safe to conclude that had he written of York State he would have concluded that it was as much below the optimum of challenge (represented by Massachusetts) as Maine was above. Applying his tests to New York, sometimes called the Empire State, we find in its favor that it once had the advantage of being a challenging "new country." It was not a "hard country" as compared to Massachusetts nor has it been penalized or felt blows or pressures. In four out of the five types of stimulus listed on the Toynbee chart it fails to meet the requisites of a country of "optimum challenge." From Toynbee's point of view, then,

Dark Trees to the Wind

York State life has been so prosperous and easy as to promote indifference and other faults that might eventually make it unimportant. . . . Yorkers take warning. . . .

When Al Smith was governor, all the folks—and the cottagers too—on both sides of Keuka Lake were complaining about the dusty road and asking for a hard one. But Al said that the budget wouldn't let him pave but one side and he didn't know which side to choose. So they asked Al to come over from Albany and spend a day on each side.

He spent the first day at the Keuka Hotel on the east side, and the rich folks there took him for a ride in a speedboat and they gave him a big dinner at the hotel and he had a wonderful time and things looked bad for the folks across the lake.

Next day, Al went over to Deer's Point and the folks there gave him another big dinner but they had it set outdoors in the shade of the big trees and they chose the place so that the wind would be blowing across the road toward them.

All day long that road was busy. There wasn't a farmer on that side who didn't have to go to Hammondsport for somethin' and by the time he got back he'd remember that he forgot to get what he'd gone for. The dust rolled off that road in clouds right onto that dinner and I reckon everybody includin' Al et more than his peck o' dirt by the time it was over.

I bet you know who got the hard road.

There was a young city fella from Buffalo. He used to sculp statues and things. He was pretty good at it, but he never got no orders, never won no prizes, so he asked his teacher why that was and his teacher said: "You sculp pretty good statues, but they don't have no style."

So the fella quit and went to farmin', and he had a herd of sheep. He raised 'em careful and when the County Fair time came round he paid his entrance money and he took 'em to the Fair.

Well, his sheep was as fat as any there. Their wool was as long and clean and curly as the wool of the sheep that won the blue ribbons, but he didn't get no ribbons at all.

So he went to the judge and he says: "My sheep were as fat as those that won the first prize blue ribbons and they had just as long and clean and curly wool. Why didn't I get no prize?"

And the judge said, "The trouble with them sheep of yourn is they ain't got no style."

Upstate is much more enthusiastic about culture than it is about politics but it sticks to conservative patterns. Its old colleges maintain educational traditions established soon after they were founded and with a tenacity that prohibits progress in educational philosophy. None of its private schools is so unconventional as the bold Putney School of Vermont, none of its colleges so experimental as the same state's Bennington or Ohio's Antioch. The old ways of schooling have proved in many respects good ways, Yorkers say. Let the other regions do the pioneering. If they find something better, we will adopt it.

Yorkers believe in education, nevertheless, with unshakable conviction, and they know that it does not end with graduation from an institution of learning. They organize reading clubs and historical societies and they crowd the museums that have been provided for them by rich and grateful fellow citizens of the state. Unfortunately, they are inclined to accept the judgments of these men with regard to the arts, partially because the prosperous patron has been materially successful, partially because they share with him a Victorian folk belief that the creative worker, being an original in his own field, is apt to be disturbingly original in economics, politics, and society. To the disgust of the living artist, the Yorker, whether rich or poor, refuses to look upon him as a natural product of the people of his region but insists on regarding him as a biological sport, a not-to-be-expected growth from the soil of upstate civilization.

The only sure way to further the cultural development of the community he would bless, the patron believes, is to give it the opportunity of looking upon works accomplished in the past by artists on whom posterity has conferred the accolade of the word "immortal." The upstate philanthropist, therefore, gives the public some sort of show place for the exhibit of works by artists who may now be safely mourned. This enhances his reputation for noble giving, while it takes nothing from him that the income tax would not have taken.

Meanwhile the Yorker artist starves while the public appears in crowds to test its appreciation of rare incunab-

ula, Italian primitives, or early English opera. Not that as a rule the creative worker wants the rich man's direct patronage. A rich man's money comes too high. It must be paid for with overdone gratitude, with treacle in music, propriety in verse, sentimentality on canvas. The wants of any artist at work are, for the most part, simple and few—respect from his fellow citizens as a person and as an artist, relief for the time being from annoyances, both domestic and financial, opportunity for undisturbed concentration, stimulating companionship.

Occasional efforts on the part of upstate patrons to improve the culture of their loved land by aiding in the production of art by helping at its source, the living artist, have been deserving of pity when they were not ludicrous. They were, of course, always generous and well meant.

One of these was a project established about 1913 in the picturesque hill country southwest of Rochester by the wealthy and autocratic Mrs. Coonley Ward. At her Hillside Farm in the little town of Wyoming—once known for the manufacture of good whisky—she gathered as her guests at her "summer school" and at other times a surprising number of able artists. A woman of great kindness and indefatigable energy, she was so concerned with arranging and organizing the lives of her guests—who could not protest, since they were accepting her hospitality—that few of them had either the quiet or the leisure to do the work she constantly urged them to do. She had planned to make Wyoming a center radiating a cultural influence throughout the upstate region and she expected local residents to find as much joy in it as her guests. But the Wyoming citizens and their wives were lacking in appreciation and the instructors were reduced to swapping attendance at the several classes. At the town hall that the bountiful lady had given to Wyoming, painting classes and dance classes were somewhat more popular.

The day at Hillside Farm began with Mrs. Coonley Ward, white-haired and patrician in a white gown overlaid by a blue silk scarf and wearing a flat piece of lapis lazuli on the gold chain about her neck, at the head of the breakfast table. In summer, on the plate of each of the assembled artist-guests was a bouquet of flowers symbolizing his personal qualities. In winter, a handful of unset jewels was scattered on the plate. Before anyone could begin to eat the food, which was extravagantly good, the hostess would ask all to rise and repeat with her the first ten lines of Robert Louis Stevenson's *The Celestial Surgeon:*

> If I have faltered more or less
> In my great task of happiness;
> If I have moved among my race
> And shown no glorious morning face;
> If beams from happy human eyes
> Have moved me not; if morning skies,
> Books, and my food, and summer rain
> Knocked on my sullen heart in vain,—
> Lord, thy most pointed pleasure take,
> And stab my spirit broad awake . . .

At this point the hostess always insisted on her guests' ceasing to quote because she disliked intensely the last four lines, which read:

> Or, Lord, if too obdurate I,
> Choose Thou, before that spirit die,
> A piercing pain, a killing sin,
> And to my dead heart run them in!

· 25 ·

Dark Trees to the Wind

The instructors at the summer school, creative artists of some achievement, were expected when they were not teaching to keep the vases of the big house filled with flowers, to do a little light gardening, consisting mostly of clipping off dead blossoms, and to assist in shelling peas, husking corn, or stripping string beans outside the kitchen door. Since, during these Brook Farmish activities, the artists were given the company of a tall handsome Russian prince and his secretary, a count said to be a lineal descendant of Lord Byron, they found the hours passing pleasantly if not creatively. The count had brought with him to America five large bronze wreaths, planning to lay one on the grave of each of the five greatest deceased Americans. His choice leaned toward Edgar Allan Poe, Theodore Roosevelt (who was not yet in a grave), Mark Twain, Buffalo Bill, and the Indian chief Osceola. The artists, unable to get at the work they had planned for the summer, exercised their creative talents in inventing for his edification Americans greater even than those of his selection.

The afternoons were gay, with swimming parties and teas given by charming and well-to-do neighbors; the evenings were filled with romantic German melancholy by an excellent string ensemble—the Zoellner quartet. There was a week of performances by Stuart Walker's Portmanteau Theatre—all fifteen players being guests at the big house. One long-remembered production was *Gammer Gurton's Needle* in front of Hillside's blue-watered pool.

The guests who spent appreciative if unproductive days were many and certainly varied. Edwin Markham had more luck than most and he wrote his hostess, temporarily absent:

York State Is a Country

I am moved to melody and this is taking form
in verse more abundant than I have ever
produced in the same stretch of time in
any other region in the East. Hallelujah!
Blow bugles of the Resurrection!

Another writer of experience wrote to a friend succinctly,
"It was not for writers."

There were occasional visits from Edmond Vance Cooke,
Henry Turner Bailey, Percy F. Boynton, Lydia Bush-Brown
—all well-known names in the days before World War I.
And there was the record of at least one protest—that of
the impeccable English dramatist Lord Dunsany, who on
being interrupted during dictation to a secretary who was
needed to play the piano for dancing, was reliably reported
to have replied to the messenger of his hostess, "Will you
get the hell out of here?"

The story among the irreverent was that when Elbert
Hubbard heard the noon train whistle for East Aurora
station he would hastily remove his coat, grab his hoe at
the back door; then as the cars were slowing up all passengers could see him in his garden proving the dignity of
manual labor, his wide-brimmed Stetson shadowing his
noble head from which his long hair fell about his face, his
coarse white shirt a proud background for his wide and
careless Windsor tie, and his narrow galluses. As soon as

the train had passed, the cynics used to say, he would return both his hoe and his body to its accustomed leisure.

There was more than a little envy in such talk, for Fra Elbertus, as he had named himself, was in his day and in his way a genius. Only he, of all advertising men, had the inspiration to retire to a little upstate town, found a noncommunistic community of which he was lord, master and prophet, and make his carefully planned eccentricities so well known that they contributed mightily to the sale of community products.

A friendship with William Morris, English poet who advocated a return to the proud craftsmanship of the guilds of the Middle Ages, gave Hubbard the idea. After visiting Morris, twenty years his senior, at the Kelmscott Press in Hammersmith in 1896, he retired from the soap business, established the Roycroft Press (named after Samuel and Thomas Roycroft, seventeenth-century London printers) at East Aurora, and began to emulate the older man's labors in printing and hand binding. Soon he added pottery, copper smelting, furniture manufacture, publication of a magazine—the *Philistine*. He prospered at once, and there were over five hundred Roycrofters on his payroll—mostly the sons and daughters of farmers in Erie County, never famous for fertile acres. "Our motto," wrote the picturesquely dressed prophet, "is 'Not How Cheap But How Good.' "

The *Philistine*, pioneer of the pocket-size magazine, seemed to readers of the early twentieth century a daring experiment from its rough brown butcher-paper cover right through every word of its contents. Hundreds of thousands of potential rebels from the dictates of Victorian convention read it with shocked delight—and today their children wonder why. Hubbard, like most gifted advertising men, had a way with aphorisms and slogans and he did a rousing business in them. The fillers at the bottom of the pages seemed to all friends of American capitalism (as then practiced) both the last word in bold originality and the epitome of inspired common sense. For Elbert Hubbard was the loyal friend of Big Business and his best efforts were directed at idealizing it. Strongly opposed to the unions, which had dared to question the big bosses' qualifications to determine the merits of their employees and to reward them accordingly, he set down in fancy type exquisitely printed with a red capital letter at the beginning of each word such sayings as:

People Who Never Do Any More Than They Get Paid For Never Get Paid For Any More Than They Do.

An Ounce Of Loyalty Is Worth A Pound Of Cleverness.

Any Man Who Has A Job Has A Chance.

Success Depends On Loyalty And Co-operation.

Industrialism, As It Changes And Betters Human Environment, Is The True Civilizing Agent.

A Man's Measure Is His Ability To Select Men And Materials And Organize Them.

Business Is Human Service. Therefore Business Is A Divine Calling.

Dark Trees to the Wind

The Only Prophet Without Honor Or Mazuma Is The
One Who Does Not Know How To Advertise.

I Am Not In The Business Of Defaming America *nor*
Using As A Doormat The Things That Are Building It
Up: I Believe In Big Business *and* More Of It!

There Is But One Way To Win, And That Is To Do
Your Work Well And Speak Ill Of No One, Not Even As
a Matter Of Truth.

Those thinking Americans who did not consider the
works of Fra Elbertus vulgar, crude, blasphemous—and
they included most of the prominent men of the nation
at the time—made pilgrimages to East Aurora in such numbers that Hubbard was obliged to build the Roycroft Inn
for them, a tavern decorated with the framed proverbs and
witticisms of the prophet. His humor was of the broad and
practical-joking variety no longer popular in sophisticated
magazines but heartily enough applauded by the public to
sell thousands of copies of the *Elbert Hubbard Scrapbook*
year in and year out to this day. His wisdom was for the
most part expressed in restatement of obvious truisms in
his own advertising language. His genius was for showman-
ship. His artistic taste resulted in making countless homes
and hotels in America uncomfortable with "Mission" furniture, countless "Turkish corners" a hodgepodge of burnt-
leather decorations, countless parlor tables a hazard of
hand-bound books by Shakespeare and Elbert Hubbard,
Elizabeth Barrett Browning and Elbert Hubbard again.

He made much money on the lecture platform, much in
vaudeville. And while he preached democracy and love of

one's fellow man he cultivated the society of "worth-while" celebrities, made worshipful obeisance at the shrines of robber-baron gods, assumed with a greater show of arrogance than most prophets his own infallibility. His biographer, Felix Shay, wrote in his *Elbert Hubbard of East Aurora* the best argument ever made for him but ruefully admitted his one great fault:

"He considered most people children, who needed a Little Father to tell them when to go to bed and when to get up; when to work and how much and at what! how much to spend and how much to save! . . . he always saw himself as judge, jury and chief executioner."

When Elbert Hubbard died in the waters of the Irish Sea after the torpedoing of the *Lusitania* in World War I, York State lost its most popular, if least consecrated, prophet and Roycroft its great factotum. Despite efforts to carry on, it was doomed. Now the cozy stone buildings, the chapel in which the boys and girls of the countryside, released temporarily from their labors, used to gather to laugh and applaud the gospel of the prophet and his friends are the property of others. Only the Roycroft Inn keeps the name of the Utopian project of Fra Elbertus.

There was also Yaddo—cluttered, spacious, Victorian Yaddo—sitting heavily upon its hill near the outskirts of Saratoga Springs and looking darkly down from its many windows on its formal rose gardens, its informal rock gardens, its little statues very white in the dark shade of its groves. Spencer and Katrina Trask were rich and eagerly intellectual and they bought this land with its two ponds from which Alexander Hamilton and others of the Revolutionary Army's smart and youthful officers used to catch trout to be cooked as only old crotchety Dutch Barhyte— eccentric tavernkeeper—could cook them.

The Trasks wanted to be different from their friends of the Newport Set and so they built this home at Saratoga and in the early 1900's were giving house parties at which the conversation was at the same time more philosophical and more brilliantly gay than the Rhode Island millionaires could manage. When a small daughter insisted upon being taken to one of the ponds in order that she might see her "yaddo" in the water, her unintended invention was hailed with glee and the big place was formally christened Yaddo.

The Trasks were very happy in this refuge of poetic contemplation and mad repartee—this happy contrast to the emptiness of society and the vulgarity of the racing gentry so evident in other vast buildings nearby—the Grand Union and the United States hotels of Saratoga, but tragedy was soon to descend upon them. By drowning and by fever, they lost their children, and as the years wore on they faced the fact that there was no one bound to them by blood ties on whom they could call to feed with fresh fuel their bright flame of the north barrens. They dreaded the thought that Yaddo conversations might cease, that the words of Henry Van Dyke scratched with a diamond on the glass of Katrina's tower-room window would be read by irreverent eyes. Since they were very rich they felt that they could provide against such a violation of the tradition of the place and they planned a foundation which would provide the funds for a perpetual house party of brilliant and congenial minds at Yaddo. America's most distinguished painters, writers, and composers would be their guests after they themselves were gone, would gather at their dinners in the high-ceilinged dining room to eat viands provided by a chef of distinction and to trade bons mots in an atmosphere of happy but intellectual abandon. Stimulated by the companionship of one another, freed from worry over expenses and other mundane affairs, they would create works of art of an excellence and profusion such as no group of artists had ever before produced.

The Trasks at once set about accomplishing their high purpose, and not even Spencer's tragic death in a train accident handicapped them. A suit for damages against the New York Central Railroad added considerably to the ample sum already available, and Katrina's later marriage to her husband's closest friend and his business partner, the millionaire philanthropist George Foster Peabody (to whom she and Spencer had given land for his beautiful home on the estate), made the realization of the lovely dream appear to be a certainty.

Only a quality within Katrina herself caused difficulty. Perhaps she was more spoiled by her riches than she realized—the idea would have horrified her for, like Mrs. Coonley Ward, she said she recognized no social distinctions—but the simple delight which she took in a play-ceremony was possibly indicative. In royal robes she descended the great staircase into the big hall and in the presence of many guests and almost as many servants was seated in a tremendous becanopied and becarved bishop's chair (two such thrones still make the room awesome) and was there crowned "Queen of Yaddo." This so pleased her that some

· 33 ·

time later she arranged for still another coronation and she treasured no possession more than an invitation sent to her later by the prime minister of Canada, who had been an impressed guest, in the name of "Your Royal Sister, Victoria."

Perhaps Katrina's innocent love of show and the panoply of high position, her quite explicable lack of understanding of the creative artist's life, had its psychic influence on administrators of the foundation, perhaps not; but whatever may have been the truth, after her death the dream of the perpetual house party on a high plane of philosophical thought and subtle merriment was not at once achieved. The foundation proved so lavish that tales of the early days of Yaddo sound more like fancy than sober fact. One of these, not easily authenticated and perhaps a product of the folk fancy of successive groups of creative minds, goes that artist-guests were served their ample and tasty breakfasts in bed by no less than eighteen comely Swiss serving maids of a sweetness and amiability not usually discoverable by creative workers in this country. Wednesday evenings were set aside for gatherings in Katrina's tower room, where the Van Dyke inscription was eyed with proper respect and where representatives of the patrons, artists, and servants were for a precious hour or two all considered to be on the same democratic plane, regardless of their daily employments. No one knows how long this Utopian idyll might have continued had not the directress of the establishment taken a turn through the grounds of the Saratoga Racing Association on a sunny day in the middle of what is known to mundane Saratogans as "the season." There, according to this doubtful and tawdry story, she beheld exactly eighteen artists, whom she had supposed to be wrestling in their rooms with the problems that only genius can solve, each parading proudly with a pretty Swiss maid on his arm. The incident is said to have ended Yaddo's Golden Age.

Yaddo carries on today with surprising usefulness to upstate's creative culture, considering its limitations. As the thick entrance door swings open to the artist-guest he sees before him a nude stone maiden kneeling in a wide shallow basin and he hears the trickle of water. A stained-glass window above her head depicts in radiant colors a number of lightly clad American Indians bearing off a beautiful white girl-captive whose yellow hair falls in a gleaming cascade to their feet. As the new arrival turns to face the window that fills most of the wall at the far end of the long room he sees two painted Dutch sleds, the huge carved-walnut bishop's chairs with hanging carved-walnut canopies, a gleaming white cupid with arched bow about to let go an arrow from a dark corner, the great staircase, a Virgin and child peering down from the mantel above the huge fireplace, and two more than life-size portraits. One is of Spencer Trask in tight golf knickers standing on a pillared terrace. The other is of Katrina in a high waisted white dress, a single rose held in her hands.

The rest of the house is in kind. There have been artists who have been so sensitive that, on approaching a dining-room chair, they have been given a sudden turn and a cessation of appetite by the all-too-realistic carving thereon of Salome offering the head of John the Baptist on a tray. There was one, a Communist poet (the administration has tried to keep a nice balance between points of view), who spent most of his allotted time pacing up and down the bedroom that had once been Katrina's, grinding his teeth

in rage at the cupid-ringed marble tub, the exquisite wood-
work, the expensive furniture, and a plethora of other examples of the wickedness and bourgeoisie of American life.
There have been guests who were too tired at the end of a
day of strenuous "creating" to toss the glittering ball of
conversation lightly about as those who remember Katrina's
desire for a perpetual house party would encourage them
to do. There have been others who have gradually overcome a feeling of oppression occasioned by unwritten rules
and written, by signs in the library demanding "Silence,"
by the central lift-top desk that contained the mail and
perhaps an admonition from the management, perhaps the
message known to be the equivalent of a final separation from
free living, good food, stimulating companionship: "We
fear you are not happy here."

One other residence for creative artists in the state lived
a short life on Long Island. It was for painters only. The
nice old man who founded it with the best intentions had,
nevertheless, eccentricities. Observant resident artists, who
saw him start out for church on Sunday morning with all
his grandchildren like a flock of yellow butterflies about
him, made deductions and soon the canvases along the
line of studios, which the patron often patrolled for evidences of progress, began to blossom as yellow as Van
Gogh sunflowers.

The money that supported the painters while they indulged in these orgies in ocher is now more wisely employed in a foundation to aid deserving artists to paint their
pictures wherever they wish and Yaddo is the one remaining subsidized residence for working painters, composers,
and writers in the state. Governed by a distinguished board

of directors, it is gradually becoming more functional, more like the most effective of such institutions, the MacDowell Colony at Peterboro, New Hampshire, where the widow of composer Edward MacDowell, a comparatively poor woman who is now ninety-two, established and managed for forty years the only simple and sensible institution in aid of the creative artist at work in the nation.

The most distinctive quality of the true Yorker is the witch's brew of humor and whimsy that, despite his tendency to obey conventions most of the time, occasionally comes to a boil in the kettle of his being. Since the creative imagination, at least from the point of view of objective agnostics, has had more than a little to do with the asseverations of York State's founders of religions, perhaps the same essence, less seriously at work, is responsible for the wild deceptions practiced by Yorkers upon their fellows. Whatever the underlying reasons, the hoax has never found more ardent devotees than among the natives of the hills around Syracuse and Ithaca. How long ago they began trying to give each other delusions is uncertain but at least by 1820 the definite pattern of the typical York State hoax had been established.

In the summer of that year, Philo Cleveland, clearing a stony field to make a meadow, upended an oval-shaped boulder with his crowbar. Holding it on edge with his hands at the top of the bar, his back against a stump, he rested a moment from the arduous effort of raising it. As he was about to continue his heavy labor his glance rested on the flat undersurface of the stone and he saw, or thought he saw, strange lettering beneath the dark earth that clung to it. Paying little attention to this unusual circumstance, he moved the boulder, which was about fourteen inches long, twelve inches broad, and eight inches thick, to a pile nearby and would have thought no more about it had he not passed the pile a few days later and seen that a hard rain had washed away all dirt and that the lettering was indeed a reality. It read as follows:

Leo X De   L. S.
VI 1520-   + ∩

Between De and L. S. was a crude thin serpentine line.

Philo got help and carried the stone to Cy Avery's blacksmith shop at Oran, where it became at once a popular curiosity.

It was taken thence to the museum of the Albany Institute and the archaeologists of the time were soon at high noon of a field day. The inscription, they said, could be interpreted as "Leo X by the grace of God, sixth year of his Pontificate, 1520." The date was unquestionably correct, they said, since Leo X was elected pope in 1514. The authorities agreed that the stone was designed as a sepulchral monument, that L.S. signified the initials of the deceased, a cross (noticeable under these) that he was a Roman Catholic, and an inverted U beside and below that he was a member of a Masonic Order. Most felt that the person buried had been a native of Spain.

"Possibly," wrote an eager scholar, "some adventurer of this nation, allured by the story of a lake at the north whose bottom was lined with silver [the salt at Salina Springs] traversed this region in pursuit of the darling object . . . the survivor or survivors may have placed this monument over his remains."

The distinguished scholar H. R. Schoolcraft—to whom the world owes much of its knowledge of the Six Nations of the Iroquois—went further. Pointing out that Florida was discovered by Ponce de Leon in 1512, he advanced the theory that a straggling party of his men had wandered north to this spot, and added this disturbing thought: "As a mere historical question a claim to the discovery of the interior of New York by the Spanish crown might in this view find something to base itself on."

More creative was the lecture in 1879 of Henry A. Holmes, librarian of the New York State Library, before the Oneida Historical Society. This learned man said he thought the stone a memorial to a European, probably a Spaniard, and on this premise he built a story of the capture of the wanderer by Indians, his winning such favor with his captors as to be adopted into their tribe, his eventually arriving at the status of an important sachem.

Against this thesis Father John F. Mullaney preached in Syracuse in 1897 (three years after the stone had been proved a hoax) a sermon in which he stated that missionary priests of the Roman Catholic faith had visited central

York State a hundred years before the landing of the Protestants at Plymouth Rock and that the stone had probably been carved by one of them. The inscription, he pointed out, was carved in characters of the ecclesiastical usage of Catholic prelates alone, and the design on the stone obviously depicted "an old Spanish emblem symbolizing reward and punishment."

These happy ventures in speculation delighted the reading public but not quite so much as the report of the state archaeologist, the Reverend Dr. William M. Beauchamp, a shrewd scientist who stated bluntly that the letters and figures on the stone were purely modern and that they and the other marks had been made by two cold chisels "of good quality," and a hammer, and a smith's punch, a combination which, he remarked dryly, "would make a pretty good kit of tools for a wandering Spaniard."

This shattering report emboldened John E. Sweet, respected citizen of Syracuse, to write a letter that effectively ended all claims to the authenticity of the stone and had York State archaeologists making thin and embarrassed explanations to a laughing citizenry for a decade.

My uncle Cyrus Avery, born in Pompey, lived there during the early part of the century, and told me the last time I saw him, in 1867, that he and his nephew William Willard of this city cut the figures on the Pompey Stone just to see what would come of it. When the account appeared in Clark's history, so much had come of it they decided it was best to keep still altogether. . . . The tools were exactly the ones most likely to be at hand in Grandfather Avery's blacksmith shop at Oran. . . . Mr. Avery was given to just that sort of thing. The Pompey Stone is nothing more or less than a joke. It can hardly be called a fraud, as it does not pretend to be anything, nor did the makers ever do anything to make it appear that it was. Really I hardly think the stone worth sending back to Albany, and Mr. Beauchamp may congratulate himself upon having sized up the inscription so accurately.

(Signed) John E. Sweet, June 11, 1894

Almost a half century later another hoax, the Cardiff Giant, was uncovered at Cardiff, only a few miles from Pompey. Though more elaborate and purposeful (profits from displaying it are said to have been over a million dollars), the procedure followed was so close to the previous pattern that it would seem to have been suggested by it. The story of the "Great Stone Sleeper" has been too often told for repetition here and it is mentioned only as perhaps the strongest of all evidences of the delight of Yorkers in fooling one another.

Even Cornell University, great institutional seeker of truth, has been seduced by the humorsome spirit. A number of years ago announcements appeared in Ithaca that a renowned Austrian professor of psychology would deliver in one of the college's larger halls an important lecture revealing his most recent discoveries. The response on the set evening was gratifying and the young impresarios who had arranged the event were delighted to see that the wife of the president of the university, a coconspirator, was seated on the platform as a sponsor. The wildly bearded professor made a startling appearance as he marched down the aisle and when he stated emphatically in his thick dialect, "Eet ees not enough to know that you know. Eet ees necessary that you know that you know that you know," all the graduate students in psychology, seated in the front row so as not to miss a word, nodded their heads and solemnly copied this wisdom into their notebooks. Indeed the fact that the famous scholar's contributions to knowledge were to be compared in spuriousness only to his beard was kept from a gullible college public for several days before the horrid truth leaked out.

This hoax was so successful that in May of 1930 a group of earnest undergraduates on the board of the *Cornell Daily Sun* (one of whom is now a distinguished clergyman) invited a number of leaders of the Republican Party then resident in Washington to a dinner honoring the sesquicentennial of the late and very distinguished Hugo N. Frye, native of Elmira, veteran of the War of 1812, outspoken opponent of the Mexican War, and founder of the Republican Party in the state of New York. Though none of the party moguls were, unhappily, able to attend the dinner, the hosts assembled anyway at the appointed time and place to read the harvest of replies. The Republican national chairman greatly regretted his inability to attend, the vice-president of the United States sent a genial and chummy wire, and a member of the Cabinet filled their cup to overflowing (though it might already have been emptied a few times) by stating "I find it a pleasure to testify to the career of that sturdy patriot who first planted the ideals of our party in this region of the country."

Not until a southern senator pointed out that possibly "You go'n fry" might be a profane translation of the great man's name did the high political factotums realize that they had been duped. Even telegrams of apology from the collegians did not entirely soothe their ruffled feelings.

Now comes a strange story that is a possible continuation of the chain of deceptions that have made Yorkers skeptical of archaeological findings in their own countryside. For years it has been a legend in the Helderberg Hills near Duanesburg and Delanson that Knox Cave had at one time been the refuge of Moroni, sole Nephite survivor of the battle between his people and the Lamanites at Cumorah Hill, site of the discovery of the Book of Mormon, the golden pages of which had been written by his father and hidden in the earth of the hill.

About fifteen years ago, Mr. Delevan C. Robinson, owner of the cave, and two men, one being William Beyer, owner of a gasoline station in Cleveland, Ohio, were in the cave when Mr. Beyer, who had lagged behind, cried out to his companions. They retraced their steps and found Beyer pointing in amazement at the wall of the cave. They could see a plaque about two feet wide and three feet long. On it were characters that looked like some sort of strange writing.

The plaque was removed from the wall and imprints of its characters were made. These imprints have been shown to scholars, one of whom has said that the characters resemble Egyptian writings. A section of the reproductions was sent to Salt Lake City. It was returned by the curator of the museum of the Church of Latter-day Saints, who suggested further investigation by sympathetic scientists, and by the Smithsonian Institution at Washington, whose representative also urged further study.

Mr. Robinson has expressed the theory that the former

occupants of the cave, whoever they may have been, used pine torches for illumination and that the "writings," which were on the walls of the highest dome room of the cave, were made by resin. A hard substance of some kind, he feels, has covered them in the years since they were written.

Mr. Duane Featherstonhaugh, who lives in the big pillared mansion of a distinguished ancestor who lived in the days of the American Revolution, is the most accomplished spelunker (cave scholar) of the region, and his only report is that the publicity attendant upon the discovery of the writings brought to his house an upstate devotee of certain fancy-fed pulp-paper magazines who claimed that these strange inscriptions might have been written by very little, very intelligent people who live in a land in the far depths of the earth and are quite aware of the existence of men on its surface. To guard their country from invasion, he said, they employ huge morons who stand guard in all caves and deep places where men might obtain ingress.

With these illustrations the case for the imaginative whimsy of the Yorker must rest.

This chapter is, of course, a very incomplete essay on the qualities of the typical Yorker. Further discoveries are possibly to be made from the chapters that follow, narratives from which the reader may obtain general conclusions which the author has found it difficult or impossible to express.

"You see that farm," said my white-bearded grandfather, leveling his whip at sunny rolling meadows beside the road. "It went down your great-grandfather's throat."

Sometimes it seems to me that the rectitude and respectability of our artists borders on the quixotic else I would have certainly met at least one in here with whom I could have exchanged ideas.

> From a letter of No. 22818, a talented artist
> who is a life inmate of a York State prison.

When Ed inherited his father's money he took a trip abroad and one day arrived in Cambridge, England. He went for a walk among the colleges and asked of a polite bobby:

"Isn't this the campus of Smith College?"

"This is Christ College, sir."

"Oh, yes," said Ed hastily. "*That* was the name."

Yorker Proverbs:

Don't trade no horses with a preacher.
It's as bad to slop over as it is to leak.
A farm won't run by itself 'ceptin' downhill.
A farmer needs a Dutch purse.

Poem on William Wright's House the Frame for Which was Hewn, Cut, Spliced, Fitted by Two Rochester Carpenters from a Monday through a Friday and Raised by

Dark Trees to the Wind

His Neighbors on a Saturday Night of a Full Moon at Rich's Corners in 1810.

> For William's convenience
> And Phoebe's delight
> It was framed in six days
> And raised in a night.

> There, in the warm days, we listened
> To trees whispering in the wind,
> Making us glad of summer, and of hills.

From *When the Grass Was Tall*, by Lansing Christman

2

Hometown Revisited

LIKE ALMOST EVERYONE WHO GOES BACK AFTER years of absence to a town where he has lived, I was going back to a time as well and expecting to find it waiting in the familiar streets. To pass the limits of Albion and be the person I was forty years ago in that western York State village as it was then, I knew to be impossible, but something in me unreasonably demanded that special and private miracle.

As it had been four decades ago, Albion was big houses and deep tree-dominated lawns, heads of families—and families. South Main Street began with the town's beginning when those entrepreneurs who had planned a man-made waterway from the western fresh-water seas into the Hudson named quintuplet huddles of buildings along its unfinished banks Spencerport, Brockport, Newport, Middleport, Lockport. Albion was Newport on the Erie Canal and the bridge that connected the banks separated South Main Street from North Main Street, and "canawlers" howled at their mules along the north-side towpath and howled at each other in the south-side saloons. But there were other Newports—even in York State—and some lover of England got the name of the place changed to Albion, and perhaps the distinction of a classical name had at least something to do with the kind of town Albion became.

There were other influences on the community's growth, and when a section of the region round about was officially designated a county and some lover of France got it named Orleans, these influences were at work to make the town the seat of the county government. Having heard that the deciding dignitaries, before a promised visit, looked upon Albion with disfavor because of its lack of water power, these influences effected repair of two abandoned sawmills on Sandy Creek—a streamlet never watery enough for a good swimming hole—had its trickles efficiently dammed for some weeks before the arrival of the great men, and on the day of inspection gave their guests, in a fleeting interval between toasts to their health, such a vivid impression of log-laden wagons, shouting teamsters, whining saws, and roaring waters (just undammed) that conversion was instant, and Albion was county seat and deserving of a courthouse before the immediate moment when the millrace ran dry.

The building of a courthouse, white pillared and white

domed, meant the coming of attorneys and magistrates, new units in the growing number of professional men who were giving the town an air of solidity and dignity. These citizens looked to be men of judgment and proved their appearance undeceitful by investing their savings in a company that was building a toll bridge of the suspension type at Niagara Falls, fifty miles west, and in a company which was manufacturing small cameras called kodaks at Rochester, thirty miles east.

While the men of Albion were making these satisfactory transactions, the farmers of Orleans County were discovering that the sandy loam of the coastal plain of Lake Ontario on which they lived was particularly suited to the growing of apples, and they had covered thousands of acres with low-spreading trees that offered wide seas of bloom in the spring, and in the fall millions of hanging juicy spheres, red stained and shining. Baldwins and Northern Spies, Rome Beauties and Ladies Blush, Ben Davis and McIntosh. A man might make a fortune if he had two good successive harvests on an orchard of two hundred acres, and some men did, and sold their farms and went to live in Albion.

The houses of South Main Street, paid for by tolls, canal trade, dividends, and apple profits, were set apart, each on a spacious lawn. Those which were of wood were dark green, clear white, brown that was the color of a winter leaf, and pumpkin yellow. They were elegant but there were greater elegances—that of red brick, which turned a weathered pink, and that of cut sandstone, deep rust at first but paling with age. Porches were piazzas and verandas and they were wide and railed. Windows were tall and panes were large and some of them were of plate glass, shimmering with reflections like a clear pool. Cupolas sat on the roofs of many of the frame houses, giving them a height sometimes not at all suited to symmetry. Towers rose along the corners of the brick houses and sometimes shot up above the roofs. The most admired house in town was brick and painted baby blue and its towers wore an intricate wrought-iron crown. In its front yard, rising from the center of a small round pool, was a liver-colored fountain—a boy and girl under a spread umbrella—and from the end of the shaft of the umbrella water spouted a few inches and fell like rain.

The men who were the heads of families living in the big houses desired to be known as heads of families and citizens of worth even while still young. Unlike their sons, who, having passed their thirtieth birthdays, pathetically indulged themselves in college boy follies as the twenties sped them into middle age, these men wanted to be considered mature as soon as possible. Once twenty-five, they affected long mustaches or short beards, bought Prince Albert coats, stretched gold chains from gold watches in pockets on the left of their waistcoat buttons to gold toothpicks in pockets on the right. They spoke judiciously and they walked in a portly manner—even the thin ones.

Churches and secret societies gave them the high offices that satisfied their thirst for prestige and they were deacons and vestrymen and members of the session and Sunday-school superintendents in their denominational associations, while at the same time potentates, shriners, archons, and knights templar in fraternal orders.

The men were the owners of the usual shops of a town of five thousand people or they were associated with one or another of the few industries in Albion. The very quiet business of buying apples and holding them in high windowless "cold storage" until prices proved advantageous was the most profitable. But sometimes prices did not reach the height expected and then the owners, having waited too long, lost great sums. Quarries just outside of town furnished the sandstone from which some of the big houses were built. A small factory was buying and canning peas. A stamping company had once established itself in a big brick building by the railroad depot, but it had failed and thus provided a high-ceilinged hall for high school basketball games.

The wives of the heads-of-families took little active interest in their husbands' businesses or in town affairs. They spent the mornings at their housekeeping duties and attending to the children, their afternoons at duplicate whist, their evenings for the most part in the family circle. They oh'd and ah'd at concerts (which were rare) and they hung reprints of Watts's "Hope," Landseer's "Stag at Bay," and Reni's "Aurora" on their walls. They talked a great deal about friends at the moment mercifully absent, about high society as reported by the Rochester papers, and about recipes for cooking special dishes. Many of the latter they tried out on an expectant public at church suppers and once every few years the ladies of one denomination or another would put their recipes together and have them printed in a cookbook.

Before the idea of a book club had flashed into the brain of a publisher they had established their own, buying the books most favorably recommended by *Harper's Magazine* and the *Atlantic*, passing them among the members, selling them at a reduced price to the ladies who, having read them, wanted to own them.

These ladies were, for the most part, virtuous. It would seem hard to imagine how they could be otherwise and maintain their schedules, but there were a few who received lovers after making such elaborate arrangements for secrecy that the town was aware of their liaisons as soon as they had been established. It was the code of Albion society to reserve delicious conversations on such subjects for intimate moments between friends or spouses, and in public to make self-conscious pretense of a complete ignorance of them. No strong social pressures were brought to bear upon the erring ones and their affaires d'amour, if they lasted for a long time (as most of them did), came to be recognized as part of the town pattern and regarded with tolerant though sorrowful acceptance.

As for other sexual unconventionalities, they were few. Though the one girl generally known to be a prostitute was by far the prettiest in the community, she came both literally and figuratively from so far below the tracks of the Niagara Falls branch of the New York Central Railroad that most of her patronage came from her own neighbors and I never heard of her associating with any of the South Main Street blades or their fathers.

The ladies of South Main and their friends who lived near them felt themselves socially a cut above their sisters who lived in other areas, and many cuts above the wives of "Polack Town" whose husbands worked in the quarries and whose daughters "hired out" to work in the better kitchens, and the wives of "Little Italy" or "Dago Town" whose husbands sold fruits while their daughters worked in the stores but never the kitchens. The prejudice against the Irish (born during the building of the canal) was wearing thin, though many of the older townfolk still spoke of them with disdain as "Shanty Irish." The Albion men, however, even the rich and the well born, held no snobbish ideas and often profanely denounced their wives' pretensions.

Many of the men were college graduates, the largest body of alumni being that of a small and not distant institution with classical traditions—Hamilton—and they and their wives were serious in their desires to follow intellectual pursuits. They read "papers" on subjects of the day to the Historical Club and the Conversational Club before the hostess's best recipes were tested, they listened to Sunday sermons with the air of connoisseurs, they attended "lectures" given for respectable fees by such well-known figures as Elbert Hubbard—Fra Elbertus—the sage of nearby East Aurora, and Thomas Mott Osborne, warden of the state prison at nearby Auburn.

In politics the town was like most of upstate New York, strongly Republican. Theodore Roosevelt passed through, stopping long enough to win the heart of my mother and all other Republican ladies with his irresistible "deelighted." Governor Charles Evans Hughes made a point of visiting us to make a speech in favor of his bill to outlaw gambling on horse races and, since our gambling on horses consisted of an occasional quarter risked on a trotter at the county fair, we pledged him our support in the largest auditorium in town—that of the First Presbyterian Church. But when Eugene V. Debs spoke from a baggage truck down at the depot, only a dozen men stood about listening embarrassedly as the tobacco-stained teeth flashed in the lean, jaundiced face and taut ideas tumbled on the air— twelve men and a small boy who had come to see how a man could be a man and at the same time such a monster as he had heard described.

When matters of importance to the bumbling Republican machine of the town were voted on, a slick politician who had the knack used to deliver as many votes as were necessary to swing the election, marching voters of doubtful eligibility up from Polack Town and paying each one a dollar after his ballot had been cast. When the question of local option on the sale of alcoholic liquors came up, however, no bribes were necessary. I was in high school then and as a horrified watcher for the anti-rum forces heard the last vote counted, heard the great roar in the town hall, saw the bottles tilted as the celebration of the drinkers began.

The formalities of holidays were the town's favorite recreation, and there were many holidays and the formalities always ended in a baseball game. It seems to me now that every long-awaited morning of celebration began with the massing of dark clouds just beyond the white dome of the courthouse and the soft feel of anticipated rain. By eleven o'clock, though, irregular spots of blue would appear behind the curving gray masses above, and the squeal of a fife and the beat of a drum were an irresistible call to the courthouse. I cannot remember the fifer or the drummer because, towering between them and lifting the flag of his country far above his own incredible height, a white-bearded old veteran looking like Michelangelo's Moses in a blue brass-buttoned uniform was marching up the steps as steadily as ever he marched with the same banner up Missionary Ridge, and all eyes were inevitably upon him.

A quartet sang "Tenting Tonight" and a frightened little girl recited the Gettysburg Address, and then the town's lawyer-orator, corpulent and elegant in his best blue suit and white waistcoat, stood on the platform and with calculated deliberation began his patriotic oration. Twenty minutes later his rich deep voice was pouring out his devotion to his country and his flag with all the poetry and rhetoric born in his Irish soul. His audience was spellbound. When he had ended his concluding paragraph, we all stood and sang the first and last stanzas of "My Country, 'Tis of Thee," and as we roared out "Great God Our King" the fife suddenly took up "The Girl I Left Behind Me" and the snare drum was imparting a great bounce to it, and the tall old flag-bearer was lifting his feet right smart.

Down across the canal bridge we marched and there on the baseball diamond the visiting team was warming up with the snap and grace of a team in the Eastern League. They had arrived at the depot early that morning in their special car which bore their name printed in gilt letters. They were often the Cherokee Indians or the Cuban Giants or, best of all, the Bloomer Girls. The Cherokees emitted war whoops and did Indian steps around the bases, the Cubans were screamingly funny but in dialect more influenced by Alabama than Spain, and the Bloomer Girls shocked us by being hard and businesslike and playing win-

ning ball as soon as their girl-pitcher had been relieved by
a man at the end of three innings.

I was going back, as I said, and I have been trying to
suggest what the town and the time were like forty years
ago in order to say how they have changed. I chose midsummer for my return because when I begin to think of
the town I think of it as it was in midsummer when the
maples in full leaf arched over South Main Street and
blobs of sunlight dropped through them to the dark asphalt. When I approached the hill that slants into the
street, I saw at its summit a black water tower—we all
called it the standpipe—that used to rise above a net of
gnarled and lichened limbs woven by an old apple orchard,
but that was gone and the black cylinder stood naked
now in a loneliness of no trees. Wondering if this might be
an omen, I was cheered by the sight of the maples still
sifting the sunlight and encouraged to believe that the
time I was remembering was waiting for me after all. It
was not until I reached the four corners where East and
West Avenues meet South Main that I knew this was not
to be. South Main had been a symbol of the town, and
those corners, austere in the dignity of massive houses set
back on green and level lawns, had been the symbol of
South Main.

But East and West Avenues are a part of a brick-paved
pike, called the Million Dollar Highway, and where the
Swan house had stood serene in the assurance of its red-
brick towers lay a wide cement-covered yard decorated only
by the garish protuberances of a gasoline station. The Shel-
don house, a brick box, was a reminder of things as they
had been, but set back on its spacious yard the huge white-

pillared Burrows house now offered small apartments for
rent. Across the street the dark-green Bruner house, elegant
with piazzas, bay window and staring cupola, had disappeared except for its foundations, which seemed pathetically small for the edifice that rested on them.

I lived in that house from 1901, when I was eight, until
I had graduated from college and found a job, and all my
hometown memories are bound to it. Behind its back yard,
big enough to play one old cat, lay Mrs. Bruner's rose garden with its fifty-three varieties of lush and fragrant blossoms. The bright determined old lady had reserved a
two-room apartment on the second floor and the satisfying
of her needs for scuttles of coal, library books, and groceries
was the source of much of my spending money. I rebuilt
on those pitiful foundation walls not merely the house itself but the time when I was picking pears on one of our
Bartlett trees and my father and I decided that rich skin-
flint Uncle Al, who had made a famous escape from Libby
Prison in the Civil War, would be more likely to give me
a farewell present if I stuck at my work instead of seeing
him off on the cars and I could still hear my father's laugh
as he reported the old man's tart "I was going to give Carl
a dollar if he'd come to the depot."

I reconstructed, too, the day before the high school dance
when my parents refused me money for flowers for my girl
and my best friend had his dozen florist's carnations packed
in two long green boxes so that I might deliver a dozen of
Mrs. Bruner's roses in one of them and not lose face with
Althea; the happy day when the Hamilton College Glee
Club came to sing a concert and my pretty mother was
gayer and prettier than I had ever seen her; and particularly
those Saturdays when, after mowing the lawn (now seem-

ing less limitless than then), Bobby Clarke—the wildest pitcher in Albion's baseball history—turned in a good game and won it with one tremendous swing that took the white ball up above the diamond's green and out against the blue sky and dropped it *plop!* into the yellow waters of the canal.

Of other big houses along South Main Street I found that the Sawyer house, once distinguished by striped awnings outside and darkly gleaming "Nubians" within, advertised for overnight guests; the Taylor house was a cafeteria; the Dye house was a funeral home; the Cornell house still boasted a lovely Georgian-colonial shell but sheltered equipment of a food company's laboratory. The Wage house was gone and its big barn, which once had sheltered the first horseless carriage in town, to the dismay of the occupants of nearby stalls, was now a restaurant and night club known as Marti's. Here a chromium-striped modernistic bar welcomes the patron, and behind it, dimly illumined by concealed but lurid red and blue lights, a huge booth-lined dance hall resounds to glittering juke boxes by day and name bands by night.

Looking into its dark depths I remembered a party I had attended only a few yards away when, after a rich old lady had died and left her money to her daughter, the daughter and her husband moved in and gave a ball that was rumored to have cost a fabulous thousand dollars. White crash had been tacked down over the precious carpets and, though others had employed them singly, it was the first time that both Teall's Caterers and Dossenbach's Orchestra had been imported from Rochester for the same affair. The guests had danced until four in the morning and all the children of the neighborhood had come the next afternoon to eat up the leftovers and dance to the gay fiddles of the Luttenton Brothers, who played behind the same palms that had partly concealed Dossenbach's tony musicians.

Perhaps that party was the beginning of Albion's metamorphosis; perhaps the change of the town's collective mind came later. Whatever the date of its origin, the differences, which must have occurred gradually, struck me with sudden force as such alterations always affect the returning who, aware of it or not, are seeking the good old days.

The time I was going back to meet and had probably idealized, perhaps even constructed from my affectionate imagination, was not waiting for me. It had died with the big houses. Albion had been contented and busy, but not ambitious. It had been easygoing, moving comfortably, stopping at times for the joy of contemplating itself with a not-too-smug narcissism. Separated from the nearest cities by long miles of fertile earth, it lived a rich independent life of its own. Today those same miles are short. Albion had been a country-minded town. Now it is a city-minded town.

You can tell the difference in many ways. The tailoring firm that had once displayed dark and sumptuous serges and broadcloths for men's suits is no more. Rochester is forty minutes away by motor and a suit by a city tailor has prestige woven into it. The select shops of Rochester's East Avenue sell certificates of respect from her neighbors to the Albion matron who buys their wares.

Grass grows on the half-mile track at the fairgrounds of the Orleans County Agricultural Association where the hoofs of trotters and pacers used to beat a fast tattoo and where the county farmers tried to beat each other in the "hitch-up and once around" races. The city of Batavia is only a half hour away and the crowds that speed every night of the summer season to pour dollars into the pari-mutuel windows at Batavia Downs include a surprisingly large percentage of Albion's population.

The County Fair—great folk festival of my youth—is now only a memory of a blaring midway filled with joy rides and tent shows, of dignified slow-moving cattle parades, of the "art department" filled with painted china and canvases depicting winter sunsets and forest fires, and trays of big apples polished until they blazed with light.

When the citizens of Albion cannot be lured into the cities, the cities come to the town. Some of the men who would in the old days have owned their own stores now work as employees of chain stores controlled in distant metropolitan offices. The canning factory, once owned by a man we used to see every day on the streets, is now a tremendous frozen-food "operation," property of a generous and paternalistic nothingness, a composite of many John Does—mostly city folk. The Saturday night gatherings in the drugstore at the corner of Bank and Main, where a man could get a sampling of his neighbors' opinions on matters that influenced their lives, have adjourned to the Town Club, where amid comfortable appointments ("like those of a city club") and the jangle of those gambling machines known as "one-armed bandits" the same kind of talk goes on.

Albion is a boom town now, alert, progressive, dynamic. It is about the same size as it was forty years ago, but it believes in growth as it never did then, and it will grow. It has a local "Committee of Economic Development," which was sponsored by the Albion Chamber of Commerce, and that committee has worked hard and with intelligence and foresight. Aided by the ladies of the Auxiliary of the American Legion, it made a recent survey of the postwar desires and plans of its citizens. Of the 600 families (out of a possible thousand) interviewed, 390 wanted automobiles, 336 wanted electric refrigerators, 225 wanted washing machines, 85 wanted to travel. A fifth of the factory workers preferred to do something else. Popular vocations were office and construction work, owning one's own business, keeping house. Farming was losing in favor. The survey indicated that two-thirds of the people were dissatisfied with the stores of the town. One out of every seven persons interviewed expressed a wish for a new industry in Albion.

The town has lived through a crisis. It saw death on the way as swift transportation, radio advertising, and recreational opportunities drew its people to the cities to buy. On the way to its own funeral, its hearse met the triumphal coach of returning prosperity as city industries decentralized and moved out to the towns.

There are disturbing factors. School attendance was reported by the survey to be losing in popularity among children old enough to have the choice of staying away. The Conversational Club has died and only the Historical Club, with but thirty members, remains. More than a third of the town's families are not sure that they want to continue to live there. The people are less interested in cultural activities. And the aisle of arching maples, which was the place where all could see the life of the town parading, is lined by fading ghosts of big houses. They are the symbols of the end of an epoch. They are now a liability, a handicap. The old shells must be replaced with ranch types and pre-fabs, more business must come with more money, a new cycle must be well begun, before the town can have time and inclination to build for itself another and a different cultural pattern.

It was raining when, after happy reunions, I drove south out of Albion. The traffic light at the corner was blinking and I remembered it was an arc light when we children used to watch for the man who changed the carbons so that we might capture the crayonlike used ones and draw smudgy pictures on the sidewalks.

As the green light snapped on it reached out into the dark to show a sudden veil of heavier rain sweeping toward the spot where our bay window had been and it made me remember the last time I saw Lon Whiteman. Lon had been a worshipful idol when I was seven and our acquaintance had been interrupted by the Carmers' moving from Dansville to Albion. My close association with the genial Lon, whom the president of the Pinkerton National Detective Agency once described as "beyond all question the

ablest criminal in the United States," had ended fittingly
on just such a black, windy, watery night and in that very
house. My parents, my sister, and I had just come from
the dinner table and were settling down for a comfortable
evening made cozy by the sound of rain on our windows
when the old crank bell on the front door rang a single
note.

My father went to answer while my mother wondered
who would be calling at such an hour on such a night and
my sister and I listened for the sound of voices.

"Perhaps it's a telegram," said my mother fearfully.

We soon knew this was no usual visitor, for my father's
loud and hearty voice seemed muted and the words of the
man who came into the hall at his bidding were indistinct,
high pitched, and strained. After perhaps two minutes,
which seemed longer, my father strode swiftly through the
living room where we sat and opened the door of our only
downstairs bedroom—our best guest room. As soon as he
had turned the knob a tall slim man wearing a dripping
dark topcoat and carrying in his right hand a dripping
derby walked swiftly from the hall door across the inter-
vening space and into the bedroom. My father immediately
closed the door, turned to us, and said:

"I'm going out for about ten minutes."

"What on earth are you thinking of?" said my mother.
"You'll catch your death. And who's that man and why
is he in our best guest room?"

"I'll be back in a few minutes," said my father.

"If you think you're going to leave us alone and unpro-
tected on a night like this with a strange man in the guest
room—"

"Minnie, shut up!" said father sharply, and we all knew

that when he said that something serious was going on and he was not to be annoyed or interrupted. We heard him putting on his rubbers and stomping his feet firmly into them in the hall and a moment later the front door opened and closed with a bang.

"I know who it is," I said with the triumphant assurance of an eleven-year-old taking part in grown-up affairs.

"Who?" said my mother.

"It's Lon," I said. "Lon Whiteman."

My mother's blue eyes went wide open and round with surprise. A muscle in her chin tautened.

"I'm going in there to see him," I said.

"You'll do nothing of the sort. You and your sister take your books and go upstairs at once. You can read in your rooms."

"What about you?" said my sister Katharine.

"I'm coming too."

It was a half hour before my father returned. We heard his loud tramp into the hall and the drop of each of his rubbers. In a moment his kindly, deep voice was coming up from the guest room. After a short pause we heard him say good night and plod up the stairs.

I went to the door of my room and looked out. My sister was peeking too. As soon as father went in where mother was, we both tiptoed down the hall and listened.

"Is it really Lon?"

"Yes," said my father firmly. "It's Lon."

"Oh, Willis," said my mother despairingly.

"He graduated from Hamilton the year before I entered," said my father defensively. "Besides, there's not a family in Dansville that wouldn't do what we've done."

"But we're not living in Dansville any more. We're in

Albion and people here won't understand. Why did you go out?"

"I had to let the presidents of the two banks know—and I couldn't phone from the living room where he could hear me."

"It'll be all over town in the morning—and you the superintendent of schools."

"Goddam it, Minnie. I couldn't turn him away on a night like this."

"Well," said my mother coldly, "if you're going to swear at me I will say no more."

3

The Next Happiest Man in the World

DANSVILLE IS, NEXT TO LON WHITEMAN, THE MAIN character in this story. It is the kind of upstate town that makes people say, when they drive through it on their busy way to Corning or Elmira or Binghamton, "When I quit business this is the kind of little place I'd like to live in." Actually Dansville has some thriving businesses of its own and has always been reasonably alert and industrious. Its inhabitants look upon it as unique but few other people think it is. Set in the center of it you would not, without the aid of place signs, be able to distinguish it from hundreds of other York State towns of about the same size.

The Next Happiest Man in the World

Its lawns are level and green in summer, snowy and white in winter. Its houses are solid and comfortable—some more impressive than others, none more impressive than the turreted, red-brick mansion decorated with white stone trim and wrought iron, known for years as the Whiteman house. Many of the present residents are descendants of the town's first settlers and names that I still remember after leaving it a half century ago aid in suggesting the town's quality—Fielder, Edwards, Dyer, Snider, Sweet, Ward, De Long, Rowe, Woolever, Oberdorf, Burgess, Hedges, Klink, Bastian, Bunnell, Woodruff, Crisfield, Readshaw, Welch, Brettle.

I am describing the town in a little detail because, as I have said, it is a character in a story—a kind of composite or mass character—but definitely to be considered as a unit, a human unit. I do not suppose that it recognized itself as a character until gossip about a Dansville youth began trickling back from Hamilton College in the late 1870's. The townfolk had always thought Lon Whiteman a real nice boy and smart—gosh all hemlock, he was smart. His cleverness was no more than was to be expected though. Everybody looked on Lon's father, Reuben Whiteman, as maybe the town's first citizen. He was a first-rate farmer, he'd built a paper mill and made it into a going concern, he owned thousands of acres of midwestern real estate growing in value every day. He was, moreover, a simple God-fearing man, regular in attendance at the Lutheran church, pious in speech, humbly Christian in manner.

His wife was just as religious, though she was a Methodist and would not give up her faith to follow that of her husband. She was a busy church worker, an intelligent, modest, affectionate woman, a sweet woman whose smiles

and thoughtful actions made her a leader in Dansville social circles. Sometimes she had sort of absent-minded fits
of picking up things she was attracted to in the Dansville
stores and hurrying home with them without going through
the formalities of actually buying them; but Reuben
Whiteman had told the tradesmen to watch her and send
him the bill for what she took, and so whenever on in-
ventory day something was missing it usually was listed
on Mrs. Whiteman's bill and promptly paid for.

After Lon had prepared for college at the Geneseo Nor-
mal School, ten miles down the valley of the Genesee, the
Dansville neighbors were pleased when his parents sent
him to Hamilton—a fine old-fashioned college of Presbyterian origin where boys were drilled in the Bible, the
Greek and Latin classics, and especially in public speaking. It would have a good influence on Lon, they said to
each other, and Lon was beginning to need a good influence. There had been a good many chuckles down at
Gambles's Blacksmith Shop and around the hot stove at
Bailey's Hardware Store about his climbing out of his window after his strict parents had gone to sleep, to join the
all-night poker games of the Dansville fast set. A boy as
smart as Lon couldn't help being bored cooped up in his
room at night. At Hamilton those brains of his would get
some real exercise. He wasn't really a bad boy. He didn't
smoke and he didn't drink and he went to church and
Sunday school every Sunday.

But the story that came back from Clinton, seat of
Hamilton College, as the town was at that time always
described, was enough to shake the town into conscious-
ness of the emergence of its individuality. Apparently in
the respectable bosoms of conservative Dansville dwelt an

appetite for the picaresque and it was soon to be whetted by a taste of joys to come.

Seated at a table on the second floor of the old Butterfield House in Utica, John Bender and Con O'Brien, notorious in the eastern states, happily contemplated the ideal gull of the criminal gambler—a rich college boy with pretensions to slickness. As the fall of the cards continued, however, the careful arrangements of the older men to separate freshman Alonzo J. Whiteman from his money went steadily awry. No matter what exceptional groupings they held, the boy held sequences declared more favorable by the laws of poker. At the end of a particularly disastrous hand when the collegian gathered in a sum that set his total winnings at over $3,000, Con O'Brien casually gathered the cards and suddenly turned them face up on the table. Like so many eyes, six aces stared up at him.

"Out the window with him," said Con, and the two criminals advanced on Lon.

"After you," said Lon politely and drew a revolver. "Suppose we go down by the steps."

Holding the gun at their backs, the young man marched his victims into the street and to the most elegant restaurant in the city. In the safety of its dining room he returned the gun to his pocket and ordered for them and himself the best dinner the place afforded. After the brandy he paid the bill and said a courteous good night, and the three went their separate ways—John eventually to life imprisonment at Auburn for a killing in Utica; Con, "King of the Green Goods Men" and "Greatest Bunco Steerer in the World," to an unmarked grave on Devil's Island for the murder of a pal in a Paris railroad station; Lon to a destiny to be here described.

The Next Happiest Man in the World

Though Alonzo J. Whiteman had graduated from Hamilton a year before my father entered in 1881, the tales of his college exploits, many doubtless of folk origin, still delight its undergraduates. They tell how he "busted" the bank at Dink Davis's famous faro game in Utica and used the funds so obtained and others as ill-gotten to defray the college expenses of worthy college mates (particularly fraternity brothers in DKE) who were preparing for the ministry; how he submitted one of Emerson's essays to his English professor as his own and was flunked on it; how he wrote home in handwriting purporting to be that of one of his instructors asking for funds for a worthy educational purpose and when the money was forthcoming intercepted the faculty mail and abstracted the money. When his rich and pious old father knelt to pray for the regeneration of his son the object of the petition bent down to pluck from an exposed hip pocket a bulging wallet, acquire most of its contents, and return it unobserved to its previous situation. Though his grades were not exceptional, he found time from his intercollegiate poker contests, which rendered "Dekes" at Cornell and Syracuse continuously fundless, to write for the *Hamilton Literary Magazine*, to sing in a quartet, to be a prize orator, to be treasurer of a political club devoted to the interests of Samuel J. Tilden, and to superintend the schedule of the baseball team in a costume sartorially so remarkable as to win him citation from the Utica *Observer* as "Noblest manager in the country."

When Alonzo J. Whiteman received his first degree from Hamilton College his father gave him a check for ten thousand dollars and sent him to Columbia University Law School for a brief period. Apparently Alonzo, whom later events proved to be naturally gifted as a lawyer, found this dull and his father ordered him to Duluth, Minnesota, where he knew, from profitable experience, the real estate business was booming. The old man must have been proud of his judgment and of his son in the three years of life that were left him, for in that period Alonzo amassed a fortune in the pine lands and dock holdings of the "Zenith City of the Unsalted Seas," achieved the Vice-presidency of Kitchi Gammi, the town's one exclusive men's club, and won a seat in the State Senate, the only Democrat and the youngest candidate who had up to that time been elected to that body. Exultant Hamilton awarded him an Honorary M.A. and after commencement, where only the opposition of the distinguished Elihu Root prevented his being elected a member of the college board of trustees, he returned to exultant Dansville to make the Fourth of July oration and to tell his father that he had made his first million. Rich, powerful, and the "most popular young man in Minnesota," he wrote to his classmates, "I like politics. It is a luxury, however, and from a financial standpoint is not profitable."

Alonzo's mother received the bulk of her husband's million-dollar estate when he died in 1888. Senator Whiteman received $60,000 in cash and felt himself prosperous enough to marry the wellborn daughter of a Civil War general and to indulge in running for a seat in the national House of Representatives on the Democratic ticket. Realizing that he was pitted against a skilled and able Republican, the clever young man persuaded unambitious and pessimistic Kittel Halvorson to be a candidate for the same office on the ticket of the Farmers' Alliance, thus splitting the Republican vote and assuring, he believed, his own election. Whiteman twice contributed sizable sums to Halvorson's campaign fund and, when the gloomy Swede tried to retire from the race a few days before election, persuaded him not to do so. Halvorson was elected by less than two hundred votes.

Humiliating defeat obviously had a searing psychological effect on the young political genius. He had reached his turning point. Society had rejected him—let society beware. Bad luck dogged him. His wife obtained a divorce, he lost every bet at the races and the gaming tables and his last dollar on the Chicago Board of Trade. He had left only his salary as a Duluth bank employee.

Out of the East at urgent invitation came Robert Knox, Hamilton '81, son of an Elmira Presbyterian minister, Alonzo J. Whiteman's best friend in college and after. The mere statement of this information won him hearty welcome and unlimited credit at the Kitchi Gammi. The town's blooded blades were cursing their luck at the club's tables and Whiteman and Knox were explaining apologetically that in all their years of playing together they had never held such successful cards when, as on a memorable previous occasion, a skeptic turned up the cards. This time there was no gunplay. Knox left town, Whiteman resigned, and club members tried to suppress the scandal.

Soon letters to Whiteman from Bob Knox and his attractive young wife, daughter of a minister in Bath, New York, began arriving in Duluth from Mexico City. They were buying jewelry and had given the jeweler drafts on the bank where Alonzo was working. The drafts were honored and, as they expected, the jeweler was growing more and more friendly and trusting. Now was the moment. Bob was to purchase diamonds valued at $20,000 with a draft on the bank and the Knoxes were to dash for the border. Alonzo was to delay refusing the draft until his accomplices had had enough time to reach the north side of the Rio Grande. The beginnings of the plan worked beautifully. The jeweler pressed the glittering stones upon the charming Knoxes and accepted the draft with Latin ardor. Whiteman postponed refusing it as long as he dared. But neither he nor the Knoxes had foreseen the delays of travel in sunny, sleepy Mexico. The gem-laden fugitives were still south of the border when officers overtook them. For the next few years the Sigma Phi fraternity at Hamilton sent food packages to Brother Bob Knox and his bride, who had tired, after their first meal at their enforced residence, of Mexican prison fare.

At his trial in Mexico City, Bob Knox testified that he and his wife were honest folk who had been led astray by the smooth talk of an experienced sharper named Alonzo J. Whiteman. This in no way alienated the affection of the man whom he accused and Lon worked untiringly for the release of his friends. Annie Knox was freed in six months and Bob at the end of a year. For the next thirty years of arrests and trials, each of the two college chums charged the other whenever the occasion seemed to call for it with being the cause of his downfall.

In the year of the Mexican debacle (1892), Lon left Dansville, where he had taken up residence with his mother after Duluth became unfriendly, for a few days of gambling at the Sheepshead Bay Race Track. Already apparently he was a marked man, for on his way back to his hotel he was accosted by William A. Pinkerton of the famous agency. The detective suggested that Whiteman had sent a telegram to Joe Ullman, bookmaker at the track, directing him to pay three hundred dollars to Alonzo J. Whiteman and had signed it with the name of a rich owner of a racing stable. Whiteman admitted that he had got the money by this forgery and Pinkerton was about to arrest him when he added casually that he had stolen and burned the bogus telegram, destroying all proof of his crime.

In the following months, whenever Lon left the quiet dignity of his mother's home for the gayer life of the leading American race tracks he paid his way with drafts that were not worth the paper on which they were written. A handsome, winning man of gracious manners and reserved good taste in dress, he won the confidence of whatever company he chose to adorn. He neither drank alcoholic liquors nor smoked tobacco and from his blue eyes emanated a friendly and amused light that attracted all the people of background and culture among whom he moved. When talk of his illegal activities grew annoying he suggested to his mother that he was being persecuted by his enemies, particularly the Pinkertons, and that a year or so in Europe would be advisable. She gladly paid his way and a Dansville Bank was soon thereafter explaining embarrassedly to a similar London institution that the draft for £700, which a British cashier had honored at the request of an American who was obviously a rich man of affairs, was drawn upon an account that did not exist.

Before Scotland Yard could find the engaging stranger, a young couple, obviously English by their dress and speech and more obviously on their honeymoon, entered a jewelry shop in Paris and made a few inexpensive purchases which they paid for. A few days later, to the delight of the proprietor, they returned to his shop and selected a bauble worth many thousands of francs. The young man, whose name had been recognized by the owner of the shop as that of a popular member of the British Parliament, offered a draft for the required payment written on a check which bore the imprint of that name. Before an embarrassed M.P. in London could explain to many pained owners of the more exclusive shops of Paris that his checkbook had recently been purloined and that he had not recently visited the continent, Alonzo J. Whiteman had sailed for New York. He was met at the pier by officers who arrested him for an alleged forgery committed in San Francisco.

Held in the Tombs awaiting a hearing on extradition to California, Alonzo wrote a letter home and to the rescue rushed Sheriff McNeill of Livingston County with a warrant from a Dansville justice of the peace charging his fellow townsman with perjury in a civil case. This device only temporarily delayed removal to California. There, after conviction and a sentence of ten years, Whiteman obtained a new trial and as his own counsel defended himself so ably that he was acquitted.

Three years later the New York *Times* for March 7, 1897, was moved to publish the following headline:

He Started In His Life With Bright Prospects
But Is Now Accused of Many Crimes—The Story
That He Tells In His Own Defense.

Beneath these words the *Times* reported a crime so thoughtfully engineered that it has been hailed generally by police officers and private detectives as a Whiteman masterpiece. On February 21 a gentleman of prepossessing manner, well dressed and obviously prosperous, stepped into the Columbia Bank at 501 Fifth Avenue and said that he wished to open an account. When received by the proper official he introduced himself as Dr. J. H. Williams, a physician of Brooklyn, and said that since he was moving his practice to Manhattan and opening an office on West 40th Street he would like to transfer his account from the National City Bank of the city across the river. He presented a check for $3,700, which was gratefully received, and left.

Since banks were closed on Friday, the 22nd, Washington's Birthday, and on Saturday and Sunday as well, three whole days had elapsed when the distinguished-looking depositor appeared at the cashier's window of the Columbia Bank on Monday morning. He first asked for a safe-deposit box and the courteous employee guided him to the vaults of the American Savings Bank. On the way he asked to be introduced to the teller of that bank and the three men spent a cordial few minutes before the Columbia cashier went back to his bank. Soon the genial doctor reappeared at his window, this time with a check for $580. Since his account was now several days old and its owner was so evidently trustworthy, the cashier paid out the money without realizing that the transfer could not yet have been made. Shortly after the doctor left, however, the cashier lifted his telephone receiver to hear an excited bank officer sputter that no one named J. H. Williams had ever had an account at the Brooklyn National City.

There was no doubt in the minds of the high-ranking New York and Pinkerton detectives when they met in the next few minutes at the Columbia Bank. This was a Whiteman job. No other criminal would have had the ingenuity to plan it, the courage and savoir-faire to complete it. The Pinkertons, who were employed by the American Bankers Association, were represented by the agency's assistant superintendent, George S. Dougherty, who immediately furnished a photograph of a handsome man wearing rimless eyeglasses and a drooping mustache. The frantic cashier said yes that was the man.

A general alarm at once disclosed that a gentleman answering Alonzo Whiteman's description had spent several February evenings happily playing cards and pool at a fashionable hotel in nearby Lakewood, New Jersey, using as his initial stake money he borrowed from willing guests. But from Dansville, good old loyal Dansville, came the dismaying information that Lon had been living there continuously for a considerable period.

"This charge is merely one of a number that have been made against me by Pinkerton detectives as the result of a conspiracy to persecute me," said Whiteman to the reporter from the *Times*. . . . "I considered the actions and persecutions of the Pinkertons so outrageous that a few months ago I published a small book (*The Great Conspiracy*) giving a history of these charges and cases with the opinions and decisions of the court. The truth told in this book nettled the Pinkertons. . . . Now as to this latest arrest. I knew nothing of this charge until this morning when the detective arrested me as I left the ferryboat from Hoboken. I have been in Dansville for six weeks. . . . I will prove easily that on the dates I am charged with being at that bank I was hundreds of miles away from this city. I have never been convicted of any crime and every charge that has been made against me has been trumped up by the Pinkertons. . . . I have too much at stake to indulge in the petty tricks and schemes with which they have charged me."

As the true facts are now pieced together (and even the Dansville witnesses to his alibi eventually came to believe them), Lon Whiteman took a night sleeper from Hoboken to Dansville on the evening of the day he got the money from the Columbia Bank (the 25th). The First Methodist Episcopal Church of Dansville, his mother's church, was giving a church "Bazaar and Entertainment" that very night. Lon was on the streets of Dansville early the next morning.

"Fine program, last night," he was saying. "Enjoyed every minute of it. And that talk by Reverend Sykes—you'd have to go far to find a better one."

When the good preacher himself walked downtown, whom should he run into but the son of his most faithful and generous parishioner, Mrs. Whiteman, and the younger man hailed him with respectful delight and went over his speech at the bazaar sentence by sentence, approving it heartily. Buying rolls at the baker's, Lon had said, "Fine warm day for the twenty-fourth of February, isn't it?" and the baker had put "Feb. 24" on the sales slip which he later produced as irrefutable evidence of Lon's whereabouts on that date. By the end of the day, Lon had referred to the events of yesterday so knowingly and so often that he had performed the most difficult kind of mesmerism, a gradual mass hypnosis upon Dansville. So, on March 6, when the town received the shocking news that its favorite son had been indicted for a crime committed at about 10:30 A.M. in New York City on February 24, there was hardly a citizen who did not honestly believe that he had seen Lon in Dansville that day. And

since there were no New York to Dansville trains from
10:30 A.M. until evening, Lon could not possibly be guilty.

With cries of honest moral indignation Dansville rallied
to defend a Dansville boy. In America a man was innocent until proved guilty, wasn't he? Lon had had hard luck
all right but he'd never been convicted of anything, had
he? And since even the beloved Pastor Sykes had seen him
at the bazaar, those smart Pinkertons couldn't use one of
his good Methodist congregation as a scapegoat for their
own inefficiency—not by a jugful. When Lon's lawyers
sent up to Dansville for witnesses to prove his alibi they
could have had most of the town if they'd been willing to
pay expenses. And the trial came out just as his Dansville
friends said it would. Indeed, so good was his fortune that
it almost seemed as if the New York district attorney had
been bewitched into incredible errors.

The reminiscences of the one still living witness, Pierre
Ward, who lives in Geneseo now and seems much too
young to have been there, and the published memoirs of
Detective Dougherty agree as to the main goings-on. The
prosecution made out a good case for a while. The cashier
of the Columbia Bank identified Lon and won the undying
enmity of all Dansvillians. The Pinkertons told why they
were sure the forger was Whiteman and they gave good
reasons.

But as the court was adjourned for lunch, the prosecuting attorney left his desk. Lon saw that it had not been
cleared of several samples of his own writing and surmised
these would be used to prove that the forged check for
$580 was in the same hand. He therefore persuaded his
own attorney to write out some copies of these writings
and add them to the collection. After lunch, a great hand-

writing expert, called as a witness for the prosecution, swore that the questioned check and all the writings on the table were written by the same hand, thus destroying at one and the same time much of the state's case and his own career as an authority.

The kindly Methodist preacher had his firm say, and so did the Dansville undertaker, the mayor, and a sweet yellow-haired young girl. And just to make assurance doubly sure, as if fatefully compelled, the district attorney asked a quiet, reserved Dansville man *why* he felt so sure he had seen Lon on February 24.

"Did you say 'why do I know'?" asked the man.

"Yes," said the district attorney, remembering with a sinking sensation that most books on trial procedures advise strongly against letting down one's guard with such a question.

"I was in the telegraph office sending a wire to my sick brother when the telegrapher gave me a message that my brother had died," said the man. "I started home to tell my mother and outside on the street I met Lon."

The jurors were obviously impressed with the truth of this pathetic statement and there is little doubt that the witness himself believed it. Whiteman was acquitted and, according to a generally accepted story of the time, immediately threatened the Columbia Bank with a suit for false arrest which that institution avoided by paying him $3,000.

This successful crime set a pattern on which Alonzo J. Whiteman worked successfully for the next few years. Though living quietly in the elegantly furnished brick house in Dansville, he was the busiest criminal in the

United States. While the number of his crimes mounted, police and courts alike grew nervous, cross, testy. Occasionally Lon made a vacation trip to New York.

"In court yesterday," said the New York *Times* for May 30, 1899, "there were representations from the Stewart, the Tuxedo, the Cadillac, Martin's, Burn's, Shanley's, the Murray Hill and other hotels and restaurants mulcted by Whiteman. . . . Whiteman was arraigned Sunday morning before Magistrate Pool and was held in $500 bail for examination at 9:00 A.M. yesterday. . . . When his name was called there was no response. It was called again and again and still there was no response. Then Detective Reidy excitedly turned to Magistrate Pool and said:

" 'I warned you yesterday that if you let that man go he would make good his escape.'

" 'You did not tell me anything of the kind,' said Magistrate Pool. . . .

" 'I tried to tell you . . . but you wouldn't listen to me.'

" 'I don't care a damn what you told me,' shouted the Magistrate."

Six months later it developed that Whiteman had mixed business with pleasure on his Maytime holiday. Posing as W. L. How, cashier of a bank at Lawrence, New York, he had stopped in at the offices of Maverick and Wissinger, lithographers, of 176 Fulton Street and ordered 10,000 drafts bearing the imprint "National Bank of Lawrence" made up into checkbooks. He paid cash for these and ordered them sent to him, "Care of Mrs. Whiteman" at Dansville. One of these books became detached from the shipment and dropped from a ferry into the North River on its way to Dansville by way of the Delaware and Lackawanna Station at Hoboken. A ferryboat dockhand picked up the soggy mass and, apparently of a deeply suspicious nature, sent it to the Pinkertons. The Fulton Street lithographers gave the detectives a description that all of them had known "by heart" for many years. Anticrime forces waited anxiously for something to happen.

It happened at Woonsocket, Rhode Island, on October 3 of the same year. A bank there paid $3,000 on a worthless draft for $10,000 drawn on the National Bank of Lawrence, Lawrence, Kansas. Once more to quote the New York *Times*, the issue of November 15, 1899:

"Four out of five members of what is declared by police to be the most accomplished and successful gang of bank swindlers in the country are locked up at Police Headquarters in this city. The fifth man of the quintet is a prisoner in Pittsburgh. . . . The police say the proof of their guilt is so complete that the only question is where they shall be punished for their crimes as prison doors are yawning for them in many states. The leader of the gang in the opinion of the police is Alonzo J. Whiteman, ex-senator. . . . He has been arrested innumerable times and at least twice has been convicted and sentenced but his extraordinary cleverness, for which the police give him full credit, has stood him in good stead and he has never yet worn a convict's stripes."

Despite New York police claims, Whiteman was extradited to Chicago to answer a charge of having swindled the Grand Pacific Hotel out of $250. As soon as he arrived there he gave the Chicago *Times-Herald* reporter an interview:

"Most of the stories about me are ridiculous. Every morning after I am arrested I read accounts in the papers and make up my mind if I get off with a life sentence I will be lucky. . . . If I have committed all these crimes . . . why is it I am brought a thousand miles to answer to a misdemeanor instead of being convicted somewhere for a felony? . . .

"For the last fourteen months I have been living quietly with my mother and sister in Dansville, New York, and the police . . . as well as the Pinkerton people knew where I was . . . they would not have troubled me had I not been with a man named Knox for whom they had a warrant."

The "man named Knox" was extradited to Pittsburgh, Pennsylvania, where police were clamoring for him, convicted of forgery, and sentenced. But when, in a few years, he was eligible for parole, the story is that a New York lawyer who said he was a member of the Empire State legislature, appeared at Harrisburg before the parole board and spoke so movingly of his client's distinguished and pious family, his long connection with the church, the high regard in which he was held by his Hamilton College classmates, the sincerity of his repentance, that release on probation was a foregone conclusion. Soon the convict and his champion, said to have been a tall, slim, clerical-looking man whose costume included a frock coat, striped pants and rimless eyeglasses, were on a dining car bound happily for New York and its better restaurants.

In the meantime, Whiteman was busy amassing and spending considerable sums and, not without pride, contributing to the Alonzo J. Whiteman legend. On a visit to his old western haunts, according to report, he persuaded a Denver bank to cash a large check in gold coins, which he placed in two leather valises. As he was walking to the railroad station, a bag in each hand, he was overtaken by two detectives but had enough presence of mind to heave both burdens into an alley. The two officers dashed for the money and Whiteman dashed for the train. Locked in a hotel room in Montana for nonpayment of his bill, he rang for a bellboy, seized and tied him, and walked out, a free man, in a rather tight uniform.

A dispatch from Boston published in New York read: "A pathetic scene was enacted in the Superior Court this afternoon when the mother of Alonzo J. Whiteman pleaded with Judge Bell to give her 'boy' another chance. . . . She was alone in the world, she said, with no companion on the old farm in Dansville and wanted the court to let her son go back with her. 'Oh, your Honor, I ask for your clemency and mercy,' she exclaimed. 'I have talked with my boy and he has promised faithfully to change. I know he is sincere. At last he sees himself in his true light and he is ashamed. Give him a chance, Sir, I beg of you.' " Three days later the accused was placed on probation.

Charged with swindling at Binghamton, New York, Whiteman told the judge that he had repented and had become an evangelist. The work of the Lord would be interrupted if His servant were obliged to serve time in prison. Sentence being again suspended, he actually made a tour of the towns around Binghamton as an evangelist and was so articulate, rhetorical, and obviously sincere that many came down the aisle to grasp his hand and sit in the pews of the repentant. Unhappily a good Presbyterian sister was so impressed with his work that she entrusted to his keeping some $4,000 from the funds of her church and his eloquent nightly pleas to the sinful were silenced by his absence from south central New York State.

At about this time (1901) Eddie Burke and Sol Leichenstein, well-known bookies at the Saratoga track, received in the second week of the racing season identical telegrams reading "John Kerr deposited this day to your credit $300" and signed "Bank of Amsterdam." Though neither of them could remember a John Kerr, they were satisfied that the wire was authentic and, on receipt of a wire signed by that name directing them to place the money on a certain horse and their winnings, if any, on another, they complied. Both horses won. Two days later, Mr. Kerr, a very prepossessing gentleman, appeared and collected in all something over $1,700 from the bookies. A week later each received a wire informing him that $500 had been deposited to his account, again signed "Bank of Amsterdam" and a later wire directing the wagering of the money. "Why not wire the bank? Maybe you're betting against wind," said Burke's cashier. The Bank of Amsterdam answered that it held no such accounts, and William A. Pinkerton, chief of the Western Division of the famous agency, at once identified the swindle as one that could have been planned only by Alonzo J. Whiteman.

"Honest John" Kelly, finding an old friend who had lost thousands at his tables temporarily embarrassed, gave Whiteman $300 with which to make good a bad check. Whiteman was effusively grateful, promised to pay back the debt, asked for the gambler's card. Some time later he came to Kelly's Long Branch, New Jersey, gambling house and used the card to obtain credit from the manager. Having lost $2,000 in a few minutes, he gave a worthless check for the amount, then won $1,100 and departed with it.

The class records of the Class of 1881 of Hamilton College have the following notation under the date 1902: "A. J. W. Dansville, N.Y. Whiteman writes that he is living quietly at Dansville and is well and happy. Decoration Day orator. Elected Superintendent of the Methodist Sunday School last April."

By this time the criminal organization that Whiteman had been building had reached the height of its effectiveness. None of its members had been particularly well known to the police before he cast them in their respective roles but Pinkertons and police alike were in agreement that they were putting on frequent and perfect performances. Whiteman planned the crimes and took care of all legal complications. Bob Knox, now a gentle, well-dressed, glib widower, was the best "scratcher" in the country, and elderly, benign, corpulent, confidence-inspiring Charles Stewart, alias Charles Ward, was the "layer-down" who presented the checks at cashiers' windows. There were occasional other members of the organization but these were the debonair three on whom success most often depended.

The amount they mulcted from the banks, hotels, and race tracks of the United States has been variously estimated. Herbert Asbury in the *American Mercury* for September, 1915, while Whiteman was still alive, reckoned their illegal gains in ten years at "between one and five million dollars of which Whiteman got and spent the major portion." This is probably an exaggeration, though court records show them to have taken many thousands a year from the 8,000 member-institutions of the American Bankers Association. The chief of San Francisco police told a reporter, "Whiteman is probably the cleverest forger and confidence man living. He feloniously obtains more money from banks than any thief in his class that I know of, and he is polished enough to deceive anyone." The Chicago

Record-Herald reported him as having stolen "upwards of a million dollars."

It was during the middle years of this decade that I knew Lon, as almost everybody in Dansville called him. Reminiscences are tricky and colored by hindsight but I believe I recall that his manner with children was confidential and charming, that he never talked down to them but met them as equals, that he frequently stopped to chat with them, particularly on the many occasions when he walked out from 35 Elizabeth Street with his sweet, elderly mother. Though I was very young (we moved from Dansville to Albion when I was seven), his hearty voice and genuine manner definitely attracted me—the more so for my having heard my elders whisper about him or talk forthrightly of the outrageous persecution to which that band of tough city detectives, the Pinkertons, subjected him. There was about Lon a glamorous aura that gave his neighbors an intuitive affection for him and Dansvillians preferred to trust their intuitions about a friend whom they had known, man and boy, for forty years, rather than such vague accusations as his outsmarted enemies, desperate for proof, might bring against him. The impression he made upon me must have been very strong or I would not have been able to tell my mother who he was when, in Albion four years after I had last seen him, he asked my father for shelter. I still recall my bitter disappointment when I dashed downstairs the next morning and found that he had risen early and left without breakfast. I remember, too, that my father made an anxious tour of the Albion banks and seemed much relieved at noon when he reported to us that our guest had not visited them. Our family never saw Lon again.

The Next Happiest Man in the World

It was natural that law-enforcement officers and the press of other towns should resent Dansville's loyalty to its notorious resident and comment on it. This thoroughly pleased the people of the community. When a big city newspaper, the San Francisco *Examiner*, devoted a whole paragraph to their attitude they felt important. "Lon's putting Dansville on the map," they said, and read the paragraph aloud to all visitors:

"The people of Dansville absolutely refuse, men, women, and children, to believe that Whiteman is a swindler or a criminal in any way. They claim that detectives are hounding him to death. In Dansville Whiteman is as free to walk the streets as any man that ever lived. There the people would stick by him through thick and thin."

Even when detectives were searching for him and broadsides were being distributed throughout the nation stating that he was "wanted," Lon was a welcome visitor in many of the quiet, elegantly furnished homes of Dansville's first citizens. His anecdotes were the delight of their Victorian parlors, his travel talks instructive and amusing, his charities generous, his church work ardent. He was considerate of servants and of poor people, a free spender, a hard worker in good causes. He frequently borrowed money from his neighbors, meticulously returning it in brand-new bills. "He makes it," they used to say, but only as a joke because they resented any serious implications of his dishonesty.

Even the few Dansville people who had not known Lon well had a feeling of understanding and sympathy for him, a feeling that has persisted. The townspeople spoke of him, as they do now, as of a child, stressing the good points and ignoring others not so good. The sophisticated would laugh a little and say things you can hear in the streets of the town today—"There would be more crooks if they could be as smart as Lon" or "He was born just as goddam crooked as he was smart," while the innocent would declare, "In spite of all the talk, a fine man" or "If he had only put his brain to something worth while he could have been President of the United States."

Few speakers could outdo Lon on a patriotic occasion and he was much in demand to declaim appropriate truisms at holiday "exercises." He also uttered many an aphorism in the semiprivacy of Dansville's card parlors and poolrooms (he was an excellent billiard player). These were, and are, happily passed about as samples of his worldly wisdom:

"Be liberal in prosperity, it brings good returns."

"I never knew a man to win a pot by laying down his hand."

"When you see trouble is inevitable, meet it halfway and you have it half beaten."

The epitome of his philosophy, however, was contained in a teaching he repeated more often than any other:

"The happiest man in the world is the man who wins a bet. The next happiest is the man who loses."

To the people of Dansville and the whole valley of the Genesee Lon had become, for his own lifetime and thereafter, a folk hero to be remembered and loved. "He never crooked a friend," they said, and their grandsons say the same. "You could always lend him money and get it back."

It was easy for the storekeepers of the little town to spot strangers and when they did word was passed along.

"Couple of suspicious-looking characters got off the after-supper train last night, Lon."

The Next Happiest Man in the World

Lon always thanked his friends gravely and kept to the house until somebody stopped by to say that the detectives had gone. The grocers and butchers—and the visiting detectives too—always knew when Lon was hiding out at home because his mother would be coming to the stores to order delicacies foreign to her own simple tastes—sweetbreads, mushrooms, caviar. Lon was not self-conscious about his arrests or convictions, never hesitating to speak of them frankly and to tell friends he was relieved to be out of jail and glad to be back home. As an undergraduate he had once been attentive to a charming girl from Perry, near Dansville, at a Hamilton prom. Years later, when she was a distinguished matron, she saw her now notorious old beau coming toward her and ducked down a side street but to no avail. "Well, May," he said, "have you done something you're ashamed of that you can't speak to an old friend?"

It is a commonplace now in Western York State to say of Lon "He never got his comeuppance until he operated in home territory. If he'd kept on working the New York City banks he'd have been O.K." His neighbors had not minded his activities in Binghamton—that was reasonably near the Pennsylvania line. But getting busy in Buffalo—that was pitting his wits against folks as smart as he was and therefore dangerous.

When, in September of 1904, newspapers reported the arrest of Alonzo J. Whiteman in St. Louis, no one who read them, except possibly the Pinkertons, considered the incident more than routine. The Chicago *Sunday Record-Herald* gave the Whiteman story a full-page Sunday feature treatment but many American city papers were doing the same thing about once a year. It said that Lon was wanted in over forty cities including, besides thirty-three in the United States, Vienna, Paris, Marseilles; and in England—London, Southampton, Exeter and Manchester. He had been arrested, the story said, 43 times, indicted 27 times, convicted and sentenced 11 times to a total of 51 years and had so far been incarcerated a total of 12 months.

Whiteman had been on the way to the St. Louis World's Fair exhibits when arrested in the company of a girl whose name, he gallantly asked, be withheld. "She is young and innocent," he said, "and knows nothing of my history." Two detectives were sent to bring him to Buffalo for trial. Lon must have had a premonition of the fate that awaited him, for he now performed the uncharacteristic and violent feat that resulted in scare headlines in most of America's city newspapers and caused the conservative New York *Times* to exclaim: "There has never been such a man, outside of fiction, in the bank swindling game."

The train stopped in the September twilight at Dunkirk, New York, pleasant little Lake Erie city south of Buffalo. The detectives and "Lonny," as they had come to call him out of mingled exasperation and affection, walked up and down the station platform to break the tedium of their almost completed journey. At the cry of "All Aboard" they reboarded the train, Whiteman in the lead. "Suddenly as he reached the door of the stateroom," said the Buffalo *Evening Telegraph* on the next day, "he sprang inside, slammed the door shut, caught the spring lock and dived headfirst through the window.

"There was a shower of splintered glass and the forger was seen rolling down the embankment beside the track. A moment later he was seen to spring to his feet, wave his hand jauntily to the detectives and disappear in the bushes at the side of the road."

Women in the car fainted, and the frantic detectives demanded that the train be stopped, but Conductor Rogers unsympathetically refused to give the order because the train was carrying United States mails on a fast schedule.

With frayed tempers the frustrated Pinkertons began again their search for the man against whom, patiently and ably, they had built up a case calculated to end his criminal career. Their handbill, distributed throughout the country, began with the adjuration "ARREST ALONZO J. WHITEMAN," and after reporting his escape and describing his physical appearance, said that at the time he made his highly publicized jump he was "dressed in a dark frock coat, striped trousers and a straw hat."

Rumors flooded the country. The fugitive had been seen in the West, in the South. A Philadelphia paper reported that he had left the city on the steamship *Noordland* but that police had not found this out until the ship had passed the breakwater. Confidently it prophesied: "Whiteman will be arrested in Liverpool." All police forces were alerted. No trace could be found.

The truth was, Whiteman later told the Pinkertons with pardonable amusement, he had walked back to the Dunkirk depot, mingled with the crowd awaiting another train, gone to the Erie Hotel, and had a good dinner. Later, on approaching the hotel register he had seen signed thereon the names of the detectives he had escaped and realized that they had returned to Dunkirk. Unperturbed he had signed an assumed name below those of his recent escorts and gone to bed. After a leisurely breakfast in the morning he had gone by rail to Dansville.

Two groups of interested persons, the Pinkertons and the people of Dansville, felt that they knew during the weeks that followed exactly where the fugitive had sought refuge, and they eyed each other with extreme distaste. Public opinion was so strong against the detectives that they determined not to risk the ridicule that would be heaped upon them if they raided the house and did not find their man. They waited. Dansville waited too, not without passing audible and scornful comments in the presence of strangers, all of whom they assumed to be Pinkerton detectives. In November tension relaxed and the officers suspected correctly that their jailbird had flown. Lon had taken a vacation trip south.

Christmas was coming soon and Superintendent Goodwin of the Pinkerton office in Buffalo felt sure that sentimental Alonzo would be spending the holiday at home with his dear old mother. Tension returned to Dansville, and he knew he was right.

Humanely Goodwin waited until after the Christmas and New Year merriment was over. Then, toward the end of a cold January day, the number of idling strangers in the little town was augmented by a considerable infiltration. One by one they drifted in—seven of Pinkerton's picked men, six of Buffalo's sharpest detectives.

Late that night the house was surrounded and the trap was ready to spring. Mrs. Whiteman's maid, "hired girl," we used to say in those days, was expecting a call from an admirer who had been delayed. He arrived about midnight and knocked on the back door. As the door opened he was surprised to find that he had thirteen companions.

Mrs. Whiteman, awakened by the noise, rose and denounced the intruders, denying that Alonzo was in the

house, though a rumpled bed seemed to indicate other- wise. After presenting their search warrant, the detectives brushed past her and made a thorough search of the house without finding her son. Again and again they went through every room and closet, with no result. As they were coming down the steps from the cupola one of them heard a sound like that of a cup being returned to a saucer. It seemed to come from the wall. Examination disclosed a concealed entrance and the officers were soon in a small secret room built into the chimney. Dishes and food indicated that Alonzo had been calmly satisfying his hunger while they were searching for him just a few feet away. They heard a window open and rushed to it in time to see the fugitive, sitting on the ridgepole of the house, start a precarious slide to the gutter. They rushed down the stairs and outside just as the hunted man dropped safely into a big snowdrift. The world's cleverest criminal was once more a prisoner.

Western New Yorkers considered the trial in Buffalo in March a thrilling drama. To the large majority of them the Pinkertons were the villains and the judge had some difficulty in keeping spectators, including a large percentage of the defendant's fellow townsmen, from expressing their opinion vocally. When the case finally went to the jury, there were twenty-eight hours of sleepless suspense that ended in an unquellable ovation when the foreman of a panel of twelve peers of Alonzo J. Whiteman pronounced him "Not Guilty."

While the crowd taunted them with those familiar words the Pinkertons smiled politely. The freed prisoner had been reindicted and rearrested and they had reason to expect that the subsequent trial would have a different outcome. The new charge seemed to all the countryside only further evidence of the vindictive persecutions of the Pinkertons, and the members of that admirable agency were astonished and hurt by the bitterness they engendered. They now realized that a conviction must be obtained if they were to keep their standing, and though the crime with which the defendant was charged was so obviously a Whiteman undertaking that it seemed to bear his notorious signature, they made ready for the ordeal of the trial with characteristic thoroughness.

The plan of the crime had worked perfectly. A $9,000 draft of the National Hudson River Bank of Hudson, New York, raised from a mere $51, had been sent by messenger to the Fidelity Trust Company of Buffalo by a depositor who signed himself F. H. Hubbard on stationery indicating he was a businessman of East Aurora. Soon Mr. Hubbard appeared in person and the Buffalo bank, having heard nothing from Hudson to cause suspicion, cashed checks totaling $3,850. Then came the news from Hudson that the original deposit was worthless.

To make sure of their man this time the Pinkertons, acting through Assistant Superintendent Dougherty, persuaded a jailed Whiteman accomplice to betray him by asking him for advice in letters delivered by a fellow prisoner. After the secret incriminating correspondence had been carried on for some time, jail authorities searched both cells and seized it.

Even then Whiteman's luck did not desert him. A mistrial was declared when a juror became ill and could no longer serve. Dansville folk were giving odds on neighbor Lon's acquittal in the next trial and were finding few takers for their wagers. A famous vaudeville booking agency offered the defendant a fine weekly salary to appear in the theaters of its circuit as soon as he was free, and he accepted.

But on October 20, 1905, Alonzo J. Whiteman stood to hear a verdict of "Guilty." The jury had been divided, six to six, all night long but in the morning they had agreed. The prisoner showed no emotion. He turned to go back to his cell. The Buffalo *Enquirer* reported: "There was a slight sneer on his lips as he faced the sea of faces turned on him."

Now it was the Pinkertons' turn to celebrate but, though the press emphasized their "unbounded joy," they were too well aware of general disapproval to do so. Indeed, Superintendent Goodwin of the Buffalo branch of the agency felt it good policy to make a defensive, almost apologetic statement.

"In this case the sentiment of the general public is with the prisoner," he said. "Well, to be frank, we can't expect anything else. . . . The Pinkertons have never persecuted Whiteman or anyone else but in the discharge of our duties we may have given that impression. There are always two sides to a story. We are employed by the Bankers Association. . . . There is no question but what Whiteman is a wonderfully clever fellow. His method of swindling banks is nothing more than a science. He dotes on combating with the law. He has tried to be good, and can't."

Life was dull for Lon in the eight and a half years that followed. Auburn Prison irked his free spirit and, though his old college friends (particularly the ministers whom he had aided in the past) occasionally called, he began to break under the awful monotony of life in a cell. There were a few bright weeks when, appointed an instructor in banking and business procedure at the prison school, he taught the most crowded educational course in the prison's history, but when a judiciously placed stoolpigeon reported that he was instructing his students in an illegal business procedure known for some years to officers of the law as the "Whiteman method" even this pleasure was denied him.

At this time prison officials began to suspect what would probably have seemed obvious to their successors today, that Alonzo was "touched in the head." He was transferred to Dannemora and became a trusty in the warden's office. There he amused himself by smoking up a box of the boss's fine Hoya de Monterey cigars and manipulating the office records to show that the warden owed A. J. Whiteman a full box.

When he was released in 1914, his old enemies, the Pinkertons, were waiting. Newspapers reported him a "broken man" but the agency took no chances. The "eye that never sleeps" was always watching. He went back to Dansville, bundled up his mother, now in her nineties, and took her to live with him in Zion City, Illinois. There he became a preacher for the followers of Voliva, prophet of a cult whose creed included the belief that the world is flat, and lived a religious life until midwinter, when he left, taking with him $2,500 which had been entrusted to him by Sister Sara Conger.

After his mother's death, he applied for residence in the Livingston County poorhouse at Geneseo, ten miles from Dansville. An old Dansville friend gave him some clothes and took up a collection around the town to pay his bus fare. While he was there Bob Knox came to see him, and the poorhouse superintendent once told me he had been greatly moved at seeing the meeting of the two old men. They began to weep as they moved toward each other and when they had come close they clung together a long time, tears streaming down their cheeks.

Lon was too proud to stay in the poorhouse. As soon as he felt well enough he got a job as a cashier in a restaurant in Rochester. From Rochester he went to Georgia and, after working on the Atlanta *Constitution* for a few months, got a better job on the *Wiregrass Farmer* of Ashburn. He worked at this until illness took him to a hospital in Milledgeville, where he died on October 13, 1921.

A fitting and final tribute to what the New York *Times* called his "extraordinary fascination" appeared not long ago in the published memoirs of Superintendent Dougherty, the accomplished Pinkerton man, who had hounded him for nearly twenty years. "When he was released from prison," wrote the great detective, "he came to see me. He was broken in health and promised to quit the crooked game forever, which I am sure he did, because I gave him money from time to time to live on."

Uncle Matt McCartney was a proud sight whenever on a summer's day he set out down Main Street in Dansville in his white pants. The strut of him showed that he had an appreciation of his own elegance and that very fact gave the whole town a sense of well-being. Only a few envious folk would not be sorrowing when, as always happened, clouds rolled up over the valley and let go their watery cargo on Matt and he would stride home, shaking his Irish thorn stick defiantly at the lightning and with his pants stuck to his sturdy legs as if they had been dipped in paperhanger's paste.

Came a hot season and long drouth to Dansville and even when gray clouds hung over the town as if anchored on the high hills above it there was no rain. The Canaseraga Creek was dry as tinder even up Poagshole where the old swimming hole, "The Rocks," held not enough water to give a boy decency when a buggy passed by on the dusty road. The rain-maker prayers of Dansville's one-armed parson, George K. Ward, availed nothing and finally, as threats of fire and of a dangerous scarcity of water were mounting, the town fathers held a meeting and discussed the crisis earnestly. Among other reasonable actions taken that evening, they passed a resolution in the interests of community welfare requesting their esteemed fellow townsman, Matt McCartney, to parade down Main Street in his best white pants.

Matt paraded.

It rained.

"One fall day in 1859," said Fred Kast, "my six-foot Alsatian-born grandfather put on his long Prince Albert coat and high hat, hitched the light team to the well-polished 'Democrat,' loaded in his rapidly growing family and set out from his Rich's Corners' farm for the County Fair at Albion.

"At the fairgrounds, grandfather came to a stand where a whip salesman was doing a land-office business. The shining, many-colored whipstocks and the glib oratory of the seller broke down his usual reserve and reluctantly he parted with a dollar for a bundle of six new whips. Tuck-

ing it under his left arm, grandfather set out for the Main
Street bridge over the Erie Canal from which he hoped to
see a tight-rope performer walk above the water on a wire
stretched high between the two banks.

"Some two hundred and fifty other sightseers also chose
the bridge as the best point from which to view the event,
and the load was more than the old wooden structure
could stand. It trembled, then suddenly went crashing
down, throwing those whom it had supported, grandfather
among them, into the waters below.

"Fifteen persons lost their lives in the tragedy but grandfather fell clear of the wreckage and came to the surface.
As he set out for the nearest bank he saw that his long-tail
coat billowed far and wide in his wake and pointing out
the buoyance of his garment to a boy here and another
there he eventually reached shore with seven youths lashed
to his stern.

"After pushing his passengers out on the bank, grandfather crawled from the water and took rueful stock of himself. Though his dripping Sunday suit would probably
shrink, his high hat had ridden out the water journey like
the smokestack on a steamer. Tucked under his left arm,
somewhat tarnished by canal water, was the bundle of
new carriage whips."

*"A Tale of the Ridge Road, Known to Scholars as
the Alluvial Way, to Travellers as the Great
Western Turnpike."*

One night near Christmastime in 1813, Captain Eleazer
McCarthy heard from the west that the British had massa-

cred most of the folks in Lewiston and everybody that got away had sloped along the Ridge Road east. Eleazer got word to Bill Burlingame and Bill ran most of the four miles on foot to John Proctor's bark-roofed cabin in the Nine Mile Woods.

John had the only horse around there and Bill got him out of bed and told him the captain wanted him to ride east at once and tell everybody along the ridge as far as Clarkson that the British were coming. John didn't lose any time. He kissed Polly, his young wife of a little more than a year, saddled his horse and lit out.

He had a good sixteen miles ahead of him and there were a chain of farmhouses along the ridge. John Proctor stopped at each one shouting out the news. Some of those houses are still standing where sudden lamps appeared in windows as the farmer and his wife roused themselves at his warning. He yelled to the miller who lived beside Johnston's Creek and he made a great uproar in the little group of houses where the Ridge Road crossed Oak Orchard Creek. The sun had not yet risen when he stormed into Clarkson shouting his news.

John must have made his ride in record time, for by early morning he was on his way back west with a little company of the men he had warned. Marching with him, guns on their shoulders, were Moses Bacon, Justise Ingersoll, Allen Porter, Reuben Root, Sam Tappan, Joe Hart, Bob Treadwell, Hubbard Rice, Chauncey Robinson, Judson Downes, Amos Barrett, David Hood, and Jeremiah Brown. They picked up Bill Burlingame on their way and Captain Eleazer McCarthy took his place at the head.

It was a long hard march of nearly forty miles and dusk had come when the weary marchers saw the lights of Molyneaux Tavern gleaming ahead of them. Eleazer called a halt then and he went ahead by himself and sneaked up to one of the windows. There he saw some redcoats and Indians drinking liquor and yelling and singing and in order to yell and sing better they had stacked their rifles in a corner. So Captain Eleazer went back to his men and ordered them on.

They got up close to the tavern and when he gave the signal they dashed through the doors and jumped through the windows and made for that stack of rifles. One of the Indians tried to beat them to it but Eleazer shot him dead. Then all the rest of the redcoats and Indians surrendered and the captain made camp at Hardscrabble nearby and set a guard over his prisoners.

John Proctor must have slept well that night after his long ride and the longer march to the west. When he was an old man he used to tell the story of what folks called his Paul Revere Ride, sitting in his rocking chair in the glassed-in cupola at the tope of his high-hipped and comfortable house in the town of Childs where he could look down and watch the hired man working in his fields beside the Ridge Road over which he had galloped long ago to warn his neighbors.

"Brother," said Red Jacket, "if you white people murdered the Saviour, make it up yourselves. We Indians had nothing to do with it."

4

"I Am a Cayuga"

THE OLD CHIEF, CLINTON RICKARD, LIVES IN A LIT-
tle house near the Niagara County town of Sanborn on
the reservation of his tribe, the Tuscaroras. York State Indians and those of the Iroquois Federation who dwell in
Canada will always remember that house—not merely because Clinton Rickard, now white haired and nearly blind,
has done many good things for his people in his long lifetime, but because, at his invitation, another fine man, a
homeless exile, lived out his last days there. Though his
name is known to few white people, no loyal eastern Indian will forget Deskaheh, chief of the Young Bear Clan
of the Cayuga Nation.

Deskaheh was a descendant of Mary Jemison, whose
story appears later in this book, and he was born in Grand
River Land, a reservation of the Six Nations people who
fled or were driven to Canada from York State after the
American Revolution. They chose these acres gratefully
ceded to them by Canadian Governor Haldimand, because
the Grand with its level flats reminded them of their beloved Mohawk valley which they had tried to preserve for
the English king.

After his years of grammar school, Deskaheh, like many

other Grand River Indians, exercised his treaty right to cross the United States boundary to become a lumberjack among the lower York State and upper Pennsylvania Alleghenies, but after an accident he returned to Grand River and took up farming. He married the daughter of a Cayuga mother and white father and she bore him four daughters and five sons, most of whom live today in western York State.

By 1914 Deskaheh had reached the middle period of what white neighbors called a successful reservation-Indian life. His honesty, his sincerity, and his ability as an orator in the Cayuga language had brought him deserved election as head chief when the Canadian government, satisfied until the beginning of World War I to allow the Iroquois the status of a separate nation, decided on grounds of expediency to disregard old treaties and assimilate the Indians, by force if necessary. Deskaheh was the leader of the delegation that patiently explained in Ottawa, first, that the Canadian government had no jurisdiction over the little nation they represented, second, that, since the Indians had already volunteered in proportionately greater numbers than the people of any other nation in the world, enforced draft of its young men by a foreign ally would seem silly.

They won this argument but the end of the war brought other attempted encroachments and the red men soon knew that the majority in the legislative halls of the Canadian capital planned further inroads on their rights as citizens of the separate country known as Grand River Land. In 1921, to thwart the purposes of these schemers, Deskaheh, appointed "Speaker of the Six Nations Council,"

presented as travel credentials a passport authorized by his
nation and crossed the Atlantic to seek British aid. Since,
as he pointed out, the treaty on which his people based
their claims had been made with George III he asked its
confirmation by George V.

The English authorities refused his request, saying that
they would not deal with a Canadian domestic problem
and the Indian returned, defeated. Then the Canadian
enemies grew bolder. The creating of a fifth-column party
through persuasion, promises, and payments was easy, easier still to get the new minority to ask for protection,
easiest of all to order a detail of the red-jacketed Royal
Mounted Police to ride into the Grand River country to
protect the "loyalist" Indians and "to keep the peace." So
obvious was this procedure that Deskaheh, who had
strongly opposed it, pleading earnestly for arbitration, won
many white sympathizers among his neighbors and through
them news of the coming raid reached him in time for a
hasty flight across the border of the United States to the
city of Rochester in western York State.

The raiders arrested and jailed a number of Indians and,
though Deskaheh was known to abstain from alcoholic
liquors, they searched his house on the pretext of looking
for illegal beverages. The Canadian government then ordered barracks built for the housing of their police and
Grand River was suddenly an occupied nation.

Deskaheh now began to fight back desperately. With
the Six Nations' counsel, George P. Decker, a white Rochester lawyer, as his companion, he again used his passport,
this time to travel to Geneva to bring his people's case
before the League of Nations. He arrived in September of
1923, took lodging in the Hotel des Familles, and began

to work toward presenting personally to the Council of the League the petition of his people. Though he met with no success, he fought doggedly. Winter came and went and in mid-April he wrote to his wife and his sons and daughters:

"I have no time to go anywhere only setting on the chair from morning till night copying and answering letter as they come and copying the documents and I have many things to do."

May came to the city by beautiful Lake Leman but his thoughts were with his people beside the Grand River and like a good believer in the religion of the Long House he was seeking aid through the prayers of his people to their God. To his brother, Alex General, he wrote:

"I believe it will be a good thing to have a meeting in one of the long house, but you must be combined all the good people and the children of the long house, only those that are faithful believers in our religion and no other, and it must be very early in the morning to have this, so that our God may hear you and the children, and ask him to help us in our distress at this moment and you must use Indian tobacco in our usual way when we ask help to our Great Spirit . . . and you must have a uniform on . . . and also ask God you wish the religion will keep up for a great many years to come and the Indian race also . . ."

By June he had obtained the services of a Swiss lawyer who was preparing a statement of the case of the Six Nations Indians in French. The money the Indians and their friends had raised in America was almost gone and some means of replenishing it was necessary.

Again he wrote Brother Alex from Geneva:

"And we had a meeting of the Iroquois of the Six Nations of the Grand River Land [really the committee devoted to the interests of the Six Nations] on the 27th of June and the meeting decided to raffal off the two portrait pictures which they made, and just think of it, these two pictures of myself with my costume on it, and it is finished and it is very good pictures . . . and decided to set the price for the two pictures for a small sum of money only 6,000 Swiss francs . . . the rich lady she said at the meeting we must win no matter it takes ten years because our case is so clear and just and I may mention to you this 6,000 francs it means a little over 1,000 dollars of our money . . . and it gives me very great lift to our fight . . . very strong committee all big people of high class people, when the meeting takes place everybody looks decent of their suit and dress very well."

If these informal reports written to his loved family in an unfamiliar language seem naïve, the campaign Deskaheh and his good friend, George Decker, were waging was not. It was hard hitting, simple, direct. Continually put off by officials who found it embarrassing to deny this representative of a small nation the right to speak before the League Council, committed to the Wilsonian doctrine of autonomy for small nations, these two made the situation more awkward for the British interests by getting into the public prints distributed in Geneva quotations from treaties and documents that Canada had decided to abrogate as "scraps of paper."

The Indian was also attracting much favorable attention as a person. To the Irish woman correspondent of the *Freeman's Journal* of Dublin, who "felt as excited as a little girl of twelve at the thought of meeting face to face a real live hero of my childish dreams," he seemed "a good looking, broad-shouldered man, about 40 years of age [he was really 54] wearing ordinary dark clothes . . . and presenting every appearance of a well-to-do Canadian farmer with the one exception of his beautiful moccasins. . . ." She commented on the penetrating, searching glance of his dark eyes, his kindly smile disclosing remarkably white teeth, and finished her description with the sentence: "His beautifully-shaped but stern mouth, firm chin and heavy jaw-bones are those of the born fighter, the strong man who knows his strength and believes in it, whilst his shining eyes speak of enthusiasm and idealism." But in the middle of this enthusiastic and sentimentally feminine interview the chief had persuaded her to quote from the text of a memorial addressed to the Grand River Indians, dated as late as December 4, 1912, and filed by Great Britain:

"The Documents, Records and Treaties between the British Governors in former times, and your wise Forefathers, of which, in consequence of your request, authentic copies are now transmitted to you, all establish the Freedom and Independency of your Nations."

Time wore on and though a few Englishmen and Canadians spoke up for the Six Nations Indians, though the representatives of the Netherlands and Albania listened sympathetically and spoke of supporting his petition, Deskaheh began to suspect that his cause was lost. News from his homeland was bad. The Canadian government had announced a "free election," which would in effect determine whether or not the Six Nations government of Grand River Land should be dissolved. For this vote the Canadian government agent had taken possession of the Six Nations Council House, surrounding it with a guard of twenty police. In protest, the Indians favoring their nation's continuance did not vote. The Canadian authorities then broke open the safe holding the records of the Six Nations and took therefrom a number of wampum belts, revered as sacred by the tribes, refusing, on demand, to return them.

In November, 1924, Deskaheh wrote to the editor of a Swiss journal: "It is the heart broken that I must affirm that since several months I am against the most cruel indifference . . . My appeal to the Society of Nations has not been heard, and nothing in the attitude of Governments does not leave me any hope.

"It is in this dreadful agony that I take the advantage to cry out that injustice, by the mean of your free Review to my brothers from all races and all religions . . . Too long we have suffered from the tyrany of our neighbors who tread under feet our Right and laugh at the Pact which finds them . . . Our appeal is for all those which are animated by the spirit of justice and we ask them their benevolent help."

As if to seal its own lack of interest, the Secretariat of the League which had notified Deskaheh of the refusal to allow him to appear as a petitioner before a plenary session, aware of the embarrassment he had caused, now denied both the Indian and George Decker seats in the gallery to observe deliberations.

Despairing, the two friends struck their last brave blow. They hired the Salle Centrale and advertised in the press their own meeting at which Deskaheh would present the case of his nation to those who would come to listen. The response was amazing. The American Indian had been a popular figure in Europe since the time of Columbus and the populace, the vast majority of whom had never seen an example of the noble savage as popularized by translations of the works of James Fenimore Cooper and other romanticists, attended in thousands. All the Geneva Boy Scouts were present, but not a single League of Nations official. Members of the press of many nations, sensing possibilities of stories about a picturesque if not politically important character, were at their reserved tables, among them the distinguished Hungarian journalist Aloys Derso, now resident of New York State, who tells amusing and movingly pathetic incidents of the occasion.

"I went to the evening to see my first American Indian. He was in the dressing room already in full regalia. I drew a few sketches of him and he was a good model, sitting immobile. He had not the typical Indian profile, the nose not the aquiline nose I expected. His eyes were tired and there was a great melancholy in his expression."

When Deskaheh appeared before the great audience he walked in dignity and with no self-consciousness. There were giggles because, though in the elaborate dress of the chief of the Cayuga Nation, he carried an enormous yellow suitcase which he placed carefully on a table in front of him. Says Derso:

"One of my neighbors turned to another—'Why the hell brought he this suitcase?'

" 'Most probably,' said the other, 'he did not trust the garde-robe.' "

Smiles soon ceased, however, for Deskaheh related his story simply and sincerely. His people had heard in 1915, he said, of a repulsively homely white chief with a frightening mustache who had made war on their ally, the good bearded chief of the British people. The young Indian braves had swiftly formed a regiment and gone across the big water to fight for the government that had once so gratefully given his nation its land. Here he repeated a passage from the treaty of 1784 as worded by Sir Frederick Haldimand, governor in chief of Quebec and territories depending thereon:

"I do hereby in His Majesty's name, authorize and permit the said Mohawk Nation and such other of the Six Nations Indians as wish to settle in that quarter to take possession of and settle upon the banks of the river commonly called Ouse or Grand River . . . which them and their posterity are to enjoy forever."

Then he recited the tale of the broken pledge—the raid of the Royal Mounted, the rummaging of his own house, the building of the police barracks, the seizure of the sacred wampum. The story would be incredible without evidence, he said, but he had foreseen this and had the proofs with him.

Then he lifted the lid of the suitcase and with care and reverence drew from within the old beaded wampum on which might be read the sworn agreements of white governments with his people. Speaking with deep feeling, translating these documents slowly and impressively, stopping now and then to make clear the meanings of the bead colors and of the representations of wild animals, he made his entranced hearers feel that this was not the narration of the grievances of a small racial unit, but the story of all minority peoples—the tragedy of every small nation that is neighbor to a large one.

When he had finished there was a moment of silence— then the roar of a tremendous ovation. Thousands rose to their feet to cheer him and the great hall echoed and re-echoed with their applause. Straight, unsmiling, impassive, he waited until after many minutes the sound began to wane. Then, still expressionless, he left the platform.

As Derso was leaving the Salle Centrale a friend, whom he describes as an antiquaire and art dealer, approached him.

"Derso, have you see those Indian embroideries?"

"Of course I saw them."

"*Combien ça vaut?*" said the antiquaire.

"It is very difficult, my friend," said Derso, "to estimate the value of these things. For *me*, for instance, they have the same value as all other treaties registered in the League offices. For *you*, their value may be from 50 to 150 Swiss francs, because you expect to sell them to a connoisseur for 1,000 to 5,000. But I would advise you to leave this Indian alone with his beads."

Before the end of 1924 the Speaker of the Six Nations Council had returned to America, a beaten and discouraged man. An exile from Canada and from the nation he thought he had failed, he found refuge with Clinton Rickard in the house where the benign old chief of the Tuscaroras still lives. There, by the Niagara River, which marks the Canadian boundary, he found that the people for whom he had fought did not think him a failure. From their northern homes in Grand River Land they journeyed here to see him and assure him of their loyalty. Though his disheartening experience had weakened him physically, his spirit took fire from their words and with never-ending courage he kept up his battle.

On the evening of March 10, 1925, suffering from a serious attack of pleurisy and pneumonia, he made his last speech. It was before a radio microphone in Rochester. Once more, and more forcefully than ever, he hurled defiance at the big nations that had disregarded the claims of the Six Nations people.

"We call the little ten miles square we have left the 'Grand River Country' . . . it is just enough to live and die on. Don't you think your governments ought to be ashamed to take that away from us pretending that it is part of theirs? The governments at Washington and Ottawa have a silent partnership of policy. It is aimed to break up every tribe of red men so as to dominate every acre of their territory . . . over in Ottawa they call that policy 'Indian Advancement.' Over in Washington they call it 'Assimilation.' We, who would be the helpless victims, say it is tyranny. If this must go on to the bitter end, we would rather that you come with your guns and poison gases and get rid of us—do it openly and aboveboard—do away with the pretense that you have the right to subjugate us to your will . . .

"Ottawa officials under pretense of a friendly visit asked to inspect our precious wampum belts . . . seized and carried away those belts as bandits . . . our aged wampum-keeper did not put up his hands. Our hands go up only when we address the Great Spirit."

One by one Deskaheh told of the agreements solemnly made on the sworn good faith of each of the two big governments that had guaranteed the Indian his own land, fair treatment, independence.

"If you are bound to treat us as though we were citizens under your government, then those of your people who are land-hungry will get our farms away from us . . . We would then be homeless and have to drift to your big cities to work for wages to buy bread, and have to pay rent, as you call it, to live on this earth and to live in little rooms in which we would suffocate."

Sick, fever ridden, despairing, Deskaheh raised his voice to speak his proud last message.

"This is the story of the Mohawks, the story of the Oneidas, of the Cayugas—I am a Cayuga—of the Onondagas, the Senecas, and the Tuscaroras. They are the Iroquois.

"This story comes straight from Deskaheh, one of the chiefs . . . I am the Speaker of the Council of the Six Nations, the oldest League of Nations now existing. It was founded by Hiawatha. It is a league which is still alive and intends as best it can to defend the rights of the Iroquois to live under their own laws in their own little countries now left to them; to worship their Great Spirit in their own way and to enjoy the rights which are as surely theirs as the white man's rights are his own."

The next morning Deskaheh was in a Rochester hospital. Eight weeks later he knew he was dying and asked to be taken back to Clinton Rickard's home on the Tuscarora Reservation.

While he made ready for his journey along the Milky Way to the land of Happy Hunting, his brother, wife, and children tried to cross the border at Niagara Falls to be with him and were refused permission to do so. On June 27, 1925, alone and with his eyes set toward the Six Nations Land he had tried to serve, he died.

White Americans and white Canadians have done little to keep the story of Deskaheh alive. Few have seen the small stone that marks his grave in the burial grounds of the Cayuga long house. Fewer still care to remember his words. They make the white man uncomfortable because they bear so emphatically on contemporary thinking about the Indian, on proposed laws in the legislative bodies of states and the nation that would still, despite our agreements to (in Deskaheh's words) "protect little peoples and to enforce respect for treaties," regard Indians as incompetents to be governed for their own good by wiser neighbors. But the Iroquois remember. And when they speak of Deskaheh the white men who know his story grow troubled, wondering if they and their governments could by some unlikely chance have dealt unjustly with a great man.

Used to be an old fella over in the town of Jay near Ausable. He was real pious and he give the land for the town to build a church. When they got it built, he didn't like it.

"Heluva church," he said, and he swore he'd never go inside.

Right by one of the church windows was a great big boulder and the old man built a shanty on top of it. Used to go there every Sunday morning to listen to the sermon. When the exhorter said something he didn't like, he'd yell through the window at him.

"Read your Bible," he'd holler. "Read your Bible. It don't say nothin' like that."

5

Tisri, 5586

THE GRAND MARCH FROM *Judas Maccabeus*
ended in a roar of sound.

"Whereas," said the big man at the lectern, his muscular and portly frame seeming to fill most of one end of
the narrow auditorium, "whereas it has pleased Almighty
God to manifest to His chosen people the approach of
that period when in fulfillment of the promises made to
the race of Jacob, and as a reward for their pious constancy
and triumphant fidelity, they are to be gathered from the
four quarters of the globe and to resume their work and
character among the governments of the earth!"

He paused dramatically and the audience in front of
him, many in uniforms of varied nature, stirred and settled themselves. The large face with its big, hawklike nose
was intent. A magnificent ermine-trimmed vestment of
scarlet silk fell about his huge shoulders and rustled as he
lifted a hand to the richly embossed gold medal suspended
around his neck. Again his hearers, weary from marching
in the long parade that had preceded these exercises, heard
the resonant rise and fall of his organlike voice.

"And whereas . . . the ancient people of God, the first
to proclaim His unity and omnipotence, are to be restored
to their inheritance and enjoy the rights of a sovereign
independent people . . .

"Gather together in a land of milk and honey where Israel may repose in peace under his vine and fig tree, and where our people may so familiarize themselves with the science of government and the lights of learning and civilization as may qualify them for that grand and final restoration to their ancient heritage which the times so powerfully indicate . . .

"A City of Refuge to which both Jews and others of every religious denomination are invited to foregather and there dwell in peace and happiness . . .

"The capitalist will be enabled to employ his resources with undoubted profit and the merchant cannot fail to reap the reward of enterprise in a great and growing republic; but to the industrious mechanic, manufacturer, and agriculturist it holds forth great and improving advantages."

Members of the brass band began carefully and silently setting down their instruments. Officers of the Army of the United States, sitting very straight, stared blankly as the voice went on:

". . . aid and encourage the emigration of the young and enterprising and endeavor to send to this country such as will add to our strength and character by their industry, honor, and patriotism . . .

"Deprived as our people have been for centuries of a right in the soil they will learn, with peculiar satisfaction, that here they can till the land, reap the harvest, and raise the flocks which are unquestionably their own; and in the full and unmolested enjoyment of their religious rights and of every civil immunity, together with peace and plenty, they can lift up their voice in gratitude to Him who sustained our fathers in the wilderness . . ."

As he finished the sounding address the speaker stepped down and stood at a long table on which lay a large block of sandstone. On it was inscribed in Hebrew: "Hear, O Israel, The Lord is our God—The Lord is One," and below this legend were these words:

ARARAT
The Hebrew's Refuge, founded by
Mordecai Manuel Noah.

In the month of Tisri, 5586, corresponding with September, 1825, and in the 50th year of American Independence.

In all the men who crowded forward to see the ceremony there was no Jew. But from among the members of the Masonic lodges of Buffalo who had marched the streets to this little Episcopal Church of St. Paul rose the Principal Architect with square and level and plumb, the Master Mason with Biblesquare and compass. They moved forward to take their stations and with their instruments and his Mason's trowel did Mordecai Noah, self-described "Citizen of the United States of America, late Consul of said States for the city and kingdom of Tunis, High Sheriff of New York, Counsellor at Law and, by the Grace of God, Governor and Judge of Israel," lay the cornerstone of Ararat, City of Refuge for his people.

"In His name do I revive, renew and re-establish the government of the Jewish Nation . . . confirming and perpetrating all our rights and privileges, our name, our rank and our power among the nations of the earth as they existed and were recognized under the government of the Judges. And I hereby enjoin it upon all our pious and venerable Rabbis, our Presidents and Elders of Synagogues, Chiefs of Colleges and Brethren in Authority throughout the world to circulate and make known this my proclamation, and give it full publicity, credence, and effect."

Five years before this ceremony thirty-five-year-old Mordecai Noah, born in Philadelphia of German-Jewish father and Portuguese-Jewish mother, had dreamed of the establishment of this city which would serve as a refuge to the members of his oppressed people until the final great migration to Palestine. A playwright whose rhetorical patriotism has since led writers of the history of the American drama to dub him the George M. Cohan of his day, associate and appointee of both Presidents Andrew Jackson and James Monroe, a diplomat who at the age of twenty-eight ably and courageously handled the position of American consul at Tunis in the critical days of our differences with the Barbary Pirates, a generous philanthropist, he conceived himself as a possible Moses leading the Jews of the world, first to the city they should build in western York State in the United States of America, thence to their Promised Land.

The putative Moses had chosen as a site for his great city Grand Island, set in the waters of the Niagara River four miles below the mouth of Lake Erie and about the same distance from Niagara Falls. It was a smiling island of 17,381 acres, eight miles long, six miles wide. Its woods were crowded with wild game birds and with deer, its fruit trees were bent with the weight of their burdens at harvest-time, its soil was dark and fertile. Niagara Falls, Buffalo, Tonawanda, and the hills of Canada were pleasant views from its shores. Mordecai Noah knew when he set out for Buffalo, then a town of 2,500 inhabitants, in late August that the opening of the full length of the Erie Canal would be celebrated in October, that commercially the area would soon be prosperous beyond most dreams of prosperity. He had already persuaded a friend, Samuel Leggett of New York, to buy 2,555 acres, some at the head and some at the foot of the island, cannily believing that the remaining acres might fall into the hands of the pioneer settlers. He had for some time been publishing through his newspaper, the *National Advocate*, a summons to all Jews to come to the shores of the Niagara on September 15, day set for the founding of the city.

After the laying of the cornerstone on the communion table of St. Paul's, the Reverend Dr. Addison Searle, rector, spoke the benediction. Then the congregation of Masons, politicians, important local officers, bandsmen, soldiers, all who had marched in the parade behind Colonel Potter, its mounted grand marshal, dispersed and Mordecai Noah joined his devoted friend A. S. Seixas, who had made the journey from Manhattan with him and aided in all the arrangements. Since Grand Island was not easily accessible, the two New Yorkers had, with the aid of Buffalonian Isaac Smith, a crony of exciting days in Tunis, persuaded the kindly rector to allow the use of St. Paul's. Like Moses in one respect at least, Mordecai Noah was never to set foot on the Promised Land. Now he and Seixas said grateful farewells to Dr. Searle and to Isaac Smith and set out on their return journey.

Mordecai Noah had failed truly to judge what the attitude of the Jews of the world would be toward his project. The European authorities, the important rabbis, on whose aid he had called, refused him support, and his great day had no constructive result. Calmly he went on to other projects, ever a dreamer, ever an enthusiast. But in the days of triumphant Judaism, let September 2, 1825, and the little Christian church in Buffalo not be forgotten. There for the first time in America the great dream was given eloquent and fitting words. Be it remembered in Zion.

Part Two

Told under the First Star

These hemlock-covered hills slow
The strength of the wind . . .

From *Hemlock-Covered Hills*, by Lansing Christman

6

The Fowlers, Practical Phrenologists

VERMONT YANKEES, SEEKING FERTILE LAND BE-
tween the high ridges south of the Genesee country, looked
down into the valley of the Cohocton and decided to make
it their home. They named their village after the stream,
built homes, cleared fields, and established a school and a
church. The birth of the first white child—to the Horace
Fowlers—gave them a sense of permanence and dignity.
They rejoiced in it and prophesied great things for the little boy. But even that mixture of practicality and dream
which was their heritage could not foresee a life so struck
with the light of fame and the blackness of its eclipse.

Orson Squire Fowler was born on the eleventh of October, 1809. His parents, in moderate circumstances, were
well thought of in Cohocton. As soon as he was old enough
to understand, they and their friends instilled in the boy
a respect for religion and education. Like many an eldest
son of his time, he decided to be a preacher and prepared
himself under ministerial instruction and at Ashfield Acad-

emy to enter Amherst College, where courses leading to the ministry were particularly emphasized. When he was ready to matriculate, in 1830, he realized that his parents could ill afford to send him to college while supporting his brother, Lorenzo, two years younger than he, and his sister, Charlotte, who was five years younger. So for two years he worked his way—chiefly by carpentering, sawing wood, and doing other handyman jobs about the college.

Then occurred an event which was to set the current not only of his entire life but of the lives of his brother and sister as well. The Austrian scientist, Dr. Johann Spurzheim, delivered in Boston a series of lectures on the new science of phrenology, first expounded some thirty-five years earlier by his teacher and associate, the celebrated brain surgeon, Franz Joseph Gall, of Swabia and Vienna.

Orson Fowler heard Spurzheim talk and became tremendously excited over a teaching which denied Calvin's gloomy creed of man's innate sinfulness and proclaimed each individual endowed with certain qualities, some good, some bad, which made themselves known in the shape of his head. He was no more excited, however, than his handsome classmate, fellow wearer of the gold fraternity badge of the Society of Natural History, Henry Ward Beecher. He and Beecher immediately plunged into the reading of all that they could find on the subject of phrenology, exhibiting an energy and attentiveness which had not previously been noticeable in their studies. They learned to classify man's faculties phrenologically and to be able to tell where in the human head each is located. They spoke learnedly of the contours that indicated Ideality, Veneration, Eventuality, Amativeness, Philoprogenitiveness. It was not long (according to a contemporary account) before young Beecher was delivering to the Society of Natural History "an able address upon the subject of phrenology expressing the futility of objections offered . . . and exhibiting and defending its fundamental principles," and young Fowler was running his hands over the heads of his college mates (at two cents a head) and telling them what vocations they were best fitted to follow. Beecher was so earnest that he scolded the lovely Eunice whom he was soon to marry for wearing artfully contrived golden-brown ringlets in a bobbing fringe about her face.

"A good shaped head is a greater beauty than a wig any time," he told her, and the abashed maiden thereupon brushed out the curls and wore her hair folded close.

The new science became more than a study with these two young men. With an amusing rationalization, they announced that in order to give themselves practice in the art of preaching they had arranged a number of visits to nearby towns to explain and demonstrate phrenology. Ignoring gibes of their classmates at "the religion of bumps," they made their tour and Beecher's golden words and Fowler's sensitive interpretations convinced many a New England skeptic. They also brought in dollars—so many that, as graduation approached, the call of the Christian ministry grew dimmer and dimmer in Fowler's ears. Beecher could not be persuaded to join him in refusing it. The spellbinder already knew his destiny—at least enough of it to keep him firm on the evangelistic path. But Fowler had found his profession. His first solo appearance as a practical phrenologist had brought him forty dollars. He would not be a preacher.

When he had received his diploma the young enthusiast sought out Lorenzo, instructed him, and took him to New

York City. There, in 1835, the two opened offices at 135 Nassau Street (under the old Clinton Hall) for the practice of phrenology and the arrangement of lectures on the science throughout the United States. Thus Orson Fowler began a career which was to make its influence felt throughout the English-speaking world.

In 1835 he wrote, between lectures, the first edition of a book, *Phrenology Proved, Illustrated and Applied*, which was to have such wide popularity and steady sale that in the next twenty years it ran through sixty-two editions. I do not know that Fowler planned to write nonfictional best sellers. But if he did not he must have had a subconscious feeling for the selection of those subjects in which the credulous are always interested. The most intriguing of these being sex, he followed his first great success with a volume entitled *Love and Parentage; Applied to the Improvement of Offspring Including Important Directions and Instructions to Lovers and the Married Concerning the Strongest Ties and Most Sacred Momentous Relations of Life*. This he dedicated "To all who have ever tasted the sweets of love; or felt its sting; or consummated its delightful union; or who anticipate its hallowed cup of tenderness; or expect to enfold its dear pledges in parental arms—or more especially to women, the very embodiment of this angelic emotion—to all who would enjoy its heavenly embrace, avoid its pangs or render their prospective children healthy, and talented, and lovely."

Almost a century before the American censor's banning of Dr. Marie Stopes' *Married Love* ran it into the bestseller class, Fowler's *Love and Parentage*, unaided by censor, reached twoscore editions, none of which was less than a thousand copies. In it, for full measure, he added to his "Instructions to Lovers and the Married" a eugenic program quite different from that which John Humphrey Noyes was initiating at Oneida. Pointing out that a child conceived in drunkenness had been born an idiot, that the child of an injured fisherman had been born with "a weak and sore spot corresponding in location with that of the injury of her father," and that the child of a "retired judge on holiday" had turned out to be "one of the best-natured children in the world," he advocated the ascendancy of spiritual love over sensual and, in a section entitled "States of Mind in Parents Most Favorable to Talents and Morality in Offspring," advised that prospective parents should develop the phrenological qualities evidenced in those protuberances labeled Marvelousness, Ideality, Approbativeness, and others.

The rush to the bookshops for this book must have prompted its immediate sequel, *Amativeness, or, Evils and Remedies of Excessive and Perverted Sensuality; Including Warning and Advice to the Married and Single,* which became so popular that it was running neck and neck with its predecessor at forty editions each in 1844. Meanwhile the business had been so brisk for the Fowler brothers, "practical phrenologists," as they called themselves, that they had called their sister from Cohocton, where she had been preparing herself by giving talks about the new science, to their aid. She helped Lorenzo with the lecturing and the head-reading while Orson dashed off *Intemperance and Tight Lacing Considered in Relation to the Laws of Life, Fowler on Memory,* and *Fowler on Matrimony, or, Phrenology and Physiology Applied to the Selection of Congenial Companions for Life Including Directions to the Married for Living Together Affectionately and Happily.*

In these three volumes he succeeded in anticipating the modern dress reform, the popular "Mr. Addison Sims of Seattle" memory course, and many a psychologist's treatise on how to live happily though married. On the title page of *Fowler on Matrimony* he took a further fling at what he considered one of the crowning evils of the age with a slogan printed in capitals, "Natural Waists or No Wives," and he continued the argument a few pages later with the statement that "the object of the ladies in padding some parts and compressing others is to make themselves not better but more handsome . . . Marrying small waists is attended with consequences scarcely less disastrous than marrying rich and fashionable girls . . . Tight lacing is gradual suicide . . . besides exciting impure feelings." These attacks led to the formation of many antilacing societies throughout the United States, a fact that must have given Fowler a sense of his increasing influence.

I have put together a few of Mr. Fowler's maxims on marriage into which he launched after a description of "How to get in Love" and "How to know the character of your intended"—the answer to the latter being to have the head of your intended read by a good phrenologist. They seem to be quite as modern and quite as futile as advice on the subject from any contemporary specialist:

A man should first make his selection intellectually, and love afterward.

Let courting be done in the daytime . . . in your everyday clothes.

Marry your first love.

Never let Pride interfere with love.

The Fowlers, Practical Phrenologists

Do not marry for a home merely.

Marry to please no one but yourself; not even your parents.

Do not marry an intemperate companion.

In expansion of this last precept, Fowler echoed his eloquent appeal in his earlier volume *Amativeness*: "Ye daughters of loveliness . . . who would return again to purity, health and happiness, sip no more of the beverage of China; no more of the drinks of Java." In the same passage he reported the case of a man who, "professor though he is," was carried away by excesses after a few cups of strong coffee "returning to the straight and narrow path only when he finds himself debilitated, penniless, having squandered the savings of months, perhaps years of industry."

In this volume, too, Fowler analyzed the subversive forces that degrade civilization, and womankind in particular. He attacked the reading of weeklies which "boast 30,000 subscribers" and claim "the largest circulation in the world." Examine them and "more than half their entire contents will be crimsoned with the sign of Amativeness." He decried the reading of novels by "fastidious ladies who eagerly devour the vulgarities of Marriat and the *double-entendres* of Bulwer, and even converse with gentlemen about their contents." The novels of Scott, he said, "are full of *love*: and I maintain that this passion in man is quite strong enough without *any* artificial stimulant." Finally, after advising against stimulating food and drink, he attacks the theater and fashionable music, "especially the verses set to it, being mostly lovesick ditties or sentimental odes, breathing this tender passion in its most melting and bewitching strains. Improper prints often do immense injury in this respect, as do also balls, parties, annuals, newspaper articles, and so on."

Having discussed the ever-popular subjects of the choice of a mate, female costume, sex, diet, and contemporary literature, it might be supposed that Fowler would feel that he had put sufficient reader bait into the book. He reserved his heavy artillery, however, to blast "modern female education."

"Most of our fashionable boarding schools are *public curses*," he declared, adding in a footnote, "I am gratified to be able to except the schools of Reverend Mr. Avery of Danvers, Mass.; Mrs. Burrill, of South Boston; and Miss Lyon's Mount Holyoke Seminary." Then he continued, significantly and with apparent reference to the Emma Willard School: "Not a thousand miles from Troy, N.Y., is a mother school of this class, the baneful influences of which will long remain to curse not its own sex merely, but the other also, with fashionable wives and weakly mothers. These schools . . . only whitewash the *outside* of these rouge-painted, tight-laced sepulchres."

The response to such popularizations of pseudo-scientific theory must have outdone the most optimistic dreams of the Fowler family. Hundreds of thousands of Americans were going phrenology-mad. The Fowlers took larger offices at 308 Broadway. These were crowded daily. The trio was swamped by the demands of the public and they needed help. Fortunately that was obtainable within the family. Though Orson had put his matrimonial theories to work as early as 1835 by marrying the young widow, Martha Chevalier, daughter of Elias Brevoort of New York, apparently that lady took little interest in the business.

Not so with Lorenzo's choice, Lydia Folger of Nantucket. Lydia went to work with the rest of the family as soon as she married Lorenzo in 1844. Five years later, at the age of twenty-seven, well known as a lecturer and author, she entered the Central Medical College of Syracuse, New York, and emerged from it in 1850 with the degree of Doctor of Medicine, the second ever given to a woman in the United States. The school was so pleased with her that it gave her the first professorship ever granted a woman by an American medical college. Throughout her career, she proved herself a most valuable addition to the Fowler ménage.

There was one more to make the family monopoly complete. The Fowlers had not been slow to see that with the tremendous popularity of Orson's books the ownership of a publishing house would be a distinct financial advantage. So in 1844 the brothers formed a partnership with twenty-four-year-old Samuel Roberts Wells, graduate of a medical school and believer in phrenology, and established the publishing house of Fowlers and Wells. At about the same moment Charlotte Fowler married Mr. Wells.

Now the Fowlers were phrenology and phrenology was the Fowlers. They all wrote books. They all delivered lectures. Horace Mann wrote treatises on phrenology and Fowlers and Wells published them. Advertisements for employees in the daily newspapers stipulated "It will be necessary to bring a recommendation (a chart showing properly developed bumps) . . . from Messrs. Fowlers and Wells, 131 Nassau Street, New York." Horace Greeley was converted to phrenology, and so was Walt Whitman. Emerson listed Spurzheim as one of the world's great minds. In England, Albert and Victoria had the head of the Prince of Wales examined. Steadily, one by one, the

Fowler books covered the entire field of human thought from the phrenological point of view. They were bought by the millions.

In a new and improved edition of his *Memory and Intellectual Improvement*, published in 1848, Orson Fowler gave a list of the Developments Requisite for Particular Vocations. In this he betrayed something of his own shrewd nature: with his advice to teachers, to secure the goodwill of their pupils' mothers; to ministers, to develop large ideality that they might please by elegance of style and ease of manner and not offend by coarseness; to doctors, to encourage the growth of Amativeness to render them favorites among women—"yet not too much"; to lawyers, to favor Language that with limber tongue they might talk much and say little, substituting verbosity for argument. "I hardly know a politician," he continued, "who has a superior intellectual and moral head." He seems a little nonplused when he comes to poets: "Poetry depends more on the physiology than the phrenology"; as for artists, they "require the developments requisite for mechanics except that Calculation and Destructiveness are by no means indispensable in most of the fine arts." Boardinghouse keepers and cooks "require large Alimentativeness to give them a relish for savory dishes"; milliners, seamstresses, fancyworkers, and the like need "good Form and Size" to aid them in fitting.

In the same volume he laments in words that have had a familiar ring for a long time: "O! My country! to what art thou verging! To lawless, ruffianly demagogism, the very worst possible form of tyranny . . . it is time those who love Republicanism, not blustering logrolling, should rise, instruct the people, and renovate the government while we can." On the same page he anticipates the modern Fascist with "No individual or nation should be allowed to govern themselves until they know how to do so" and on the next, advocating education through "Cabinets of Natural Specimens" he proves certain modern governmental practices are not new ideas at least by "Give me twenty millions and I will furnish every town with a splendid cabinet of animate and inanimate nature."

Then, after taking up "Is a Collegiate Education Desirable?" and answering, "not as now conducted," he overcame his aversion to logrolling with "Books should be multiplied a thousandfold till they become the great commodity of traffic and commerce . . . Trashy novels require to be superseded by works full of sound sense, excellent instruction and scientific knowledge."

Through the late forties and the fifties, the Fowler alliance continued their rushing business. They took up the water-cure fad as an adjunct to their phrenological activities and published many a tract on hydropathy. With their rare genius for selecting popular subject matter they added such titles as *Should Woman Obey?*; *How to Behave*; *A Pocket Manual of Republican Etiquette* (forerunner of Emily Post's twentieth-century best sellers); *The Family Gymnasium*; *How to Write*; *A Home for All*, of which more will be said later.

Though their publications did not have the wide sale of such contemporary popular fiction as *Fanny Campbell, Female Pirate Captain* and *The Wide, Wide World*, and though they sold at comparatively low prices, the Fowlers prospered. They even dreamed of expanding their business to other cities. Having trained a young protégé, Nelson

Sizer, as a phrenological examiner (headreader) for four years, they sent him in 1853 to open a branch office of Fowlers and Wells in Philadelphia. At the end of two more years, however, the Fowler brothers tired of the grind of publishing. Nelson Sizer's *Forty Years of Phrenology* says Orson's main interest was in a great new house on his farm at Fishkill and Lorenzo preferred to spend his time lecturing "for pleasure and profit."

Therefore, in 1855, the two of them sold their shares of the publishing house to Charlotte and Samuel Wells, who had been the business pillars of the firm from its beginning. That necessitated bringing Nelson Sizer back from Philadelphia to read heads in the bust-decorated examining room of the Fowler and Wells Phrenological Museum at 308 Broadway. There for eleven years and in successive locations at 389, 737, 753, and 775, as business slowly climbed up Broadway, Sizer read the heads of thousands of New Yorkers, many of whom are alive today. Of those who are not, the three most distinguished met violent deaths.

Blindfolded, Sizer read the head of John Brown in 1858 and said, "This man has firmness and energy enough to swim up the Niagara River and tow a 74-gun ship, holding the towline in his teeth." Not recognizing the head of George A. Custer, because it had been shorn of its yellow curls, he made to that soldier the understatement, tragically ironic, that he was "inclined to overdo." He told a gangling youth that he had all the combativeness of a Stephen A. Douglas and that with proper development he could someday be a chief justice, without any prophetic knowledge that his client, James A. Garfield, would aspire to a higher office.

While Orson Fowler was busy rearing his architectural monument at Fishkill, the Lorenzo Fowlers and the Wellses were living in the gracious, high-ceilinged, elegantly adorned residence at 233 East Broadway. Lydia Fowler's personal charm, her unusual education, and her experience as a lecturer, combined with her husband's dignity and scientific prestige to make them one of the most prominent couples in the city's intelligentsia. When the first Woman's Christian Temperance meeting was held in Metropolitan Hall on February 7, 1853, the Lorenzo Fowlers entertained the Bloomers of Seneca Falls, New York, as their guests.

On that historic night, while upstate Yorkers Amelia Bloomer and Susan B. Anthony, clad in knee-length silk tunics and pants of the same material, waited their turns to harangue an audience which, according to the press, was "almost as large and fully as respectable as that which nightly greeted Jenny Lind," Lydia Fowler, in a "sky-blue delaine with open corsage, not differing from the ordinary attire of woman," was elected chairman, and she opened the first meeting at which women addressed an audience of New Yorkers from the public platform.

Mrs. Fowler "came forward with a pleasing girlish manner," said the New York *Daily Times* on the following day, "became flushed, and was evidently not so well trained to self-command as her more 'strong-minded' companions. She, however, acquitted herself very creditably in repeating a pretty little set speech which, were it not for the lady's declaration of being 'entirely unprepared to take part in the proceedings' we would have supposed was committed to memory for the occasion."

Amelia Bloomer's autobiography tells that, during her

visit to the "great phrenologist, N. N. Fowler," she and her hosts made an evening journey from the Fowlers' East Broadway home to 35 East 19th Street to call on Horace Greeley and of finding the great editor entertaining Charles A. Dana, and the poet sisters Alice and Phoebe Cary, with a defense of the spiritualistic Fox Sisters, who had recently been his guests.

A few years later, in 1860, Lydia and Lorenzo Fowler made a lecture tour through England and the revenue from it was so great that they moved, with their little daughter, to London, where they lived the rest of their lives. Throughout Great Britain and Ireland, Lydia lectured on "laws of life, physical culture, moral duty and social reform." She once estimated that over a period of thirty years she had spoken before two hundred thousand women in America and Europe. She and Lorenzo, Fowler-like, brought up their daughter Jessie to help in the phrenology business. Lydia Fowler died in 1879, and Jessie, at the age of twenty-three, was called on to take her mother's place in the work her father was carrying on. This she did so successfully that in ten years she was editor of the London *Phrenological Magazine*. In 1896, however, Lorenzo Fowler having just died at the age of eighty-five, she returned to her native America.

Orson Fowler, with distinguished, flowing beard, high forehead, strong nose, and piercing blue eyes, continued meanwhile to expound his phrenological and moral ideas from the lecture platform. But by this time he had found a new hobby, housing, and was putting into practice the theories expressed in *A Home for All* by building for himself and his prospective family a great new dwelling near Fishkill.

In his travels in the West, Fowler had been impressed by the building material of a house known as Goodrich's Folly at Jaynesville, Wisconsin. Like modern concrete in appearance, it was made of lime, small stones, and sand, and it was called "gravel wall" or "grout." "The stone should not be too coarse," says *A Home for All*. "Oyster shell and furnace cinders are good but middling gravel is best." As for the octagon form, which the book advocates and which Fowler adopted for his own house, that was "wholly original with the author."

The phrenologist had first become interested in building at the age of forty and he began his book and his house at the same time. The book appeared in the same year; the building of the house took nearly a decade.

A Home for All, or, The Gravel Wall and Octagon Mode of Building, published in 1849, seemed to a good many of its readers designed to prove the truth of the adage printed on the title page: "There's No Place Like Home." The more modernist of contemporary architects may well blush a little when they read it, however, to discover some of their favorite arguments pre-empted a hundred years ago. The spherical form, Fowler stated, is the most beautiful and it encloses the most space in the least compass. The octagonal, therefore, being the nearest practical building form to spherical, is by far the best. He emphasized the gain in sunlight obtained by having eight outside surfaces and pointed out that the corners of square rooms are dark and useless for furniture. Moreover, he added, distances are shorter in a house which provides opportunity to walk in a straight line to an objective rather than around a right-angled corner. The distance traversed by "a weakly woman" in bringing up wood from the basement to the parlor (he assumed this to be one of her duties) will be in a square house nearly double that in an octagonal. "What a vast number of steps will the octagon save a large and stirring family annually over a square!"

Fowler would have the entrance to his ideal house through the basement so that entry drafts would be dissipated in the passage to the stair, which was lined by storage, milk, and wood rooms on the left and sauce storage, laundry, furnace, and kitchen rooms on the right.

The floor above would contain four large rooms, the parlor, drawing room, dining room, and amusement room, arranged around the central stair well, and all capable, through wide, double doorways, of being opened together, forming one large room out of two, or a larger one, capable of receiving a hundred guests, out of the entire floor.

His third floor would contain a number of small rooms, those on the inside about the stair well being lighted from the central glass dome of the cupola and from skylights of Crystal Palace glass capable of bearing a man's weight. One of these he would make into a studio, because studios are "cool in summer, warm in winter, inaccessible to mosquitoes."

Of the necessity for warmth while composing, he wrote: "Writers will bear witness that in the all powerful exercise of the whole mind required for writing what is fit to read, the blood forsakes the extremities and skin and mounts rushing to the head, leaving all the outer walls a prey to cold, which in addition to severe mental exertion, is too much for any constitution sufficiently susceptible to write well. Most awful havoc have my own night writings made of my constitution—having almost destroyed it. Most horribly, almost as if actually dying, have I felt by the hundred times, on rising in the morning after having written most of the night and retired cold in the feet and skin but hot at the head."

The octagon shape gave plenty of opportunity for dressing rooms and for closets, particularly of the triangular variety that "are more accessible and have more shelf room."

One other requisite of a good house Fowler embarrassedly took the liberty of alluding to—an indoor toilet. This he would place under the stairs, having the rather primitive plumbing pass through one of the four chimneys that were to be centered in each of four sides of the house. Apologetically, he explained that this point was not submitted to "squeamish maidens and fastidious beaux," who would continue in their refinement to avail themselves of "the one generally used . . . outdoors." "But," he asked rhetorically of matrons and the aged and feeble, "is not such a closet a real household . . . luxury?"

Rising above the flat roof of his house, Fowler would have a glassed-in cupola, surrounded at some distance by a balustrade within whose limits clothes might be hung to dry or guests and their host might promenade.

After advocating this plan for a residence, Fowler recommends the octagon shape for both schools and churches. He argues that the shape of the rooms in an octagon schoolhouse has more sociability, reiterates his claims with regard to better light, and adds that acoustics are better also than in a room where "square angles break the sound" and create echoes. As for the octagonal form for churches, it "facilitates the congregation's seeing one another and thereby the interchange of friendly and benevolent feeling . . ." It is moreover particularly commended to ladies "who go to church to be seen."

A *Home for All* caused an immediate reaction among the people of New York State and its environs. Long before Fowler's own huge residence was completed, octagonal houses dotted the valleys of the Hudson and the Mohawk. At Red Hook and Stockport and Millbrook, at Madison and Geneva and Akron, and in dozens of other New York towns, these witnesses to Orson Fowler's reputation for wisdom still stand. On the old Ridge Road stagecoach pike from Albany to Buffalo, a coach company built a tremendous octagonal horse barn. The stalls were in a circle about a central well. Down this, hay from the loft could be pitched into every stall at once. The barn was so big that there was no necessity inside it for backing in order to turn around. The driver just continued driving around the wide circular path outside the stalls and eventually arrived at the same opening through which he had entered. Just outside of Hammondsport in the Finger Lakes wine region, Timothy Younglove built (in the same year in which Fowler completed his own house) an octagonal house, octagonal barn, and octagonal smokehouse.

Fowler chose an oval knoll just north of Fishkill on the Albany post road for his residence. People who watched it in the building thought it would never be done. They said work would go on for a while and then cease while Fowler went away on a lecture tour to earn money enough to continue the building. When it was finally completed in 1858, however, it was even grander than the plans he had detailed for it in A *Home for All*. It had four stories and a basement, and since the basement was more than half aboveground it gave the effect of five stories. From its twenty-foot square glass-roofed cupola that stood eighty feet above the basement floor, crowning the well of the stair, sixteen towns could be seen. Its nearly one hundred rooms included, besides the rooms suggested in *A Home for All*, a playroom for children, a "gymnastic room for females," a dancing room. Around the outside of all four stories there were porches with outside stairs connecting them. Around the central court or well ran a circular stairway with landings at each story from which a door opened into a hall that encircled the court and gave access to the suites of rooms on that floor.

No sooner had Orson Fowler and his wife gone to live in Fowler's Folly, as the house was inevitably to be called, than a constant stream of clients began to pour in. From all over the state, and particularly from the Hudson valley, came hordes of people asking that the great scientist feel the curves of their craniums and advise them about their lives. Hundreds of children were brought to sit beneath the prophet's hands and hear what professions they had best prepare themselves to adopt. Fowler announced lectures for certain evenings and the four big rooms of his main floor were made into a big auditorium by opening the double doors that joined them.

The phrenologist's popularity was considerably enhanced in the immediate countryside at about this time when, blindfolded, he felt over the head of the "meanest man in the county" and announced that "this man is too stingy to be honest."

Just at the height of Orson Fowler's personal success—when at least one follower in almost every New York State community was building an octagonal home, when he was spending his mornings dictating (to two secretaries) books for his brother-in-law Wells to publish, when his big residence, already the most talked-about in the Hudson valley, sheltered a large group of distinguished visitors—tragedy came. A plague raged through Fowler's Folly, bringing death to many guests. Those who survived fled in terror. For some time no one understood the cause of the mysterious malady. At last an investigation proved that one of the gravel walls, whose impermeability Fowler had praised, had allowed seepage from the cesspool into the wall. Typhoid had done the rest.

Discouraged, Fowler rented the huge place to a Professor Andrus Cassard, who established in it a military school for Spanish and Cuban boys. When Cassard disappeared in 1865, leaving behind him many unpaid bills, a Mrs. Cunningham leased the place and made it into a boarding-house. The rumor that she was the same Mrs. Cunningham who eight years before had been indicted and tried for the shocking knife butchery of a New York City dentist, Dr. Harvey Burdell, led to an exodus even more hasty than that caused by typhoid, though the lady denied, with truth, that she was the notorious suspect.

After that, though the house changed ownership thirty-three more times and was in 1880 restored for the purpose of occupancy, no one lived in it again. A Poughkeepsie newspaper account states that Fowler sold the house for $150,000. The last price paid for it was $800. In 1897 it had become unsafe, a menace to the many sightseers who visited it annually, and it was razed to the ground with dynamite by order of the Fishkill town authorities.

The coming of the plague to his dwelling seems to have marked a definite turning point in the career of Orson Fowler. Gradually, in the succeeding years, phrenology was discredited by the bitter attacks of the medical fraternity, most of whose members declared it to be utterly fraudulent. (Modern specialists now point out that he and his associates were on the right track in assigning separate functions to different areas of the brain.) Still believing, still an itinerant apostle, Fowler continued his lectures and demonstrations, offering readings at cut-rate prices, before ever-dwindling audiences. In 1865, after his first wife died, he married another widow, Mrs. Mary Poole, daughter of William Aiken of Gloucester, Massachusetts. After her death, he at last risked wedlock with a lady of no experience of that state, and at the age of seventy-three married a forty-two-year-old maiden, Abbie Ayres of Osceola, Wisconsin. She bore him three children and must have had a well-developed bump of Amativeness, for thirteen years after Fowler's death, when she was sixty, she secretly married her twenty-nine-year-old private secretary in Kansas City and bore him off to St. Louis on their honeymoon.

From 1863 to 1880, Orson Fowler lived in Manchester, Massachusetts, writing unsuccessful books with titles and contents similar to those he had produced in his youth, lecturing occasionally, interpreting the bumps on people's heads for modest fees. Then he moved to a little farm near Sharon Station, Connecticut. He died in August, 1887, of a cold and chill resulting, according to the obituary published in the *Phrenological Journal*, from working in his garden on a warm afternoon and sitting down to rest in the shade without putting on his coat.

As for Charlotte Fowler Wells, she had taken over the business of running the publishing house when her husband, Samuel, died in 1875. She ran it for nine years unaided, for a dozen more as president of the stock company known as the Fowlers & Wells Company. Its ownership, but not its name, was changed in 1896. The last time a Fowlers & Wells advertisement appeared in *Publishers' Weekly* was in 1904.

America had not heard the last of phrenology and the Fowlers, however. Nine years after Orson's death, his niece, Jessie, Lorenzo's daughter, returned, as I have said before, to America. She at once became editor in chief of the *Phrenological Journal*. Like her mother, Lydia, Jessie was strong in her desire for education. While in London she had studied brain dissection at the School of Medicine for Women. Though she held a responsible position in America, she took the time to enter New York University Law School and was graduated in 1901 at the age of forty-five. She was for many years vice-president of the American Institute of Phrenology and she wrote several books on the subject, of which *Brain Roofs and Porticoes* provides the most intriguing title. At the age of seventy-six she died at her New York City residence, 843 West 179th Street, on October 16, 1932.

In York State, even around Cohocton whence the Fowlers came, phrenology has declined to the level of palmistry and fortunetelling. Head-reading still goes on—but mostly in little tents which display on outside billboards Fowler's design of the human head showing the locales of various characteristics. Sometimes, too, the persistent practitioner has posted also, in large type, the words of Orson Fowler's ever-loyal classmate, the late world-famous exhorter, Henry Ward Beecher:

"If I were the owner of an island in mid-ocean and had all books, apparatus and appliances, tools to cultivate the soil, manufacture, cook and carry on life's affairs in comfort and refinement, and some dark night pirates should come and burn my books, musical instruments, works of art, furniture, tools and machinery and leave me the land and the empty barns and house, I should be in respect to the successful carrying on of my affairs, in very much the same plight that I should be as a preacher if Phrenology and all that it has taught me of man, his character, his wants and his improvement, were blotted from my mind."

Joe Corey is a house painter, and a good one. He's more than a little cross-eyed and folks that don't know Joe very well sometimes get the idea that his brains are not as well baked as they are.

One day Joe was testifying for the defendant in a case that the State held involved unnecessary violence.

"Have you ever been at an institution for the mentally defective?" asked the District Attorney, whose case Joe had severely damaged.

"No," said Joe.

"Are you sure of that?"

"Well," said Joe, "I was at the Utiky Hospital for the Insane for a while."

"Just as I thought," said the District Attorney triumphantly. "And now will you tell the ladies and gentlemen of the jury the reason for your residence at that institution?"

Joe turned his double-slanted gaze on the intense panel of twelve,

"It needed paintin'."

Dark Trees to the Wind

We have companioned together, you trees,
Flesh, blood and bone in me,
Cambium, sap and wood in you—
Something elusive in you too, that escapes
    the tube of the chemist;
Something that baffles science in man's body;
Something that staggers comprehension in the body
    of a woman;
Something mystic and sentient in you,
That makes you whisper and rustle and press
    together in the twilight.

From *Toward Life*, by W. W. Christman

7

The Irish Wonder and the Swedish Nightingale

THE BURKE HOUSE IN THE TOWNSHIP OF ALEX-
ander on the banks of meandering Tonawanda Creek, just
north of Batavia was until a few years ago the sort of place
that gave passers-by the comfortable feeling that owning
land in this part of the country and working it was a profitable idea. Its walls were the exact yellow of the goldfinches
that described bouncing arcs over the meadows around it
and the six tapered columns of its deep porch (spread clear
across the long front and enclosed by a wide rail set on
well-turned spindles) gleamed white and cool behind the

green shrubs and the tall maples of the front yard. There was, of course, a "bay window" forming an alcove of brightness at one end, and a fancy iron grille set in the small attic window under the ridgepole. A tall poplar pointed its limbs skyward in the back yard and the "driveway" curved from the Alexander pike past the front steps and into the wide doorway of the red barn in one uninterrupted lovely gesture.

"Summerville Farm" was the name of the place but the people who lived near just called it "Joe Burke's place" or maybe "Burke's Sugarbush." The town of Alexander was proud of the farm because Joe Burke obviously made a good living there, it had belonged to the Burke family for about a hundred years, and, crowning glory, Joe made such good syrup from the stand of sugar maples about half a mile back of the house that even the presidents of the United States bought it to pour on the breakfast buckwheats at the White House. When you considered that one of the presidents to whom Joe sold his syrup was Calvin Coolidge, native of the sugarbush state of Vermont and a connoisseur in such matters, Joe's neighbors felt that the town had reason for self-congratulation. They did not connect the sale in any way (as some outraged Vermonters did) with the fact that Joe's brother, Charles H., was commissioner of Indian affairs, and, as a contemporary journal described him, "an old-time fighting politician, coldly practical, always regular." They were proud of Charles H. too, and always happy when he came to the yellow homestead for a visit.

Not many of the people of the region remembered the man whose money had bought the Burke acres in the first place, and their knowledge of him was meager. Until recently there was a picture that might have given a clue. It hung in the dining room where the Burkes and their many cousins, the Gilhoolys, used to celebrate the first sugaring off of the season by pouring hot syrup on big slabs of ice and popping the resultant sugar cakes, at the moment when they began to wax and snap, into eager mouths. But upstaters do not, as a rule, stare at pictures on the wall, at least not at family photographs, for fear the host will consider the stare an invitation to elaborate on his genealogy.

The money that bought Summerville Farm had been earned by a small boy named Joseph Burke and it was his story that Joe Burke (named after him) told on the few times that curious visitors happened to read the handwriting on the photograph. The picture showed a short bald man with Gladstone whiskers leaning elegantly, gloves in hand, on one of those cardboard walls photographers once used to give their products atmosphere, a rather dumpy-looking woman seated beside him, braided hair piled on top of her head, cameo at throat, wide flowing skirts, and a boy and girl stiffly posed in elegant attitudes. Below it in a slanting feminine hand were the words:

> To Joseph Burke
> From his old and
>   faithful friend
> Jenny Lind Goldschmidt

Oak Lea
Wimbledon Park
July 1873

The Joseph Burke of the inscription had been born beside the waters of Galway Bay in Ireland. His father had been a successful doctor and both parents had been delighted when their son, at the age of three, had shown a precocious interest in the violin. His performances on the little instrument his father had ordered made for him had shown not only musical talent but so much histrionic ability that the proud couple decided perhaps he did not need the violin to be an entertainer. So when little Joseph was five, they had presented him to a dumfounded Irish audience at the Dublin Theatre Royal in May of 1824 in the title role of a play named *Tom Thumb*. That he was a tremendous success is attested by the fact that he was immediately re-engaged, this time to play *Hamlet*. In the succeeding seasons he played Irish comedies, Shakespearean tragedies, and the popular heroic melodramas of the time throughout the British Isles, including performances at Liverpool, Margate, Brighton, and at the Haymarket and Surrey theaters in London; giving his audiences full measure for their money by including solos on the violin, piano, flute, accordion, guitar, flageolet, clarinet, and trombone.

By the time Joseph's mother felt that he was ready for an American tour he was eleven and a seasoned trouper of six years' experience. He made his debut in New York at the Park Theatre on November 22, 1830, acting Young Norval in Home's popular melodrama *Douglas*, exhibiting on the same evening his versatility by leading the orchestra in the overture to the opera *Guy Mannering* "and concluded by playing *Terry O'Rourke* in which he sang a comic song."

He was at once the idol of the New York stage. The mayor of the city, that discriminating and inveterate playgoer, Philip Hone, went to see him prepared to scoff but became his ardent supporter. "His self-possession and knowledge of his part is admirable," wrote the mayor after attending many of his performances. "He is graceful and handsome, plays sweetly on the violin and dances well and is only twelve years of age—and in his natural dress and appearance seems even not so old. He brings full houses every night." Drama critic Joseph N. Ireland wrote of him in his *Records of the New York Stage* (published in 1866) that he was "unapproached by any other child prodigy . . . his readings were always discriminating and forcible and entirely free from the drilled mannerisms of most child actors and his attitudes and gestures were easy, striking, appropriate." His playing in the roles of Richard III, Shylock, and Sir Giles Overreach were recommended as having been so good that "none sneered at a child's taking these parts." A few months later the boy had become a playmate of Philip Hone, Jr., and an intimate of the mayor's household. Private diaries and public journals were giving over many pages to descriptions of the little boy who was so precocious and professional in the theater and yet a thoroughly natural and unspoiled child off stage.

On October 13, 1831, Philip Hone's diary related that a well-known English actor named Anderson was to make his New York debut in the character of Henry Bertram in *Guy Mannering*. Evidently Anderson on his journey across the Atlantic had behaved so badly that the first mate on the vessel had sought him out at the end of the voyage and given him a thorough beating, causing postponement of his first appearance until Thursday evening. The mate had let his Manhattan friends know that the motivation for his action had been the actor's stated antipathy to America and a mob of them had bought seats in order to let Anderson know that no one of his character was welcome in the land of the free and the home of the brave.

Hone reported that there were few ladies in the audience and that the rough bully-boys prevented Anderson's entrance by showering apples and eggs and other vegetables on the stage and shouted down all efforts to calm them. In despair the managers sent for Burke and the small boy, violin in hand, walked bravely out of the wings. At once the disturbance ceased. "The only interval of order," wrote Hone, "was during the time that little Burke was brought forward and played on his violin in the overture to *Guy Mannering* at the unanimous call of the house."

Master Burke's successes in New York were even excelled by his reception in Philadelphia and at the Tremont Theatre in Boston where he played a two-month engagement to packed houses. He ended his first triumphant year in a return Boston engagement for which the program announced that besides playing the melancholy Dane in the third act of *Hamlet*, Shylock in the trial scene from *The Merchant of Venice*, and Richard in the fifth act of *Richard III*, he would direct the orchestra in a Musical Rehearsal, compose an overture on the stage, play Rhodes's air on the violin, "accompanying himself on the piano."

By the time the little fellow was booked for an upstate engagement at the Pearl Street Theatre in Albany he was a popular American institution, reported by Albanian Henry Dickinson Stone in a volume of *Theatrical Reminiscences* as having "in point of precocious musical and dramatic talent and genius, eclipsed all juvenile aspirants that ever appeared in this or any other country" and as performing "in a manner that excited the wonder and admiration of the play-going public of the two hemispheres."

In the state capital Master Burke performed an even more difficult miracle than he had accomplished in New

York. There the Irish citizenry had been aroused on the report that Dr. Burke, the boy's father, had spoken disrespectfully of the great Irish patriot, Daniel O'Connell, and was prepared to see to it by violence, if necessary, that no child of a man so obviously a traitorous rogue should be welcomed to Albany. The rest of the town's folk, particularly its stubborn Dutchmen, regarded making the son pay for the sins of his father a disgraceful inconsistency that should be prevented by force, if necessary, and only the winning ways and amazing precocity of the young performer turned what might have been a first night free-for-all into an ovation in which all agreed that to have produced such a paragon the Irish must be a remarkable people. "One would scarcely realize the fact," wrote Henry Dickinson Stone, "after witnessing Burke's remarkable delineations of the most difficult characters at night; characters belonging to actors of riper years and longer experience—and the next day meeting the boy in the street cutting up all sorts of boyish pranks, rolling his hoop, flying his kite, playing marbles, etc., utterly regardless of the remarks as well as astonishment of the passing crowd, and apparently unconscious of the enviable and important position he occupied before the world, we repeat, that it could not be realized that this mere child who was seen the night previous rendering, in the most artistic manner, the difficult character of Sir Peter Teagle in the *School for Scandal* was really the young Roscius, Master Burke."

The stage life of a prodigy is perforce a brief one. The Burke parents made the best of the half dozen years when their son's youth was an asset. But they, and their child, were sensible people, and when in 1837 New York critics reported: "A New Year's gift for which I feel no gratitude was the return of the irrepressible Master Burke, now in his 17th year, therefore neither man nor child" and "Young Burke, no longer Master, came back as a sadly diminished attraction, in his old favorite—*The Irish Tutor*," they all realized that, if young Joseph Burke was to continue to make the stage his career, it would have to be not as a prodigy but as an accomplished adult artist. Since his earnings as a child have been reckoned at about $80,000, a more than considerable fortune at the time, employment of distinguished teachers was quite possible and it was decided that, of his many talents, he should follow that for the violin. Notices of his professional appearances as an actor in New York ended in 1837 but in November of 1844 he gave a benefit performance in Albany "prior to two years study of the violin in Europe."

In a year he had returned and at the age of twenty-six was making his second debut before American audiences in New York on December 5, 1845. This time there were no cheering throngs, no rapt idolaters, as in the days when he was eleven. If there was disappointment in this, there was comfort in the fact that he was at once recognized and accepted by New York critics as an accomplished musician.

"Who is this coming out of the years behind us? Who but Master Burke, the dramatic phenomenon of the early 30's who now, as Mr. Joseph Burke, made his appearance in the Apollo Rooms . . . and very well played upon the violin . . . Now a pupil of de Beriot, he returns as a full fledged virtuoso." Within the next twelve months Burke had twice appeared as honored soloist with the New York Philharmonic and had been widely praised for his concerts at Gothic Hall, Brooklyn, and in Manhattan at the Apollo

Rooms, the Tabernacle, Chinese Assembly Rooms, the Opera House. He was immediately in demand among orchestras, he found pupils eager to pay for instruction, he was a respected, well-to-do man of affairs. Photographs of him at this time show him to have been very handsome and his good looks, combined with his Irish wit, volatile temperament, actor's grace, and an easy manner acquired by his stage experience and his European travels, made him much sought after by a New York society which at that time placed a very high value on these attributes.

Like other New Yorkers of means, the young man had considered acquiring a country property where he might find surcease from the hurly-burly of the city in the hot months, "to rusticate" was the fashionable phrase, and after a visit to western New York had chosen in the township of Alexander near Batavia a comfortable dwelling surrounded by level acres and sugar maples, which he called "Summerville Farm." His mother had gone to this retreat early in the summer of 1850 and her busy son had finally found time to join her there for a few weeks of rest.

Then arrived a telegram which proved to be of importance. It offered Joseph Burke a considerable salary if he would complete, as violin soloist, a concert group scheduled for a tour of the major cities of the United States. The group that had already performed with great success in New York consisted of Benedict, a pianist, two well-known Italian artists, a tenor named Salvi and a bass named Belleti, and its main performer, the world-famous soprano, Jenny Lind. The telegram was signed with the name of America's nonpareil showman and impresario, P. T. Barnum.

The emotions of Joseph Burke, violinist, formerly the

great Master Burke, child actor, must have been strangely mingled in the eighteen-month tour that followed. Accustomed himself, as a child, to the sentimental adulation of tremendous audiences of Americans, he was now merely a formal and minor adjunct to the greatest show on earth, the incomparable Jenny. No matter how well he played, to the audience he was a necessary evil, filling in the too-long interval between those moments of ecstasy when the Swedish Nightingale was singing. But if the impressions of the members of the Burke family of Alexander, New York, are to be believed—and there is no reason for doubting them—the jealousy that most naturally might have developed in Burke was tempered by a quite different emotion.

Jenny Lind was about a year younger than Joseph Burke. She, too, had been a child prodigy, singing her first concert in Stockholm at the age of nine. In European music circles they had many mutual acquaintances. Both knew and loved the music literature of the world. Burke had a tremendous fund of entertaining material to draw on to keep the little band of performers happy, anecdotes of his own adventures as an actor in the cities of the British Isles and in America, monologues from his impersonations of comic Irish characters in the short farces that usually had concluded the programs of the child actor. His years of experience as a trouper in America must have been of practical value as well. There is no doubt, from the evidence of Jenny Lind's later letters to Burke, that a strong and lasting friendship developed between the two artists. The Burkes of Alexander used to say that there was more than this—that the handsome Irish violinist fell in love with the rather stodgy, pious, homely girl whose voice had won general homage. They said that, probably on account of her importance as the world's greatest living artist, he never summoned the courage to tell her of his passion. If this is true—and there are evidences that indicate it—Burke must have felt the situation's irony. The most articulate little boy ever known had lost his tongue at twenty-six. The child who had surpassed his professional elders for some half dozen years in expressing the deep emotions that possessed the complex characters of Shakespearean tragedy could not even tell a girl he loved her.

He did manage, during a hiatus between concerts when he was away from her, to write Jenny Lind suggesting that she might enjoy seeing his country home. Her reply was warm and encouraging: "If only I knew where that little home, sweet home, is that you tell me of, how gladly would I go there." Not long after that, on her way to Niagara Falls, she and her party left their train and were driven to Summerville Farm. Burke's mother welcomed her heartily to the cool, large rooms, the maple-shaded lawn. If the violinist was really in love with her, no time could have been more opportune. Here he might wander with Jenny along the summery Tonawanda while sunset died over the western woods and left in its yellow afterglow a yellower amber that marching shadows proved the evening star. Here he might show her himself, not the public's artist, but a man at home restfully enjoying the familiar company of his mother and his cousins, happy but incomplete.

A few days later Mrs. Burke was reading the wholesome Jenny's prosaic bread-and-butter letter postmarked Niagara Falls: "We arrived safely and in good time at Buffalo and there we got mush and milk and a very sweet sleep." Obviously, as western New York housewives are still wont to say in their gossiping, "Nothing happened."

At about this time accompanist Benedict left the troupe and Jenny, always generously eager to help a protégé, sent to Germany for Otto Goldschmidt, young Jewish pianist whom she had befriended. He joined the company just before the 1st of June, 1851. Jenny married Otto at Boston in the following February, and Northampton, Massachusetts, papers in the spring exultantly announced that Mr. and Mrs. Goldschmidt were to give in that town their first concert together since their marriage. It would take place on May 6 and Mr. Joseph Burke, violinist, would assist.

Joe Burke, maple sugar purveyor to the White House, used to say that his uncle Joseph told him of a visit to the Goldschmidts in England and of his having said to his hostess, "If I had thought you would marry a mere musician, I would have proposed to you," and of her replying, "Oh, why didn't you?"

This conversation seems to have set the pattern of the heartbroken suitor in which Joseph Burke moved for the rest of his life. Not since Washington Irving had a distinguished American so closely adhered to the romantically sentimental and very popular concept of faithfulness to a lost love. So well did he play his last role that all those about him recognized it and even the public prints hinted delicately and archly at his secret—as in Henry Dickinson Stone's *Reminiscences*:

"Is it not somewhat remarkable, that, with the many rare qualities Burke is admitted to possess—and doubtless the numerous advantageous opportunities presented during his many years of experience in female society, he being deemed what the ladies call 'a good catch,' that he should so long remain a bachelor—which we understand he still is."

The Irish Wonder and the Swedish Nightingale

The musician lived a long and useful life, though he was a "changed man" after Jenny Lind's marriage. He was a tower of strength in the days when the New York Philharmonic Society was young and struggling, and he served three terms as its president. He became a revered teacher of aspiring pianists and composers and some of his students dedicated their compositions to him. It was said that he would not teach the violin because he could not endure the uncertainties of pitch and tone with which the inept tortured him. He spent an increasing amount of his time at Summerville Farm, however, unhappily brooding over what might have been, pacing the floor at night, playing to his family on the fine violin Jenny had given him (which he tuned in the barn so that his hearers might be spared the raucous sound) the songs that she had sung, the solos he had performed when she had been the most fanatically adored woman in American history.

Sometimes he showed the genuinely friendly words the great diva had written him, among them a revealing letter dated Dresden, 1853:

My dear Mr. Burke:

It was with a very great pleasure that I received and read your kind, friendly letter of the 1st of January and many thoughts wandered through my head when I reflected upon the many changes that have taken place since our first new year's eve together in Charlestown. It is a beautiful thing in life to find persons we can esteem and feel friendships for and you are certainly one of those, who have many times cheered me up and made me to believe in solid friendship so for my part I shall always feel interested in your welfare and happiness.

I very often think of America it is the new world that is true. There is active life and room to take breath in. Europe is old, quite a grandmother to the rest of the world—here are thousands of beautiful things, certainly and life in Europe is full of art and poetry but—except England—there is here everywhere great *infidelity*—great want of moral activity. People here misunderstand life's clear object and end—and this makes me to feel a stranger, surrounded though I am by kind people. I feel clearly as if I was to spend my whole life in serving my soul and faculties would remain undeveloped of want of such good examples as I have seen in England and in America—and yet—how many good qualities do the Germans possess but pride makes them blind to the great want, and pride is our most dangerous foe . . .

I wished you might have some nice *sensible* music pupils that could cheer you up in your fatiguing labor as a music teacher but I know from experience how seldom we find a little more than commonplace *mediocrity* in the musical geniuses of the family celebrities . . .

Mr. Goldschmidt desires to send you his best compliments. He continues to make justice to my opinion of a true uninterested friend of mine. He is very kind and faithful to me, bears with great patience and mildness my many infirmities, and my impulsive character gets smoothed by his equal and dignified temper. God bless and lead him on in the right way, as I have every reason to love and respect him . . .

I expect that you like Albenes's singing (although she is rather fat as a person!) she sang beautifully with feeling, taste and understanding. Pity that she has spoiled, broken her voice by making it a high soprano, she is by nature intended a *contralto*. And now God help and protect you my dear Mr. Burke. May you remain in good health and spirit until we meet again!! Give my best compliments and kindest regards to your family. Mr. Goldschmidt also begs to be most kindly remembered to you all and I remain now and always your old, new acquaintance and friend

Jenny Goldschmidt
born Lind

Readers of this letter, allowing for the period's characteristic reticence with regard to *affaires d'amour*, have read many and varied meanings between the lines and may continue to do so, for the only man who could satisfactorily have interpreted it died in 1902. Joseph Burke was buried wearing at his own request the gold signet ring Jenny Lind had given him. The older people of the countryside in which he lived his last years remember the bearded old man driving alone in his old-fashioned buggy along the dusty roads of the Tonawanda valley. His old house has been made into apartments now and the photograph, dated twenty years after the letter and proof of Jenny Lind's unchanging affection, no longer hangs on its walls. Few now pass Summerville Farm who know that once the Swedish Nightingale enjoyed these American meadows in the company of their young and talented owner.

8

Yorker Turned Whaler

Ira lakey of the town of marion in york State and later of Canandaigua was one of many inland Yorkers who followed the sea. In 1853, Ira became captain of the whaling ship *Siren Queen* and on October 29 of that year he set sail from Fairhaven, Massachusetts, for Pacific waters. Three years later, this time as captain of the *Arctic*, he was cruising the same waters.

In his unpublished log there is a love story. Because Ira tells it better than any one else could, it is here presented in his words:

Sunday, March 9, 1856: This day we are twelve miles from our last port and owing to calms and head winds we are only about 700 miles on our passage but we, now for the first time, have got a good wind from Westward and are going along finely. At 10 o'clock Mr. Evans my chief mate came to me and stated there was a woman on board the ship.

By making some inquiries I find he stowed her away on board himself and in fact when I came to question him he owned up to it. She is half white by the name of Sara Corsell. Her father is a farmer in Monganui who furnished us with garden vegetables. I presume all of the officers and in fact everyone living in the after end of the ship has known of this circumstance but myself for some time. She has got quite out of health from living so closely confined and that is probably the reason I have been informed of her being here. She looks very miserable. I don't know which feeling predominates with me, pity or disgust. Mr. Evans expresses much regret for his conduct in this matter and she, poor thing, is too sick to say much anyway. I gave advice as to her health &c and leave the care of her entirely to him for the present. What I shall do with such a case finally I will leave to the future.

Monday, March 10, 1856: The more I think on the subject of our woman passenger and from seeing such anguish and despair pictured out in her face I thought possibly she might not be so abandoned a person as I first supposed. Her health is much better today. So I took an opportunity this afternoon and questioned her in the presence of Mr. Perkins (our passenger) as follows, viz:

"What is your name?"

"Sara Corsell."

"How old are you?"

"Twenty years old."

"How come you to come on board this ship?"

"Because I like Mr. Evans."

"On what conditions did you come—as a virtuous passenger or to be kept mistress of Mr. Evans?"

"I came intending to live with Mr. Evans, but I should like to live as honest a life as I could until I get to America. I expect to marry Mr. Evans when we get to America."

"Did you ever say you would dress yourself in boy's clothes and stow yourself away on board of any ship and go to America?"

"No, I never did."

"Do you want to know whether Mr. Evans intends to marry you when he gets to America?"

"I do very much."

"Did you ever have any connection with any man but Mr. Evans?"

"I never did."

"How come you to let Mr. Evans have connection with you?"

"Because I thought he loved me and would marry me."

(To Mr. Perkins) "Can you believe she has never had connection with anybody before—twenty years old and half white too?"

(By Mr. Perkins) "Why! That is the reason you may depend. She is so devoted to him and has followed him so."

I now called down Mr. Evans and read to him the above questions and answers. And he pronounced the answers all correct in his opinion and stated further as follows, viz:

"I did not say to Sara positively I would marry her when I got to America but still if she understood it so and insists upon it, I shall do it. I told her had I money to buy a farm in Monganui, I would marry her and live there. I have felt very bad on her account ever since I first seduced her. I did not once mistrust that she was a virgin until I had accomplished my wishes. My plagued tongue had infatuated her, owing to her being so innocent and ignorant. She took on so and clung to me so that I could not have a heart to leave her or turn her away. So I stowed her away on board and I find the more I see and become acquainted with her, the more I like her and I don't know but I love her as well as I am capable of loving anybody."

I then stated to Mr. Evans that if after proper deliberation he should conclude to marry the girl I thought it could be legally done here on board, and I would let him and his wife have my cabin and stateroom and I would take his stateroom for the remainder of the voyage. And as I believed she was at heart innocent though ignorant and certainly very devoted to him, I would respect her as his wife and would use my influence to have all others do the same. He takes until tomorrow to decide on it.

Tuesday, March 11, 1856: This morning Mr. Evans says he is fully satisfied that he loves the girl and he will marry her as soon as we can make it convenient. So I have employed myself in making the wedding ring. The poor girl looks much happier. "All's well that ends well."

Wednesday, March 12, 1856: This day fine weather and fair; winds; steering away for Cape Horn and home. After 4 o'clock P.M. having got everything ready beforehand we had our wedding come off. I drew up a marriage contract to the best of my ability considering the emergency of the case and Mr. Evans and Sara Corsell signed it in the presence of witnesses and all of the afterguard signed as witnesses: after which we all kissed the bride and hope they will live happily and beget sons and daughters.

COPY OF MARRIAGE CONTRACT, VIZ.:

On board ship *Arctic* at sea March 12, 1856. Lat. 42.30S: Long. 158.00W.

To all those for whom it may concern:

I, Charles A. Evans and I, Sara Corsell do this day in the presence of all these witnesses bind ourselves in every point and particular in the solemn bonds of matrimony the same as tho' it was performed in the presence of a Gospel minister or a lawfully appoint-justice of the peace. Our reasons for being married now is that we are so situated we cannot live here in a manner proper for civilized beings only as "Man & Wife". Therefore these documents are drawn up and signed in good faith in duplicate and the original placed in the hands of Captain Ira Lakey to be by him deposited in the town clerk's office of Fairhaven, Mass. USA.

I, Charles A. Evans take thee Sara to be my wedded wife; to have and to hold from this day forward for better, for worse, for richer, for poorer, in sickness and in health to love and to cherish till death us do part according to God's Holy Ordinance and thereto I plight thee my troth.

C. A. Evans

I, Sara Corsell take thee Charles A. Evans to be my wedded husband to have and to hold from this day forward for better, for worse, for richer, for poorer, in sickness and in health to love, cherish and to obey till death do us part according to God's Holy Ordinance and thereto I give thee my troth.

Sara Evans

Now, Sara with this ring which has been made expressly for the occasion I thee wed, with all my worldly goods, I thee endow, in the name of the Father, Son and of the Holy Ghost. Amen.

C. A. E.

Yorker Turned Whaler

Witnesses:

Ira Lakey	Peter Beetman
Albert Lewis	I. B. Buclin
Amasa Holbrook	James T. Holt
Henry Lord	Andrew P. Wood
	John Perkins

Monday, March 17, 1856: This day ketched a "Goney" or "Albatross" with a fish line and hook baited with pork.

Poem on the Marriage of George, Son of William Wright, to a Bride Having a Sharp Tongue.

> The Children of Israel Wanted Bread
> And the Lord sent them Manna
> But George Wright wanted a wife
> So the Devil sent him Hanna.

Herb Pentler met his perennial summer boarder at the noon-train. The two of them rode in understanding silence behind the old mare for the first ten minutes of their journey to Herb's farm.

"My daughter's marryin' the real estate man," said Herb.

"That's fine," said the boarder heartily. "That is, if you approve of her choice."

"Yep," said Herb. "He's on the school board and he's a deacon in the church and he's sergeant-at-arms of the Grange—and—*he knows when to foreclose.*"

9

Hanging Day

THE BEAT OF A HAMMER SOUNDED OUT OF THE mist that covered the valley flats east of Cooperstown on the dawn of July 19, 1805. Early risers on the river side of town peered curiously from their bedroom windows across the soft dull gleam of the Susquehanna, for they knew that the gallows for the hanging of Stephen Arnold had been set up the day before. Only a few strangers who had chosen to camp all night beside that grim angle saw two boys at work and heard them tell they were building a platform for granny to sit on so that she could see the hanging "easy and comfortable."

By seven o'clock the sun had burned the mists out of the valley and off Otsego Lake, and the town was crowded. The taverns, the Red Lion and the Blue Anchor, had been filled long before the previous night's bedtime. That moment had hardly existed, for William Cook, host at the latter, in his usual holiday costume—drab coat of the style of 1776 with buttons the size of dollars, knee breeches, striped stockings, buckles so big they covered half his shoes, and a cocked hat "large enough to extinguish him"—had served up hour after hour such punches and flips as only a former steward on a British East Indiaman knew how to mix. There was talk of a knife fight around midnight over on Pig Alley, and some folks said that in a "wrastlin'"

· 172 ·

down in Frog Hollow a "half-horse, half-man" from the wild town of Canisteo beyond the Steuben County mountains had put a slick Onondaga Indian on his back.

By eight o'clock streams of carriages were rolling along Pink Street and Mosquito Road. From the Jams, round-topped hills above Milford, and the Twelve Thousand, steeper heights east of Schuyler Lake, from Hell Town and Dogtown and Butternuts, strings of wagons, men on horseback, and men on foot converged on Cooperstown. At the head of Otsego Lake rowboats and canoes slipped out of the shadow of Sleeping Lion Mountain and caught up with others from Hurry Harry and Muskrat Castle to make a scattered flotilla steadily advancing toward the shelving beach where Front Street rims the water. Groups of curious countrymen strolled past Otsego Hall, manor house of Judge William Cooper, whose hell-raising son Jim had been sent home from Yale College that spring; past Apple Hill, the home of Richard Fenimore Cooper; past Henry Bowers's just-completed Lakelands; past the new stone house (the only one in the region) that Judge Cooper had had built on the southwest corner of Water and Second Streets for his daughter and her husband George Pomeroy.

Although the parade was not announced to start until noon, the yard across from the jail at Main and Second Streets was spang full by nine o'clock. Folks tried out the stocks, looked respectfully at the whipping post, and stared across the street at the door that was soon to swing open for a murderer on his way to his fitting and proper doom. They said that Stephen Arnold ought to hang, all right. He had whipped his six-year-old ward Betsey Van Amburgh so hard that she died, "and him an educated man and a school-teacher." All because the poor child could not help pronouncing the word "gig" as "jig" he had taken off her clothes and seven times had driven her outdoors, where he had whipped her until the bitter cold of the night had made him go back to his fire.

The crowd got so excited talking that hardly any of them noticed when Jacob Ford of Burlington galloped up on a tired horse, dismounted, and ran into the jail. A few remembered afterward that he came out in a moment with the sheriff, who was frowning over what seemed to be a letter, and that the two went off in the direction of the center of town.

By eleven, when the sheriff came back to the jail, Cooperstown, with only five hundred inhabitants, was host to eight thousand, according to the best estimators. Suddenly there was a blare of brass and a tattoo of drums, and Lieutenant Commandant Mason's company of artillery and Lieutenant Commandant Tanner's company of light infantry marched up to take their places as guards to the wagon on which Stephen Arnold would ride to the gallows. Governor Morgan Lewis's love of military pomp was already losing him votes throughout the state, but nobody would kick at his detailing soldiers in full dress for so extraordinary an occasion as this.

Now the civilians who were to take part in the ceremonies were arriving at the jail door. In the little knot about the step stood the Reverend Mr. Williams of Worcester, imported to deliver the invocation at the exercises, and the Reverend Isaac Lewis, Presbyterian pastor whose flock was finishing up the first church in the township. Here was the loved dean of the town's physicians, Dr. Fuller, and, in old-fashioned knee breeches, the eccentric Dr. Nathaniel Gott, recently succeeded to some of the unpopularity of Dr. Charles Powers, who had been run out of town a few years before for putting an emetic into the punch at the Red Lion's New Year ball. Dr. Gott's offense had been an attempt to collect his bills by writing and sending to his debtors a poem:

> Says Dr. Gott
> I'll tell you what
> I'm called on hot
> All round the Ot-
> Segonian plot
> To pay my shot
> For pill and pot
> If you don't trot
> Up to the spot
> And ease my lot
> You'll smell it hot.

Elaborately indifferent to each other in the small group were Dr. Gott and Mr. Elihu Phinney, bookseller and editor of the Otsego *Herald or Western Advertiser*, whose pen was soon to describe the remarkable events of this day. Ever since a jovial evening when they had engaged in the dangerous game of suggesting epitaphs for each other's gravestones there had been a coldness between these two. Gott thought he had scored when he intimated that Phinney's soul was so small that ten thousand like it could dance on the point of a cambric needle. But Phinney had replied:

> Beneath this turf doth stink and rot
> The body of old Dr. Gott
> Now earth is eased and hell is pleased
> Since Satan hath his carcass seized.

They did not speak to each other after that. Gott was the more annoyed since Phinney, founder of *Phinney's Calendar or Western Almanack*, had won fame as a prophet when, through a typographical error in that popular journal, he had foretold snow for the Fourth of July, only to find on that day, to his own secret amazement and the loud-mouthed astonishment of his neighbors, that nature was heartily cooperating by fulfilling his prediction.

At almost the stroke of noon the big jail door swung open. The sheriff strode out first, mounted his horse, and waited for his aides to assist the pale, heavily chained prisoner into an open wagon. Then he rode ahead. Behind him walked the ministers, the lawyers, the doctors, and a few other important citizens. The band struck up a dirge as the infantry and artillery companies formed in front of it and began to march forward with the rolling wagon in their midst. As the slow procession moved along Second Street and turned down Main, the crowds that lined the way fell in behind. Along the aisle of witch trees, "tall and lanky—pressing toward the east," past the Main Street stores they went. Soon the boards of the Susquehanna bridge were complaining beneath the wagon's wheels. The gallows were in sight on the river flats a little below the red-brick house that stood near the east end of the bridge. High above them in the distance rose the Vision, the peak that marks the termination of the mountains that form the eastern rim of the valley. At the foot of the gallows lay a wooden coffin, and in front of both, on a tiny platform of her own, sat an old woman rocking as she knitted and waited.

A few days later Elihu Phinney's Otsego *Herald* de-

scribed the scene as the wagon drew up to the place of
execution and the condemned man, his chains removed,
dismounted to sit forlorn on his coffin:

Unconnected with the solemn occasion the appearance of such an extraordinary collection of the sexes was
beautiful in the extreme. The ground at a small distance
from the place of execution, which was a small flat, arose
towards the east in such manner as to afford every be-
holder an uninterrupted view of the interesting spectacle. It seemed when viewed from the high western
banks of the river, a vast natural amphitheatre filled
with all classes and gradations of citizens from the opu-
lent landlord to the humble laborer. The display of
about 600 umbrellas, of various colors; the undulating
appearance of silks and muslins of different hues; the
vibrations of thousands of fans in playful fancy; the ele-
vated background of the landscape interspersed with
carriages of various construction and filled with people;
the roofs of the buildings, which commanded a view,
covered with spectators; the windows crowded with
faces, every surrounding point of view occupied, and the
gleam of swords, bayonets &c. in the centre afforded,
whenever the mind was detached from the occasion,
real satisfaction to the contemplative mind; but on re-
versing the picture, and reflecting that all those bloom-
ing nymphs, jolly swains, delicate ladies, and spruce
gentlemen, fond mothers and affectionate sisters, prat-
tling children and hoary sages, servile slaves and impe-
rious masters would be, in all probability, incorporated
with their native dust in 100 years, it strongly enforced
the truth and pertinence of a maxim of one of the an-

cient sages, that *pride was not made for man*. A recurrence to the occasion increased our humility.

The Reverend Mr. Williams of Worcester opened the formal program. He climbed the steps of the platform, lifted a hand, and prayed for God's mercy on all present and particularly upon their unfortunate brother whose life must soon be forfeit to justice. Then the Reverend Isaac Lewis stepped forward. The crowd was still as he read his simple text:

"And he said unto Jesus, Lord, remember me when thou comest into the kingdom.

"And Jesus said unto him, Verily I say unto thee. To-day shalt thou be with me in paradise."

Pastor Lewis preached his sermon, a "pathetic, concise, and excellent adapted discourse." When it was over, at a signal from the sheriff, Stephen Arnold rose from his seat on the coffin and spoke. He was a man of learning, he was penitent, and he spoke well, ending his remarks with the sentence:

"It appears to me that if you will not take warning at this affecting scene, you would not be warned though one should raise from the dead."

Granny, sitting on her little platform in front of the poor man, was obviously much moved by his words. While he was speaking, her needles flashed more and more swiftly in the sunlight and she rocked back and forth more and more violently. A strained silence encompassed the crowd now. The sheriff's boots sounded loud on the platform as he brought forward the rope and adjusted its noose about the neck of Stephen Arnold. There was a single warning cry. It came too late. A feeble scream, a crack of splintering wood, and Granny had rocked off the platform and broken her neck!

The old lady's death caused only a slight delay in the proceedings. The frail wizened body had been lifted and carried away before many of the crowd realized what had happened. The crescendo of questioning voices soon died out. Once more there was silence and the sheriff, standing beside the doomed man, spoke the last words the miserable fellow expected ever to hear, exhorting him to make his peace with God and bidding the spectators take warning from his fate.

Now, at the moment when nothing was left to be done save the suspension and strangling to death of Stephen Arnold, the sheriff took a few steps forward, drew from his pocket an official-looking paper, and read it aloud. It was a reprieve from Governor Morgan Lewis. While the crowd were still quiet, unable to grasp its meaning, the reader hastily explained that he had received the governor's message that morning around nine o'clock, but, after conference with several leading citizens, had decided that he could not disappoint the thousands of visitors who had come from far and near to witness the day's spectacle. Possibly he did not think it necessary to add that the sudden departure of all these people in the early morning would not have allowed Cooperstown merchants to garner all the rewards that the day's brisk trading had given them. Simply out of respect for the town's guests, he said, he had allowed the scheduled exercises to continue thus far. Obviously they could not continue further.

The purport of the sheriff's words reached the minds of the crowd and of Stephen Arnold at the same time, but their separate reactions varied widely. Arnold slumped to the floor at the foot of the gallows. The crowd roared its wrath. "Some swore, others laughed, but all were dissatisfied." Many had come a long way, lost at least two days' time, been put to considerable expense for which they felt they had had no corresponding return. "They acted and talked as if they must have a substitute." They seemed to think that either the sheriff or the absent governor would do nicely. Toward Stephen Arnold, however, they exhibited little animosity. He had done his part well and in good faith. For a few moments a riot was incipient, but the sheriff avoided it. He ordered the band to play a quickstep, the soldiers to fall in, and he headed a noisy parade back through town. It drew the whole throng into its wake.

When it had reached the jail, the sheriff held up his hand for silence and granted Stephen Arnold's request that he be allowed to make the last speech of the day. From the wagon, before the jail received him, Arnold said he wished to thank Jacob Ford, who had brought the good news from Albany, and other friends, who had worked for his reprieve. Again he warned the multitude that had followed him on his joyful return from the gallows that they must control their passions. Anger, he said, had brought him to his shameful condition. Then he entered upon an incarceration which was to last the rest of his days, for his sentence was commuted the following year to life imprisonment.

Still enraged, shouting that they had been duped, damning the sheriff and his advisers for their cruelty in not telling Arnold of the reprieve until after his neck had felt the rope, the visitors who had swelled the number of Cooperstown's inhabitants to almost twenty times its us-

ual size turned their faces toward home. They left behind
a dazed group of villagers who did not know quite what
to think. In a few days, however, they had made up their
minds. The astute Elihu Phinney expressed their sentiments in the next issue of the Otsego *Herald or Western
Advertiser:*

"The proceedings of the day were opened, progressed,
and closed in a manner which reflected honor on the ju-
diciary, the executive, the clergy, the military, and the citizens of the county."

Red Jacket's farewell: "May you have at least a thousand children and never find whisky more than two shil-
lings a quart."

10

The White Woman
of the
Genesee

MARY JEMISON GAVE OVER THE BORROWED HORSE
proudly. Going to get him had been something of an adventure, for she was fifteen and small for her age. On the
evening before, while her brothers stabled the steaming
plow teams, her father had come from his flax sowing to

tell her that she was to walk to a neighbor's farm more than a mile away, spend the night, and come back with another work animal for the new day's labors.

The smell of breakfast cakes was in the air when she tugged the horse into the sunlit clearing. It was still early morning of a Pennsylvania April day in 1758. Her father was shaving an ax helve beside the house and the new neighbor, who had just come to these farm lands beside the Conewango and Marsh creeks, was waiting near him. He took the halter from her and she went up the steps. Inside the house the voices of her sisters were merry as she ran to join them.

Nothing in her life had prepared the girl for the next few minutes. Born on the ship *William and Mary* bound from Londonderry, Ireland, to Philadelphia, she had known only the peace of happy family life on a prosperous farm beside flowing waters. The sharp explosions of musket fire outside the door must have seemed unreal to her. Even more impossible—when the door was opened—must have seemed the sight of the new neighbor lying dead, her father bound and helpless, and Indians in war paint storming into the house, led by four white men who shouted orders in a strange tongue that she knew must be French.

The looting of the house took scarcely a minute. Then the raiders hurried their prisoners into the nearby woods and drove them desperately all day through the shadows. An Indian in the rear lashed with a whip the terrified and weary children, to make them keep up with the stumbling, half-running adults. At night the Indians made camp without fire and without shelter, and in the early morning they continued the pitiless race westward. When the sun had set, Mrs. Jemison sensed she would not see Mary again—"Remember, my child, your own name and the name of your father and mother. Be careful and not forget your English tongue. Don't forget, my little daughter, the prayers that I have learned you—say them often."

The Indians led Mary away. After a sleepless night and another day of exhausting struggle through the forest, the little girl saw the scalps of her mother, her father, and her sisters stretched on hoops beside the evening campfire—ghastly trophies drying for market—while the Indians talked of the prices they would get for them in the French forts to the west.

In the almost incredible time of a week the Indians reached Fort Duquesne, now Pittsburgh, with their little ragged prisoner. There they surrendered her to two sisters of the Seneca Nation whose brother had been slain by white settlers. The women bathed her, dressed her in Indian style, and adopted her according to the tribal custom of accepting a prisoner as a kind of recompense for the loss of a relative. They gave her the name De-ge-wa-nus, meaning "pretty girl," and they took her to a little Seneca town on the Ohio River at the mouth of Indian Cross Creek.

Now began a life in which Mary Jemison became De-ge-wa-nus. The little girl tried to remember and recite the prayers her mother had taught her but there were new and exciting religious rituals to take part in. There was the Sweet Water Festival, thanksgiving for the sap that dripped from the hard maples, the Strawberry Festival, the Green Corn Festival, and De-ge-wa-nus listened to the orators and danced the dances of gratitude to the spirits that gave such good things. She learned the tales of "the little people" who would join the Senecas in their dances only if the long house was so dark that the dancers could not see each other. In the winter months there was a great shouting of hunters along the Scioto—and many a word of thanks to the spirit of an antlered buck for the food his sturdy body would provide. In the summer camp beside the rippling waters of Swan Creek there were games to watch and from the quiet grove came a melodious tinkling as the Indian babies, hanging from low branches in bell-trimmed baskets, swung in the breeze.

When she was eighteen years old, De-ge-wa-nus had reached her full height but she was only four and a half feet tall. The braids of her yellow hair were long, and the blue of her eyes was clear and deep. Sheninjee, a chief of the Delaware Nation, saw and loved her and her Seneca sisters gave her to him in marriage.

"He was a noble man," said Mary Jemison later, "large in stature, elegant in appearance, generous in conduct, courageous in war; a friend to peace, and a lover of justice. His good nature, generosity, tenderness, and friendship toward me soon gained my affection; and, strange as it may seem, I loved him!"

A year after the grief of losing their first-born, a daughter who came and went when "the kernels of corn first appeared on the cob," a healthy son was born to the happy couple and Mary, remembering her mother's last words, named him Thomas Jemison. Life was good along the Ohio then, but the idyll of love and happy forest existence was soon to be interrupted.

The Senecas of the group among whom Mary lived were members of the large tribe living on the fertile banks of the Genesee River in western New York. Insistent messages came from them, urging Mary and her little family to come to that pleasant valley. The two Indian sisters who had adopted her were living there and added their entreaties. Three of their brothers offered to escort her, and so, while her husband paddled down the Ohio for his winter hunting, the nineteen-year-old mother set out with her baby on her back for the faraway shores of the Genesee.

Her return from the banks of the western rivers proved almost as hazardous as her forced flight to them. For six months she carried her baby through the almost pathless wilderness. From the waters of the Ohio and Muskingum on to the Walhonding, thence to the creeks of Pennsylvania, and finally to the gentle valley of the Genesee was a journey of nearly seven hundred miles. Mary began it in midsummer. The snows of the new year were blowing when she came to its end. By canoe, by horse, but mostly afoot, she struggled on. Her clothing was worn threadbare and she was drenched by almost daily showers. Night after night she slept upon wet ground with only a rain-drenched blanket for cover. Often she was so tired she could go no farther, yet she continued to fight her way eastward.

At last the little party arrived at their goal. There was great rejoicing at the family reunion and the big Seneca village was gay with shouting and dancing and feasting. De-ge-wa-nus happily awaited her husband. But before the time of the Sweet Water Festival bad news came from the valley of the Ohio. Stricken by sudden illness, Sheninjee had died.

While she mourned her husband, Mary Jemison had to make the great decision of her life. The oldest chieftain of the Seneca town decided that she should be delivered to the members of her own race at Fort Niagara, in order that he might collect a reward for her. She realized that she might go back now to her people, back to the comfort and comparative security of life in a frontier town, to the food and shelter and customs she had been accustomed to in the first fifteen years of her life. With the death of her loved husband, the ties that bound her to life among an alien people were loosened. She would be welcomed and generously treated by good people—people such as her mother and father had been.

But there were other considerations. The Indian family who had adopted her loved her dearly—and they were now the only family she had. Her little son was a half-breed who would grow up among the Senecas as one of them—but half-breeds were treated with contempt and suspicion by the whites. Taking small Thomas with her, she hid in the high weeds of an open field until the great chief had set out for Niagara without her. With more courage than many would have shown, the young widow cast her lot among the people of her son's father.

Not long after this, Mary Jemison married a famous Seneca warrior, Hiokatoo, already well advanced in years. Hiokatoo was nearly six feet five, a giant of a man with piercing eyes and a harsh and powerful voice. Until old age had begun to decrease his powers, he had not known an Indian who could keep up with him in a race or throw him at wrestling.

To this great warrior Mary bore four girls and two boys. "Hiokatoo was an old man when I first saw him," she said many years later, and she added the charmingly reticent understatement: "but he was by no means enervated."

The White Woman of the Genesee

As the wife of one of the Seneca Nation's most powerful leaders, Mary Jemison became a strong influence in the councils of the tribe. Among the Iroquois Confederacy, of which the Senecas were a prominent unit, women held high place, and the four-and-a-half-foot, blonde, blue-eyed, adopted Indian had the ability to avail herself of this fact. In the years that followed, it became increasingly evident that in her the virtues of her own race and of her adopted people had been united. Hiokatoo was one of the most cruel and dangerous of Seneca braves, yet Mary always stood for mercy and justice. With him she lived out the fateful days of the American Revolution, knowing but never excusing his unspeakable excesses in the Indian raids on white settlements. More than one fugitive from the cruelties of eager pursuers she guided to a hiding place near her cabin. She was trusted by the Indians and the whites. Her words were ever for kindness and moderation. The prayers her mother taught her had been forgotten, but the days of her upbringing in the gentle teachings of Christ had made an indelible impression upon her. So had the teachings of the Seneca Long House—sharing with one's neighbor, the inviolability of a promise, thankfulness to the spirits who gave the good things of life. No one came exhausted to her cabin who was not given rest. No one came hungry who was not fed.

After the war had ended, Mary Jemison became a well-known and influential figure in one of the strangest societies of young America. To the Genesee had come Captain Charles Williamson—a dashing real estate agent bound on selling great major lands to rich gentlemen and importing European serfs to do their pleasure. Here, too, had come the dynamic prophetess, Jemima Wilkinson, who

called herself the "Publick Universal Friend" and ruled her large colony of followers with dictatorial firmness. In the valley had developed a strange milieu of trappers, Virginia aristocrats, opera singers, art dealers, storekeepers, raftsmen, actors, and outlaws. "The White Woman of the Genesee," as they learned to call Mary Jemison, was known and respected. All these white pioneers knew that she could and would do much to avert Indian warfare.

So important a figure did she become that by the Treaty of the Big Tree in 1797, despite the opposition of the great chief Red Jacket, Indians and whites agreed to make her one of the great landholders of the valley. By the terms of the treaty, the Gardow Tract—nearly eighteen thousand acres—was granted to her. It lay in a fertile, secluded valley walled by steep cliffs five hundred feet high. Here mother and daughters planted their crops of corn and beans and attended to the wants of the aging Hiokatoo. Many of her acres Mary rented to white neighbors for meager sums.

But life had not done with Mary Jemison. She was yet to experience such tragedy as few women know. For in the year of Hiokatoo's death at the age of a hundred and three, her son John, turned Cain under the influence of firewater, murdered his half brother, Thomas, and left his lifeless, tomahawked body lying across their mother's threshold.

Acquitted by the Seneca tribal authorities on the grounds of self-defense, John turned against his young brother Jesse of whom he was very jealous and a year later, in a drunken frenzy, slew him as well. Mary was prostrated with grief over the death of her loved ones and the crimes of their brother. Years later she said: "My darling son, my youngest child, him on whom I depended, was dead . . . I was overcome with grief at the sight of my murdered son, and so far lost the command of myself as to be almost frantic; and those who were present were obliged to hold me from going near him."

Bereaved of two sons through the murderous violence of a third, widowed of her devoted husband, Mary Jemison never lost the spirit that burned within her. Beloved for her kindliness by both Indian and white neighbors, she continued her life on her acres beside the waters of the Genesee.

A last tragedy deprived her of her remaining son in 1817 when John's treacherous temper found its inevitable reward—death by violence in a brawl. Six years later she told Dr. James Everett Seaver, who wrote down for her the story of her life: "My strength has been great for a woman of my size, otherwise I must long ago have died under the burdens which I was obliged to carry. . . . I have planted, hoed and harvested corn every season but one since I was taken prisoner . . . I have been the mother of eight children, three of whom are now living, and I have at this time thirty-nine grandchildren, and fourteen great-grandchildren . . . I live in my own house, and on my own land . . . Situated in the midst of my children, I expect I shall soon leave the world, and make room for the rising generation."

The old lady cried when one day a missionary said a prayer for her and she recognized the words as those her mother had once taught her. But she was amusingly and emphatically indignant when she was rebuked by an over-zealous Christian for her belief in the "pagan" teachings of the Long House. She felt properly insulted when she was told by a Calvinist that she, like all other human beings, was a poor sinner, and it is obvious that though the missionaries of the region claimed that she died as much in the Christian faith "as could be expected of her," it was not the faith as they defined it.

Mary Jemison died in September of 1833, when she was about ninety-one years old. First buried on the Buffalo Creek Reservation, her remains were eventually moved to Letchworth State Park on the Genesee River not far from her Gardow home. Near her grave is a statue, a bronze figure representing the young white girl in Indian dress, arriving at the banks of the Genesee with her baby on her back. It stands in a clearing beside an old Seneca council house which she passed on her famous journey. At a little distance stands the log cabin she built for her daughter Nancy. Just beyond the clearing the waters of the Genesee tumble over the steep rocks.

Part Three

The Banners of Onondaga

"... a banner of beautiful white taffeta on which was painted largely the name of JESUS."

Old Voyageur's Journal

"Onondaga Hunters—Canada Liberated"

11

The Big Eat-
All Dinner

(Le Festin à Tout Manger)

THERE HAS BEEN MANY A JULY AFTERNOON CELE-
bration on the northeast shore of cool Onondaga Lake,
where Liverpool now stands, and many a program cut short
by the rain that seems to threaten every upstate Saturday
but probably the first of these occasions took place in the
summer of 1655. Two speakers' platforms made from new-
cut logs, a surging crowd gazing apprehensively upward at
the drifting rain clouds, and long lines of canoes drawn up
on the pebbly beach, all showed how important the exercises were to be. While waiting spectators yipped impa-
tiently, a little group whose elaborate dress suggested authority stood beside the gray-green water looking anxiously
down the lake. Conspicuous in their midst was a man whose
white skin contrasted strongly with the darker complexions
of his companions and whose costume was a long black
cotton robe and a big black hat.

Peter Mary Joseph Chaumonot knew, and with happy
anticipation, that somewhere just out of his sight was François Le Mercier, who had forsaken his position at Quebec

as superior of all Jesuit missions in New France to join him. There, too, would be his best friend, Claude Dablon, who had last year said him an affectionate farewell and left him to all the discomfort and anxiety of life among these unpredictable wild-men. And with these, news had come, were two other Black Hats—as the natives called him and his Jesuit brothers René Menard and James Fremin—two lay brothers, ten soldiers, and thirty to forty brave French colonists. New France was soon to be, in truth, a new France.

Barely out of sight around a point in the lake, the eagerly expected guests also were excited. They particularly wanted to make a good first impression and their commander, the experienced officer Captain Zachaire Dupuis, had a plan. His party, he knew, was very weary. They had been paddling up the rapids-obstructed St. Lawrence and along the shores of stormy Lake Ontario for a month. They had run out of food and had to live on cranberries and the salmon they could kill with their paddles until reprovisioned by a canoeload of food sent out to meet them.

The afternoon was wearing on; his fleet of twenty canoes and small boats had not entered the lake from the Oswego River until three o'clock. So that his command might rest and, further, that his ideas on establishing satisfactory relations might be put into immediate effect, Captain Dupuis ordered a halt about a quarter of a league from the spot where the welcoming populace was assembled.

There, according to a journal of one of his companions, probably Claude Dablon, the captain's men landed five small cannon, the light thunder of which they made resound along the lake. "This was followed by the discharge of all the arquebuses in the hands of our people. Such was the first salute that we sent over the water, through the atmosphere and through the woods to the Elders of the country who were awaiting us with a great multitude. The sound rolled above the surface, burst in the air, and was most agreeably echoed by the forests."

Immediately, in a column of five evenly spaced fours, the canoes and small boats of the party moved into sight of the eager crowd. Fatigue and hunger forgotten, uniformed soldiers, Black Hats, lay brothers, and colonists did their best to make their water parade a miracle of precise action in unison. Above them fluttered the flag of their enterprise, "a banner of beautiful white taffeta on which was painted largely the name of JESUS." They were French. They had an audience.

As soon as they had landed they briskly fired another salvo from the arquebuses, and the elaborate welcoming exercises began. There had been rumors before the start from Quebec that the wild-men were trying to lure the French into their country in order to massacre them and the weary travelers were delighted to see only the friendliest smiles and to hear the warmest expressions of delight at their arrival. A chieftain spoke the formal welcome, made the formal gift on behalf of his people, and then Peter Mary Joseph Chaumonot, most adept of all the Black Hats at speaking the languages of the five nations of the Iroquois Federation of wild-men, replied for his countrymen.

"It is for the faith that I take in my hands this rich present and open my mouth to remind you of the pledges you gave at the time you came to Quebec to conduct us to your country."

This sentence struck a somewhat discordant note, intimating that the speaker felt after his year among them that

his hearers needed to be reminded of an August day almost two years before when a chief representing the Onondaga Nation had stood before a representative of the governor of New France in Quebec and said:

"Place yourselves in the heart of our country since you are to possess our hearts. Show us fatherly care and we will show you the obedience of good children."

Despite their good neighbors' distrust, the leaders of the wild-men were prepared to respond with generous words and, the newcomers realized with dismay, many of them. The two raised platforms "from which to pay us compliments aloud and to deliver their harangues" were being put to a use evidently intended to be protracted when, to the courteously concealed delight of the exhausted voyagers, rain interrupted the program. "They told us that they would withdraw," says the journal describing the end of the day, "in order that their civilities might not disturb our rest—to which they wished to contribute by singing around our cabins the softest and most agreeable airs, and those most capable of sending us to sleep."

There were enough Frenchmen who were acquainted with soporific singing as practiced in the region to avert it politely but no one to protect the unaccustomed ears of the wild-men early Sunday morning from a rendering by all the French of the Te Deum. After this chanting of Thanksgiving for a happy arrival the Jesuits held a communion service and displayed the ornaments they had brought with them—"which would be considered poor in France but were thought very magnificent here." They then took possession of the whole country in the name of Jesus Christ, action partially justified by the fact that, on April 12, they had received from the governor of New

France a royal deed giving to the reverend fathers of the Society of Jesus a space ten leagues square near the village of Onondaga, and the next day all began the new week by settling down to work in good earnest at building lodgings and a redoubt for the soldiers at a high point over the lake.

A month later this work had been done, and they had found from the wild-men that boiling the water of the salt springs south of the lake would turn it into salt, that application of rattlesnake scales would cure toothaches, and eating rattlesnake meat would allay fevers. The supply of rattlesnakes must have lessened considerably at once, for at this very time a fever attacked many. The wild-men were sympathetic. "Never were seen so many bright faces," wrote the keeper of the journal, ". . . it seems as if the hearts of the savages were leaping out of their eyes and I do not think that it is possible without having seen it, to conceive the manifestations of affection and cordiality . . . If, after all that, they betray and massacre us, I will accuse them, not of dissimulation but of frivolity and inconstancy, which in a short time can change the affection of those Barbarians into fear, hatred, and treachery."

Whether they were deceitful or fickle, the wild-men in the next few months did not trouble the smiling surface of life at Onondaga. The bastioned Fort Ste. Marie that towered above the landing, walled with heavy tree trunks and thatched with twigs of ash, gave the fifty bold Frenchmen tranquil security through the winter, and after the following spring smaller buildings, huddled in a fine fall of woods, looked out on gently sloping smooth land checkered for a surprising distance with fields of grain, maize, turnips, and dotted with groves of chestnut and oak and many fruit trees. Acorn-fed hogs grew so fat that they could hardly move. A lengthening procession of wild-men entered the enlarged chapel, professed themselves moved by the Christian story, and were baptized. On nearby Cayuga Lake René Menard, who had been sent there at the request of the native population, reported a new chapel and hundreds of converts.

Religious and civil authorities in Quebec were hugely pleased that the Jesuits and the fifty bold Frenchmen were winning so much for Christ and the French Empire and felt that they should be rewarded with support. When the colony was a few days over a year old, a flotilla of thirty large boats set out upriver from Montreal. Among the twenty-odd French whom Quebec was adding to the western fellowship were two picturesque and oddly different persons, each of whom would write his own story of the trials of the following days. The courage of the first of these, Black Hat Paul Ragueneau, met immediate test. On the night of August 2, when they had been on the river just a week, one of the fifty guiding Iroquois attacked a woman member of a group of captive Christian Hurons, also being convoyed to Onondaga. A male fellow tribesman went to her defense and in a trice the cowering French heard the wild whooping of the Iroquois, the death cries of half a hundred Hurons, mostly women and children. Faced with this cruel challenge to Christian principles, Paul Ragueneau sternly rebuked the sullen wild-men for these murders despite the threat of an immediate martyrdom which his companions feared they might have to share.

Of all the Frenchmen no more unwilling victim of such a fate could have been found than a gay, hard, realistic young voyageur named Pierre Radisson, whose fears were based on personal experience since his courage during torture as a boy captive had won him adoption into a tribe of wild-men. He was a rough one, a tough one, a shrewd opportunist, a lying braggart, a poetic, fancy-inspired man of action. Radisson, some six or seven years later, remembered the Onondaga days with excitement and wrote of them not in his native French but in English. The manuscripts of his journals were found and published two centuries later with an editorial note by an English scholar stating that they "as might be anticipated, in orthography, in the use of words, and in the structure of sentences conform to no known standard of English composition."

Radisson, however, was not one to let the barrier of language stand between him and communication of his ideas or of his own blithe spirit. He told frankly how scared he was on the night of the awful massacre of the Hurons and a few sentences later forgot fear completely to tell a tale branded by all honest devotees of natural science who have since read it as unblushingly tall: "As I sat with my companion I saw once of an evening a very remarkquable thing. There comes out of a vast forest, a multitude of bears, 300 at least together, making a horrid noise, creaking small trees, throwing rocks down by the water side. We shot att them but they stirred not a step, which frightened us that they slighted our shooting. We knew not whether we killed any or no because of ye dark, neither dare we venter to see. The wildmen tould me that they never heard their fathers speak of so many together."

By the time that Ragueneau, Radisson, and their companions had reached Onondaga in early August, 1657, the whole colony had begun to feel premonitions of disaster. The folk fancy of the wild-men had turned against them.

A whispering campaign, possibly started on the banks of the Hudson by the English and Dutch enemies of the French, had traveled west to the homes of the Iroquois. Baptism, the wild-men were saying to each other, was bad magic that caused the death of children and made them vomit blood that contained their souls. It was common gossip that the Black Hats were baptizing the souls out of the bodies of their victims so that they could the more easily torture them in heaven, that Claude Dablon had even filled a box with souls thus obtained, shut it up, and walked off with it. On the shores of Lake Cayuga a young warrior of the wild-men threatened to take the life of René Menard for killing a sick man by baptizing him. Sullen and hidden resentment boiled over now and then into open hostility. The French were becoming tense and irritable. Even good Father Ragueneau, having received a complaint from safe and pleasant France that the colony was costing too much money, wrote sharply to the superior of his Order:

"How comes it that you now complain of our excessive expenditures? We are in a country where the expense is much greater than in that of the Hurons . . . We walk with heads erect amid dangers, insults, hootings, calumnies, hatchets and knives, with which they very often pursue us, with intentions of putting us to death . . . and you write us you can no longer afford to maintain this Mission. I prefer, my Reverend Father, to abide by the last words of your letter, which tells us that after all, if we do well on our side, God will on his part, do what is necessary."

Of the same trying weeks, the teller of the tall tale about the bears wrote spiritedly:

"The autumn scarce began when we heare that the lower Iroquoits contrived a treason against the ffrench . . . saying that the French were as many hoggs layed up to be fatted in their country. But O liberality what strength hast thou! Thou art the onely means whereby men know all and pierce ye hearts of the most wild and barbarous people of the world. Hearing such news we made friends by store of guifts . . . There is nothing done or said but we have advice of it. Their dayly exercise is feasting . . . songs, throwing of hattchets, breaking kettles. What can we do. We are in their hands. It is hard to get away from them. We must resolve to be upon our guard being in the middle of our Enemy."

Through all of the winter the fifty brave Frenchmen lived in an atmosphere of doom—seeing behind every wildman's friendly smile the horrid leer of a torturer. Rumors reached them that the attack was about to begin. Word came from Montreal that in November three Frenchmen, having ventured too far from the fort, had been murdered and their heads severed from their bodies and displayed on poles. Dupuis was convinced that the lives of all depended upon their making a secret escape and this seemed an utter impossibility. Nevertheless, he ordered that work be begun on two large boats, contemplating flight as soon as the ice on the lake had melted enough to allow passage. The boats were built secretly on the attic floor of the house of one of the Jesuits which was large enough for the purpose.

While the work was going on Jaluck, a Huron slave who was accustomed to bringing corn into the stockade, got an inkling of the activity and, relating it to his instruction in the Old Testament, came to the conclusion that God who, to punish the wicked, had once drowned the world except for father Noah and his family, planned another deluge and had advised the Jesuit fathers to be prepared. In a panic Jaluck raced back to the village of the Huron captives and told his news. The French had to summon much tact to quiet the uproar that ensued and to convince an Onondagan committee of investigation that they had not the least idea of building an ark in the middle of winter with the ice thick upon the lake.

The boats having been completed, the Frenchmen hid them by piling around and over them a dozen bark canoes which they had used for fishing and hunting, and waited desperately for spring. Alarms increased in number, false as well as true. A sentry was attacked. The French lived in terror, their weapons ever ready.

It was in early March that Zachaire Dupuis had his idea for a great *festin à tout manger*. Reports of that remarkable party differ as to the reasons given to those invited for holding it. Pierre Radisson, the one host who mentions the matter in his writings, says that one of the Jesuit fathers pretended that he had broken his arm after attending a more select and less elaborate preliminary function and that the invitations to the big affair were accompanied by the explanation that it was to be a celebration of the good man's recovery. Another motive was described, however, by Sister Marie, mother superior of the Ursulines of Quebec, in a letter she wrote to a friend about six months after the party. She who knew well several of those who gave it,

including Jesuits Peter Chaumonot, Paul Ragueneau, and
Joseph du Perron, and may have had the tale from one or
all three eyewitnesses, told her correspondent that a young
Frenchman so popular with the wild-men that he had
been adopted into their tribe approached his new foster
father with the suggestion for the feast. He said that he
had dreamed that he would die unless all the wild-men
would agree to come to a dinner of a very special kind in
which all the guests ate every bit of the food that was set
before them. If any guests went to sleep before all victuals
had been consumed, then, the young Frenchman said
sadly, his own life would be forfeit.

The Onondagans were the mystics of the Iroquois Federation, the soothsayers and the interpreters of omens, and
they had a strong belief in the dependability of dreams.
Hence, the paternal wiseman, as the French had anticipated, took a serious view of the situation. He said gravely
that he would be desolated if his adopted son were to die
and he felt that the rest of the tribe would be equally sad.
Eating all the food at a feast, he thought, was a small price
to pay for the privilege of continued association with him.
He would be glad to accept an invitation and so, he felt
sure, would his fellows.

Whatever the pretense actually offered for the giving of
the party, and perhaps both were used since they are not
necessarily exclusive of each other, the invitation was soon
made generally known, and the time set for Monday evening, March 20. No wild-men were admitted to the fort
that day, since, as the French explained, it was not their
custom "To shew the splendour of our banquettes before
they should be presented att table." This gave the givers of
the party opportunity for packing their belongings and

making secretly ready to leave the scene as soon as it was over.

Trader Radisson's observations on the party manners of the invited guests have a cynical ring. The chieftains of the wild-men "were sure not to fail, but be first" and they accepted the invitation "to see our fashions as well as to fill their gutts . . ." It was folly, he added, "to induce them to eat for they goe about it more bould than welcome. They eat as may wolves having eyes bigger than their bellies."

The place of the Eat-All Dinner was not far outside the wall of the fort at a level spot now traversed by the Syracuse-Liverpool road. The wild-men were served on their usual table, the ground, and there was no question of the heartiness with which they entered into the spirit of the occasion. The accounts of the two men who were there and wrote descriptions of it complement each other amusingly. In simple French prose Paul Ragueneau praised the French master of ceremonies for his skill in bringing about the participation of all guests in the merry revels and told how the wild-men yelled their glee or with pretended ferocity made the night hideous with war whoops. To the rhythmic accompaniment of trumpets, flageolets, flutes and drums, happily they ridiculed the French manner of dancing with its deep bows and mincing turns while their hosts whooped and ululated as they gave broad imitations of the running steps and animal-like postures of the dances of their guests. Prizes were given to the most successful in this satiric game and also to those of the French, who while it was going on, created the loudest noise in the effort to drown out the sounds made by their compatriots who were at the same time, as stealthily as possible, dragging the two big boats out of the Jesuit's attic and down to the landing on the lake.

Pierre Radisson, writing several years after these happenings, dwelt delightedly on the menu and its consequences:

"We made excellent bisquettes of the last yeare's corn and forgot not the hoggs that were a fatning. Att last the trumpetts blowes, put yourselves in order; there is nothing but outcryes, clapping of hands and capering that they may have better stomach to their meat. There comes a dozen of great kettles full of beaten Indian corn dressed with mince meats . . . Heare comes two great kettles full of bustards [Canada geese] broyled and salted before the winter with as many kettles full of ducks. As many turtles was taken in the season by the nett . . . divers of fish, eels, salmon and carps, which gives the wild-men a new stomach. Were they to burst heere, they will show their courage. The best is that we are sure none will forsake his place, nor men nor women . . . there comes the thickened flower, the oyle of bears, venison. To this the knif is not enough, the spunes also are used.

"We see allready severall postures; the one beats his belly, the other shakes his head, others stopp their mouths to keepe in what they have eaten. They were . . . making strange kinds of faces that turned their eyes up and down. We bid them cheare up . . . Cheere up like brave men. If your sleep overcomes you you must awake; come sound the drumme, it is not now to beat the guitar—come, make a noise. Trumpet blow to make thy cheeks swell, to make thy belly swell also."

The wild-men were beginning to protest that they could eat no more but the French, with their lives at stake, replenished the fires that lighted the wild scene and the plates of their guests.

"Have pity," said the foster father to his son, "we must sleep."

"And let me die?" asked the young Frenchman he had adopted, and so to oblige him the wild-man went back to his eating.

"But there is an end to all things," Radisson philosophizes. "The wild-men can hold out no longer; they must sleep. They cry out 'SKENON, enough, we can beare no more!' Lett them cry SKENON, we will cry HUNNAY, we are a-going, sayes we."

Eventually the young man went to his foster father and said, "It is done. I will now have pity on you. You may stop eating and I will not die. I will have a sweet instrument played that will put you to sleep; don't get up until late tomorrow. Sleep until prayer-time."

The gentle twanging of a guitar and the soft singing of lullabies by a sweet-voiced and very frightened Frenchman soon had the sated wild-men dropping off one by one into deep sleep. When the last one was motionless and snoring, the French tiptoed into the fort by the land gate, rushed through to the other side, and tiptoed out by the water gate. There were the boats "of a new and excellent model for shooting the rapids," of very little draft and capable of carrying fourteen or fifteen men and a weight of fifteen or sixteen hundred livres. As the fifty-three fugitives were about to clamber into these and four canoes of the Algonquin pattern and four of the Iroquois, which were to complete the little fleet, Radisson, whose early life as a wild-man had given him savage tendencies, the soldiers, and many like-minded had what they thought to be

a very good idea. They would go back and kill their somnolent guests of the evening while they were still so full
they were unable to budge. Then they would attack the
village of the wild-men where they were sure there were
not twenty men left. It would be no great matter to put
to the sword six hundred women and maybe a thousand
children of the Onondaga tribe. Having done so, they
"might have a great hole in the skirts of that untoward and
perverse nation." Obviously with regret the bloodthirsty opportunist reports, "The father's answer was to this that they
were sent to instruct the people in the faith of Jesus Christ
and not to destroy, that the crosse must be their sword . . ."

The military men then argued that the only good wildman was a dead one. "It was in vaine to think to convert
them but the destroying of them was to convert them."
The merciful Jesuits were firm, however, and so out of deference "without noise of trumpet or drum but zeal with
grief, we left that place."

Winter lingered on the shores of Lake Onondaga. The
water still froze every night and the party were forced to
break their way through the ice with paddles and staves as
they made for the mouth of the Oswego River, not easily
discernible under the crystallized surface. They had slow
going and were still in sight of Fort Ste. Marie when day
broke but their former neighbors were happily following
their advice to "sleep late." Once in the open water of the
flowing stream, the French, fearing pursuit, paddled frantically. They saw beneath the tumbling waters of the rapids
the white faces of three drowned comrades but there was
no time for mourning or for ceremony. With incredible
speed for the time of year they made their way to Lake
Ontario and along its shore to the St. Lawrence. Without

native guides, sometimes in icy water up to their necks for hours at a time, often deep in a channel lined by steep cliffs "where a dozen Iroquois might easily have defeated us," the desperately hurrying Frenchmen struggled on toward the safety of Quebec.

Each day the weather was a renewed miracle, for the sun melted the ice as they moved north, opening a path for them. Their boats were the first on the river at Montreal and at Three Rivers after the winter freeze . . . "God who holds every moment of our lives in his hands, inspired us so happily with all that we needed to do, that leaving our house of Sainte Marie near Onondaga toward eleven o'clock on the night of March 20th we arrived at Quebec on the 23rd of the month of April," wrote Father Ragueneau triumphantly from the safety of the fortified French town. ". . . our departure was considered impossible yet ECCE VIVIMUS—we are alive and have had the good fortune to place in possession of eternal life many of those who were preparing to drink our blood and to cast our live bodies into their fires."

Soon the story of what had happened at Onondaga after the food-drugged sleepers waked found its way downriver—to the vast enjoyment of the party givers. The surfeited bodies had finally stirred and the wild-men long after cockcrow had risen to walk about the walls of the fort within which, they firmly believed, their hosts of the night before still slept soundly. The sun moved up the sky and they saw no one come out from behind the locked doors, heard no voices within them. They knocked and, having heard the barking of dogs and noises of other domestic animals inside, were satisfied that the owners of the beasts were possibly asleep, at prayer, or in council. A light snow had covered the tracks of the fleeing French after they had embarked and the wild-men, seeing its unsullied whiteness, were convinced that no one had left the enclosure since the feast had ended.

When the sun began to go down, chiefs of the puzzled people climbed the stockade and dropped down into a terrifying silence. Father Ragueneau took especial pleasure in describing the scene that followed in a letter to a superior in France:

"Entering and finding no one they looked at one another, were seized with fear, and believed that they had to do with demons . . . that the absent walked on the waves or fled through the air, that they had made themselves invisible and that they would return to pounce upon the village just as suddenly as they had disappeared . . . Their sense of guilt, of murderous intentions, threw them into the utmost terror. They were everywhere on guard, in arms day and night."

A year later wild-men of the Oneida tribe came to Quebec in an effort to secure the release of certain Iroquois prisoners held by the French. Their spokesman had a talk with Father Le Moyne, who in 1654 had been the Jesuit brother to mark the site at Onondaga as admirable for the establishment of a colony and who in November of 1656 had joined the colony just in time to live through the torment of the suspense-ridden winter.

Said the wild-man:

"The Onondagans send thee this word . . . Thy lodges still stand. An elder of our tribe lives there to preserve them. Put thy canoe into the water and go to take possession of what belongs to thee."

Father Le Moyne answered with Christian forbearance

that the Jesuits would return gladly when the difficulties between them and the wild-men had been resolved. But remembering the winter the fifty brave Frenchmen endured in the fear that each next minute would be their last, remembering the *festin à tout manger* and the heights of gluttony and deceit that had been reached that March night, remembering that he had been compelled to put his canoe into the water and to leave behind the results of all the laborious work that had been done—the houses built, the fields cleared, the souls saved—the usually gentle priest allowed himself the luxury of replying:

"I protest that it is thine own fault if thou be damned."

Free Burley is a half-breed Indian guide. Lives with his dog in a shack near North Creek. Free can play on the mouth organ and, as he says, he "used to lilt the breakdowns and learned to dance 'em in the shanties." He can still remember *Johnston's Pond, Satan's Vision.* He says there used to be a song for every shanty.

He likes to tell of the time he took a New York tourist fishin' and told him that he'd find trout growing on the limbs of a white pine that had fallen into the water. The tourist climbed out and dropped a fly beside the submerged limbs and immediately caught a large trout. Then he started for home. "Said he wasn't going to fish this country," says Burley. "Said if trout grow on trees out here, God knows what's in the water."

Free lives alone but he says he's not a hermit like Bob-cat Ranney, the hermit of Dogtown, or Noah Rondeau, the hermit of Cold River. Speaking of Noah Rondeau makes him think of two other French Canadians he knew once who went fishing with a jug between them. When the day got hot, they anchored their boat, emptied most of the jug, and went to sleep. While they napped, a breeze came up and the boat, dragging anchor, floated into another cove. One of them finally awakened, looked around, and shouted, "Pierre! Pierre! Wake up. We ain't here."

Sukie was an Indian, had a lot of husbands, lived a long time with the last one in the pine grove up between North Creek and North River. Used to say, "I've had six men and had to support every damned one of them but this one."

One day a passer-by heard a great wailing inside her house and went in to inquire what tragedy had befallen her.

"My sister and my daughter turned over the car and rolled down the bank."

"How terrible," said the passer-by.

"Terrible," said Sukie. "Busted a pint of the God-damned best likker anyone ever tasted."

One time when her man was sent up for six months' sentence, she wheedled the judge into letting her serve half of it. On her way back from prison she got off at North Creek and was greeted by a friend.

"Hello, Sukie. Have a draw on my pint of new likker."

When Sukie told about it later, she used to say, "Comin' back from jail, me with my reputation back and all, wasn't that a heluva thing to have happen?"

Sukie saw George Conway starting out to guide old man Beck on a fishing trip. George had ten loaves of bread and five bottles of whisky in his arms. Sukie said, "Where you goin', George, with all that bread?"

When her man was lumbering in the woods one winter Sukie mourned that she had no way to send him a quart of likker.

"I'm goin' in, I'll take it to him," said a lumberjack.

Sukie said, "I don't send no rabbit with a head of lettuce."

Sukie kept house for a while for Denis O'Donovan. Soon after she left she went back when Denis wasn't around and stole some of his corn. When Denis was going by the grove one day he said to her, "How are your chickens doing?"

"Doing fine," said Sukie.

"Ought-ta be—eatin' that good corn."

Sukie went to Lawyer Little and asked what would happen if she licked him. Said she was older than he was and didn't weigh so much and she thought it would be a fair fight and they ought not to do anything to her.

Sukie said, "He's a fine one to be talkin' about stealin'— he'd steal Christ if He was loose."

Dark Trees to the Wind

Among the gifts packed away in Uncle Mart Hyde's sea chest on his journey to Rich's Corners, U.S.A., were six gallon jugs filled with old and very rare wine made by his parents in the Rhine Valley.

Came a night of waves and wind when the captain advised the passengers to make their peace with God as it would be only a few hours before the ship would go down.

Young Mart took the news stoically enough but with a troubled expression in his eyes. To one after another of his weeping, praying fellow passengers he proffered a drink of his precious cargo but not one accepted.

The next morning the sea was nearly calm and the sun was shining. Sailors repaired the damage wrought by the storm and passengers happily walked the decks. Uncle Mart sprawled in his bunk below, a seraphic smile on his face, the unmistakable odor of rare Rhine wine emanating from the depths of his being. Beside the bunk lay six empty gallon jugs.

Next day a friend said, "Martin, why did you drink all that wine?"

Martin was amazed.

"Vy," he said, "I yust couldn't see all dot gut vine vasted."

12

"Creature of a High Wrought Fancy"

IN THE EARLY FALL OF 1836, NILS SZOLTEVKI VON Schoultz, twenty-nine-year-old Polish chemist, strode into the roaring saltmakers' town of Salina near the head of Onondaga Lake. He was tall, well made, and so very handsome that later even certain enemies whom he had tried with all his great physical strength and soldierly ability to kill spoke of his noble good looks. In the rough, tough town of more than sixty salt-boiling factories it was not likely that this gentle-spoken, seldom-smiling, courtly young scientist would find congenial friends, but before long there were two—articulate, refined, sensitive Warren Green, whose farm lay on the rolling fertile acres of the Vale of Onondaga, and his sister, the lovely young widow Emeline Field.

As the hickories, elms, and maples turned to the flaming colors of upstate autumn, as the air grew clearer to bring the hills closer, as the nights grew cold and bright, the young Pole sat with these two, telling them many things. He told them of his days in the universities of Northern Europe, where he had become a scholar. He spoke, Warren Green remembered later, "of polar snows, Italian skies, burning African sands," and most of all of the city he loved beyond all others, beautiful medieval Florence on the gleaming meanders of the Arno, "its statuary, picture galleries, the gracious hospitality of its people." There had been a girl there—Anna—daughter of an English gentleman of Calcutta, and the soft romantic atmosphere of the ancient town had so enveloped them that they had married there in 1834. Then they had gone to live in Sweden, home of his mother's father, the distinguished Swedish General Grepenberg, once governor of Finland. There they had been miserable, utterly unsuited to each other. When war between his native Poland and Russia had broken out he had been glad to join his father's regiment of Cracows to fight in the defense of Warsaw.

There was a suppressed excitement and sometimes a hard tone in his gentle voice when he told Warren and Emeline of what followed. Beneath the towers of Warsaw he had seen his father die at the head of his troops, and a brother slain, and in his grief he fought so savagely that he was given his father's rank of major. He told them how his mother and sister tried to escape the city disguised as peasants, but were captured and banished to wild and frozen Siberia; how he himself slipped across the border and wandered into France, how he joined the Foreign Legion there and served for a short time in Africa. Then he returned to Karlskrona, the Swedish town where Anna was living in 1836, but only to realize how hopeless their marriage was and to say goodbye.

Once in America, he traveled to the banks of the Kanawha River in Virginia (now West Virginia) and there, because he had had experience in his father's salt mines in Cracow, he worked among the saline deposits of Kanawha County and later purchased with money brought from abroad a property called Salt Rock (still a small West Virginia community). Recently, he had been working, he said, on a new method of purifying salt before it was manufactured, and, feeling that in order to complete his invention he should study processes elsewhere, he had come to Salina, built a little laboratory, and was continuing his experiments.

Sometimes, when further news of the rape of Poland by the Russian tyrant had been published, he would become restless and taut, remembering his own hopeless endeavor to save his country and hating the arrogant conquerors. Then, and only in the presence of his dear friends, words would come with a rush.

"I have seldom heard him revert to personal achievements incident to events so memorable," Green said, "and then only under circumstances of highest excitement. But I have learnt from these occasional departures from self-reserve and incontestably from other sources that the important part he acted was brilliant with heroic adventures and hair-breadth escapes, the bare recital of which is calculated to enchain and captivate the most casual listener."

The beautiful Emeline must have listened to these tales with starry eyes and sympathetic comment. Soon she came to mean more to Nils Von Schoultz than any woman ever meant, and he told her so. In answer she hung about his neck a gold locket containing a miniature of herself and he wore it ever after. From his little chest of treasured family heirlooms he took two precious Oriental stones and gave them to Warren to be set for her, but events were to happen rapidly now and Warren was to be too concerned over his friend to discharge the instruction.

"Creature of a High Wrought Fancy"

The work in the laboratory proved successful, and in the late summer of 1837 came Letters Patent No. 298 dated July 29, 1837. Two salt furnaces were already making use of the invention in Salina and many more on the Kanawha. The trio of friends were very happy. This meant riches even as great as the Pole had known in the comfortable days of peace in his native country. The patent was valued at $28,000, a considerable fortune at the time, and Emeline and Nils were betrothed, contingent possibly on annulment of his previous marriage, for Nils was a devout Roman Catholic.

Von Schoultz went to the Kanawha country to inspect his holdings there in the fall of 1838. When he returned, he found waiting for him a citizen of Salina whom he designated in an account of his actions, written later, as "Mr. Stone, merchant." It is more than likely that this new friend was Erasmus Stone, the Salina postmaster, and the only man of this surname mentioned in the town records. Erasmus had something of a record as a liberal among his neighbors, having been disciplined by the Presbyterian Church for "Sabbath breaking and light and lascivious conduct" because he tended his garden on Sunday and attended dancing parties, and because he allowed some of the followers of the prophet John Humphrey Noyes to meet in his house and discuss the principles of Perfectionism, regarded as obscene by all good Salina Protestants.

"Mr. Stone" had some things to tell this Pole, whose soldierly bearing proclaimed his experience as a fighting man. He was, he said, a member of a vast secret organization of hundreds of thousands of members whose one purpose was to free their oppressed brothers across the Canadian border from the ruthless tyranny of Britain. This organization (he whispered) was named The Hunters for the famous Canadian rebel who had conceived the idea for it, and it was composed of grandsons of the veterans of the American Revolution, sons of the veterans of the War of 1812, and all other men who were willing to risk their lives for the freedom of mankind. The democratic people of York State, Stone said, almost to a man, believed that every citizen who put faith in his country's principles should rally to the cause of the Canadian masses.

Von Schoultz listened and his face darkened as he remembered the fate of his loved Poland. He said he would like to hear more. There was much more to hear. From the western border of York State to New England, the counties were aflame with hatred for the United Empire Loyalists (descendants of American Tories in exile), the aristocratic "Family Compact" and "Chateau" clique who composed the ruling class in Canada.

"Shall we," asked a speaker in Buffalo, "refuse the Canadians what was granted by a corrupt court of France to Franklin?" In answer the band struck up the "Marseillaise" and the great crowd went wild.

Invasions were planned all along the border. Lockport, Fredonia, and Buffalo were hard at work preparing troops to cross the Niagara River. Rochester paraded forty volunteers in uniform with drums beating, fifes squealing, cannon firing salvos. Watertown boiled with wrath against the evil despots across the St. Lawrence. Sackets Harbor had welcomed escaped Canadian refugees with a "procession, colors flying, guns roaring and shouts of 'God prosper the Patriots!'" Yorkers would never rest, said Stone, "until they had revenged the burning just after last Christmas of the steamship *Caroline* [rented by Canadian rebels and American sympathizers] in United States waters, and the murder at the same time of Amos Durfee, driver of a York State stagecoach."

As for his own county, continued the speaker, did Von Schoultz know that his own town had organized a "Hunters Lodge," that virtually next door "Hunters" were working nights to turn out bullets for crossing of the St. Lawrence in armed force, and that there was a lodge at Syracuse?

Nils Von Schoultz knew what his answer would be long before Stone had done. The fight against tyranny was ever the same. If he could not fight the oppressors of Poland he could fight the dictatorial bullies of Canada. In a few days he stood silent while the secret band of his fellow townsmen sang the rousing ballad of Andrew Jackson's victory over the British at New Orleans—"The Hunters of Kentucky"—and then in solemn voice repeated the Hunter's Oath:

"I swear to do my utmost to promote Republican institutions and ideas throughout the world—to cherish them, to defend them; and especially to devote myself to the propagation, protection and defense of these institutions in North America. I pledge my life, my property and my sacred honor to the Association; I bind myself to its interests, and I promise, until death, that I will attack, combat and help to destroy, by all means that my superior may think proper, every power, or authority, of Royal origin, upon this continent; and especially never to rest till all tyrants of Britain cease to have any dominion or footing whatever in North America. I further solemnly swear to obey the orders delivered to me by my superior and never to disclose any such order, or orders, except to a brother 'Hunter' of the same degree. So help me God."

Erasmus Stone doubtless realized that the enrollment of an able man of military ability and experience would be of great value to those who planned to rescue Canada from the British yoke, and his pleadings must have been urgent. But if Nils Von Schoultz had not been a true lover of liberty he would never have joined his fortunes with those of the Hunters. He was a successful inventor, he owned property in the South and in York State, he had gained loyal friends in both regions, and he had won the love of the beautiful and congenial sister of his boon companion. Only an overwhelming conviction of the justice of the cause and of his own obligation to act in its behalf could have moved him.

The high officers of the society confided to the important new recruit that a September congress of Hunters and refugees had elected a provisional Canadian government with president and cabinet and even a national bank. Then they took him on a ten-day tour of York State—to New York City, Albany, Utica, and many more towns where he met, as he later wrote, "25 or 30 thousand of what is considered the most respectable part of the American population." With these he met also Canadian revolutionists who assured him that the working people of their country, its militia, even the British regulars stationed there, would unite to destroy the despotism of the hated Tory aristocrats as soon as an expeditionary force from the United States had landed.

It was common knowledge among all spirited Yorkers that, since several badly led expeditions against Canada had proved abortive, there would be in the late fall a more ambitious attempt. So, as the day of the intended invasion approached, the wives of the Hunters of Onondaga County busied themselves with making a white silk banner which displayed at its center a spread eagle with one blue star above it, another below, and across the bottom, fancifully worked, the legend "Onondaga Hunters—Canada Liberated." This they presented to the handsome Polish officer in a pretty ceremony and he had it with him on Saturday, the tenth of November, when he boarded the packet that took him, his servant Frederick Meals, big florid Captain Christopher Buckley, and many other serious and silent young men from Salina, Liverpool, Syracuse, and surrounding towns to Oswego. It was to be the first lap of a fateful journey.

On Sunday morning at about nine o'clock the steamer *United States* set out from Oswego with a surprisingly large number of male passengers, rather roughly dressed in similar costumes and carrying as personal baggage wooden boxes and kegs. Waiting at Sackets Harbor a similar group, many of them from Watertown, boarded the vessel.

This second group, drilled by Colonel Martin Woodruff, had been visited a few weeks before by the officer selected (by the Hunters) to command the expedition, General J. Ward Birge of Cazenovia, who was now awaiting them at Ogdensburg. A tall slender man with a smooth face and shifty blue eyes, he had marched, spurs clanking, into the Hall of the Watertown Lodge in a uniform glittering with gold lace to declare that the invading force he was to lead would number twenty to forty thousand Americans. Then, as drummers Sampson Wiley and Phares Miller stood in the center of the hall beating the long roll, he had flourished his glittering sword and called for volunteers for the liberation of oppressed Canada. More than a hundred had stepped forward.

When the *United States* neared Ogdensburg she overtook two schooners—the *Charlotte of Oswego* and the *Charlotte of Toronto*—which had been sailing ahead of her and were also laden with volunteers. At once Nils Von Schoultz took command and the two vessels were lashed to the sides of the steamer as the flotilla moved on with all pretenses of peaceful travel now cast aside and the recruits busy opening the boxes of rifles and kegs of powder.

The ships approached Prescott in Canada at two in the morning. Von Schoultz wanted a landing made at once, but other officers persuaded him to postpone this action until after they had put in at Ogdensburg, where the eloquent General Birge awaited them. As the boats moved toward the town across the river the men aboard heard alarums in Prescott—the firing of cannon, the ringing of bells, the beating of drums, and knew that now they could not make a surprise attack.

The next morning, just off Ogdensburg, the Pole met the officers who had been designated his superiors. First, and at sunrise, the muscular sixty-year-old Bill Johnston bounded aboard. Self-styled "Commodore of the Navy of the Canadian Republic," "Island Robin Hood," "Lake Bravo," he was a howling, bragging bully-boy who augmented his great physical strength by hanging an arsenal of guns and knives about him. In his famous twelve-oared boat, twenty-eight feet long and capable of transporting twenty armed men yet so light that two men could carry her with ease, he had left his island home, Fort Wallace, to lead his four adoring sons and their outlaw associates in many raids on British vessels. As leader of the Lake Buccaneers, Bill had sworn to make his comely, pistol-decorated daughter, Kate, Queen of the Thousand Islands.

Soon after Johnston arrived, he ordered the troops aboard to seize the *United States*. Her pilot, Solomon Foster, was forced with a pistol at his head to continue at the wheel. General Birge now put in his splendid appearance and once more the ships got underweigh for the Canadian shore. In the meantime the British command at Kingston, downriver, hastily dispatched a gunboat to prevent the invasion. She arrived in time to open fire on the *United States* and her third shot passed through the wheelhouse and carried away the head of the luckless Pilot Foster.

A few moments after that Nelson Traux, a Watertown volunteer sent below decks to obtain an order from Birge, found the general "stretched out on a mattress which had been placed upon eight or ten dining stools, pale as a ghost, and so faint with horror from a glimpse of the headless trunk of the dead pilot he was unable to speak." He apparently recovered enough, however, to announce, after the troops on the ship had been landed in Canada, that he had suddenly been taken with "a griping pain in the bowels" and would have to return to the American side He remained in the dining cabin, therefore, "administering stimulants to himself for medicine" until he was once more in Ogdensburg.

With neither of his superior officers apparently capable of intelligent action, Von Schoultz debarked his troops a mile and a half downriver at Windmill Point, where the building that gave the place its name, a tall stone tower built by a West India merchant in 1822, and other stone outbuildings stood on the Kingston-Montreal highway commanding both land and water approaches. At once he ordered his white banner, on which the ladies of Onondaga had worked the blue eagle and stars, flown from the top of the mill.

Though the *Charlotte of Oswego* under command of Bill Johnston ran aground temporarily, she finally delivered her cargo. Now, despite General Birge's prophecies of a force of twenty thousand, an army of something less than two hundred had been transported to the shore below Prescott and the stricken general and the swaggering commodore had returned to Ogdensburg still mouthing solemn oaths to bring over thousands of new volunteers. That afternoon Von Schoultz worked his men unceasingly at unloading supplies and strengthening defenses. Anticipating attack, he placed a decoy six-pounder in a position where it could be raked by cross fire from four directions. "This night," a veteran wrote, "no eye was closed, no hand was idle and no heart faint, all was hurry, bustle, and confusion, all anxiety and expectation." No general, no commodore, returned with the promised comrades.

The morning of November 13 was cloudless and still. As the mists that hung low above the water burned away, Nils Von Schoultz made a short address to his men. He told them that the bright weather was an omen of success; soon the sun of Canada would rise upon a free nation. He urged them to be resolute and to stand by each other—if necessary, to the last man. He spoke to a youthful band. About half were in their twenties and thirty of them, a fifth, were still in their teens. His capacity to lead these inexperienced youths was soon to be put to the test. The British were now ready to strike.

British naval and land forces began a joint attack early in the morning. Three gunboats, which had arrived during the night, began an ineffective shelling of the windmill, while the infantry moved off from Prescott in two columns which included elements of the Royal Marines, Glengarry Highlanders, Queens Borderers, 83d Regiment and several other companies. They outnumbered the invaders by more than five to one.

When the redcoats came in sight, Von Schoultz ordered his men into position behind a stone fence which they used as a breastwork. They stood two or three yards apart to cover their front and awaited attack. The royal bugles sounded when the British were about twenty rods away. They halted to fire upon the invaders but with little effect. The redcoats came on again, and Von Schoultz waited until they were within fifteen rods before he gave the command to fire. The Yorkers' aim was so deadly that many British fell. The rest wavered and fell back. Faintly, from Mile Point at Ogdensburg across the river, came the hoarse sound of yelling voices as the townspeople crowded the safe American shore or thronged the roofs of houses to cheer their countrymen on.

Realizing then that he must conserve his forces against so large a force, Von Schoultz withdrew his men into the windmill and the stone houses clustered about it. They had hardly completed the maneuver when the British, reorganized by their officers, advanced again. This time thirty British regulars under a gallant lieutenant tried to seize the decoy cannon, but the leader was shot down and the party routed. Casualties among the British officers were heavy, for these York State men knew how to shoot, had by now complete confidence in Von Schoultz, and had overcome the first nervousness of battle.

It was three o'clock in the afternoon when, after many repulses, Colonel Plomer Young (to use the understatement of his own report) "considered it more prudent in order to avoid a further risk of life to draw off the greater part of the troops." The reluctant testimony of his report published a day later tended to bear out the Yorkers' estimates of seventy-five enemy dead and one hundred and fifty wounded. "The rifle fire of the enemy was particularly true and steady . . . I regret to say that the loss was severe."

The Yorkers lost six dead and twenty-one wounded but they knew that proportionately their loss was the greater. Moreover, they had lost more than men. Faith in the guarantees of those officers who still strutted the streets of Ogdensburg was gone. Word came that the ships they had come on had been seized by officers of the United States government, that Johnston and Birge were now or would soon be safely lodged in jail as federal prisoners. And they had seen the Canadian militia, on whose support the success of their venture greatly depended, fight against them with desperate courage. The American saviors of Canada had found Canada unwilling to be saved. Not a single Canadian had joined them.

A message came under flag of truce asking a cessation of fire for an hour until the dead and wounded could be removed. Von Schoultz assented and sent a note:

"Creature of a High Wrought Fancy"

To the Commander of the queen's troops at Prescott:

I send you two of your wounded because I cannot attend to them and give them the care they require.

In requitance I beg you to treat my wounded with kindness.

If, on your honor, you can assure me that we are not received by the people here as liberators, it depends on you to put a stop to further bloodshed.

For an hour, men in British uniforms drove a wagon about the shore near the windmill picking up the wounded. The dead they left where they had fallen. A strong cold wind had sprung up carrying snow from dark, low-hanging clouds. It drifted beside the red-jacketed bodies, almost covering some of them. Brave visitors from Ogdensburg arrived. In a tiny boat they had run the blockade of the three British gunboats to ask what help they might offer.

"Send a boat to take off my wounded," said Von Schoultz and they promised that the wounded would be moved before daylight.

"Bring them down to the water's edge so that we can put them aboard the steamboat quickly when we come," they said.

So the Yorkers carried their wounded to the shore, where they lay beside the sullen white-capped river waiting seven hours for help that never came. "The wind whistled shrilly through the arms of the old windmill," said one who years later remembered this night. And as for the white banner that had fluttered so bravely in the sunlight that morning: "Our flag flapped like the wings of a raven above our heads."

Snow that sometimes changed to freezing rain was falling when daylight came. The Yorkers lay about in a dull and hellish dream, staring more often than they wished at the smoking chimneys of comfortable homes in Ogdensburg. Von Schoultz sent an open boat with five men in it across the water with petitions for supplies and either reinforcements or a rescuing expedition to take his men back home. The occupants of the windmill saw them captured by the crew of a British boat just before they reached safety. That night the shivering Yorkers heard looters robbing the dead.

A British force of regulars and militia advanced at ten in the morning. Without the supplies that they had so urgently begged for and so desperately needed, the hopeless men in the mill decided to sell their lives as dearly as possible. Von Schoultz ordered a cannon placed in the door of the building and had it loaded with pieces of broken iron, spikes, bolts, and screws torn from doors and fixtures. He waited calmly then until the enemy were close before giving the order to fire. The salvo did terrific damage, and the Yorkers estimated that it killed twenty-five and wounded as many more. Again the enemy broke and retreated.

An American steamer, the *Paul Pry*, landed at the windmill that night to rescue the besieged men. Under command of a prominent citizen, Preston King, the ship made the crossing without opposition from the British boats and King and Von Schoultz held a council of war. What they said to each other is not known. Some survivors claimed that Von Schoultz reported that less than four of his men would accept rescue, preferring to carry on in the conviction that oppressed Canadians would still rise and fight with them. Others charged that King, nervous and fearful, went back to Ogdensburg after a five-minute talk promising to return and was not allowed to do so by federal authorities.

By this time the pluck of the Yorker fighters had carried their fame throughout the eastern states. These young laborers, tradesmen, farmers, printers, teachers, practically untrained and without a knowledge of the practice of war, had withstood for four days an infinitely greater force including professional British regulars—as brave and efficient soldiers as Europe could produce.

Two years previously about the same number of seasoned American fighting men had put up a similar resistance against a tremendous army of Mexicans (less able soldiers than the British) at the Alamo and the Yorkers were already being compared to the Texans. American newspapers did not hesitate to speak of the Battle of Windmill Point as one of the greatest in world history and a writer for the Ogdensburg *Times* reported "We have a most favorable location for observing the movements as our window affords a full view of Prescott" and added a day later: "So far the Patriot Force have sustained themselves against fearful odds with signal success." An Ogdensburg tavernkeeper booted his most affluent and regular customer out of the door, exclaiming, "By God, do you think I'll mix drinks for a damn Tory!" and a wife prevented her husband from joining Von Schoultz by dressing in her riding clothes and announcing that if he could desert his home and children she could, too.

The end came with a merciful suddenness. On Thursday afternoon, according to his report of a day later, Colonel Dundas, commandant of the 83d Regiment, came down from Kingston with four companies, two eighteen-pounders and a howitzer. On Friday he began pounding the massive walls of the mill with these heavy guns and every shot penetrated them. At dusk, when the great stones of the masonry were falling about them, the Yorkers who had been sleepless for four nights and were so dog-tired they no longer cared what became of them surrendered unconditionally.

Von Schoultz, with a dozen men, undertook the dangerous defense of one of the stone houses. He was driven outside by the shells and with two companions he slipped unseen into a grove of cedars beside the river. There the Canadian militia found them. They killed one with a bayonet. Then the men for whose freedom Von Schoultz believed he was fighting attacked him viciously. Only the intervention of the officers of the 83d saved his life. His shirt torn from his back, the rest of his uniform in shreds, he stood motionless while he and his comrades were bound to each other in a column of twos. With the Pole at the head they were marched toward Prescott.

The British band, brisk and blaring, struck up "Yankee Doodle" and in a few moments the triumphal march through the main street of the town had begun. Already lamps lighted all the windows of the houses, bonfires blazed, and the people of the town shouted in wild celebration as the exhausted men shambled by. They jeered at the Yorkers, spat in their faces, struck them with such

violence that they injured many, though the soldiers of
the 83d did their best to protect them.

Colonel Dundas marched them down to the Prescott
Dock and aboard the steamer *Brockville* lying there. He
ordered the vessel moved into the river. At midnight of
the next day, once more marching in column of twos, they
were paraded through the streets of a Kingston gone mad
with victory. Again, lights gleamed on the bare straight
shoulders of Von Schoultz as he marched. A man of the
exulting mob hit him in the leg with a heavy wooden
stake. He limped to the end of his days.

Said a Kingston journal a few days later:

"The manifestation of feeling in this town on the return of the Expedition, as might be expected, was gratifying . . . The principal street through which the triumphal
cavalcade was to pass was brilliantly illuminated; and the
orderly populace, numbering some thousands, that accompanied the cortege, spoke volumes by their alternate huzzas
of thanks to the British Grenadiers that defend us and the
groan of derision with which they saluted the pirates."

The captured Yorkers were confined in small rooms at
Fort Henry at the outskirts of the town. While Nils Von
Schoultz was with them, as one of his fellow prisoners
told the story later, "his whole bearing and conduct were
noble, unstained by any act of weakness. Ever regardless
of his own sufferings he zealously tried to render his companions in arms every service in his power. Words of kindness flowed from his lips and . . . he cheered the darkest
and loneliest hour of our bondage."

The action of the Canadian authorities was quick and without question fair and punctilious. The prisoner-leader appeared before a formal court-martial on November 26 and pleaded guilty to a charge that he did "with guns, bayonets and other warlike weapons kill and slay divers of our loyal subjects." In extenuation of his acts he stated only that he had been deceived by false informants into commanding the invaders. Warned of the possible consequences of this plea, he said that he knew what they were but, since all he could say for himself was that he had been hoodwinked and then deserted by cowardly associates, he must still plead guilty. A few witnesses were called whose truthfulness he did not question. He then asked the court to be allowed to speak. Permission having been given, he stated that his conduct at the windmill had been soldierly .nd humane. This the members of the court were convinced was true.

"As to the Pole," said the Coburg *Star* in reporting the trial, "he does not expect to live. He has made up his mind to death. He is a most determined and resolute man, did his utmost to gain the end of his landing in Canada, and he is prepared to take the consequences. He made his observations more to vindicate his character than to save his life . . . In deportment the Pole is as unmoved as a rock."

The trial lasted three days and on the last of these he stood to hear his sentence—that he be hanged by the neck until dead on the morning of Saturday, December 8, at eight o'clock.

Back in the fort, a few days before his death he sang "in a thrilling yet plaintive voice" a song called "A Maiden's Answer," which, according to one account, he said he had written. If the prisoner who copied it down was really telling the truth, it must be reported that the song was really an old sentimental ballad—"A Smile and a Tear"—published in New York City about 1830 and the Pole had merely adapted one line somewhat.

> My parents though humble were happy and good.
> We could boast of our honour if not of our Blood.
> My Lover, ah, how the sad tale shall I tell
> For Poland he fought and for freedom he fell
> He was noble and brave—to my soul he was dear
> His fame claims a smile, though it shines through
>   a tear.

On December 4, Von Schoultz was transferred from the fort to the Kingston jail, bidding farewell to his comrades of the windmill. One of them said later, "There was a double loneliness in the prison when we came to know and feel that he was dead."

On the day before his execution, Von Schoultz was very busy. He wrote a will in which he bequeathed his Virginia properties to William McComus, lawyer; requested Warren Green, his executor, to collect all moneys owed to him and to sell his patent; asked that the expenses of his burial be refunded to the Very Reverend Angus MacDonell, vice-general of the Roman Catholic diocese of Kingston. He also willed to Father MacDonell $1,600 to be divided into four parts, the interest from which was to be paid to four widows of British soldiers killed at Windmill Point, and $1,000 to aid in the erection of the Roman Catholic College then building in Kingston. To his friend Captain Eduard Townsend of Her Majesty's 83d Regiment went his gold pencil case in gratitude for humane treatment at the fort. Out of whatever would be left, and the sum might be considerable if the patent was sold, he desired a fourth to go to Mistress Anna Von Schoultz, whom he had left at Karlskrona in Sweden in 1836, a fourth to Johanna Von Schoultz (apparently his mother), a fourth to Mistress Emeline Field, "now living with her mother-in-law Mistress Field in the aforesaid village of Salina," along with the two Oriental stones held by her brother, Warren Green, "wishing that she may have them set in gold and use them as a pin box." To Warren Green he left the remaining fourth (less a thousand for his sister) and "my gold Hunter watch made by McCabe in London."

He wrote two letters also, one to John Lewis at Kanawha:

Dear Friend,

From the newspapers you have undoubtedly been informed that I am a prisoner. When you read this the thread of my life is cut and I have finished to be an inhabitant of this earth. Give my last farewell to your family, and my numerous friends. I know this will come like a thunderstroke on you all. Little did we think on Canada when we parted, but I forgive those who so treacherously brought me into this situation and to death. I have only time to write you some few words, as my Execution is to take place tomorrow . . . Many sincere thanks to you and your lady for all your kindness.

My love to your children. Let Doctor Thornton read
this. God bless you all my friends; May my death stop
further bloodshed is the sincere wish and last prayer
of your true friend.

To Warren Green he wrote:

When you get this letter I am no more . . . May
God forgive them who brought me to this untimely
death. I have made up my mind and I forgive them
. . . I wrote to you in my former letter about my
body. If the British government permit it, I wish it
may be delivered to you to be buried on your farm
. . . I have great need of communicating with my
Creator and preparing for his presence . . . Give my
love to your sister and tell her I think on her as on my
mother. God reward her for all her kindnesses . . .
Farewell my dear friend! God bless and protect you.

                                      S. Von Schoultz

Early on Saturday morning, December 8, Nils Von
Schoultz shook the hands of the 83d Regiment's officers,
men who had become his friends and had petitioned Canadian authorities not to execute him. He was then taken
to the glacis outside Fort Henry and hanged. He walked
to the gallows with a firm tread, and there gave to Father
MacDonell his gold snuffbox.

"The Pole begged those Canadians who were friendly
to him," said one report of his death, "to bury him just
as he was and not to disturb his clothing. But curiosity
made them open the breast of his coat, and they found,
hung from a ribbon about his neck, the miniature of a
beautiful girl. They quickly replaced it and buried him
honourably."

Twenty days after his execution, when ten of his officers had also been hanged and many Yorkers of his command sentenced to ten years' servitude in the British penal colony in Van Diemen's Land (now Tasmania), there appeared in the Syracuse *Standard* a heartbroken letter of eulogy signed Warren Green. It ended with these words:

> "His sympathetic soul was fired at the thought of again being permitted to strike for freedom—his enthusiastic recklessness of danger led him into its very vortex and he has perished, ignominiously perished . . .
>
> "I still think on him as the creature of a high wrought fancy rather than of sober reality—like a meteor of uncommon brilliancy which has suddenly illumined the path of my dull existence, and as suddenly disappeared forever."

Part Four

Instruments of Salvation

The pines confront me dripping like dark mermen.

From *The Old Pines* ("Winter") by W. W. Christman

13

The Famous
Female Somniloquist

To THE EAST OF MARCELLUS, HILL TOWN NEAR
Syracuse, voices of no human origin have spoken to Mother
Ann Lee, to prophetic Cyrus Tead known as Koresh, to
many a follower of the Spiritualism given stimulus by the
Fox Sisters. To the west of the little town with the big
name other voices have spoken to Jemima Wilkinson, who
called herself the "Publick Universal Friend," to Joseph
Smith, confidant of the Angel Moroni, to Barbara Heynemann, who transmitted divine words to the folk of the
"True Inspiration," and to Thomas Lake Harris, founder
of the community known as "The Use." It was natural
then that Camillus, situated as it was, should have had its
own human phenomenon, and because Camillus is a town
of individualists, one who differed radically from others
who, though more famous, were no more distinctive.

In 1803, Ezekiel and Hannah Baker of Pelham, Massachusetts, brought their nine-year-old Rachel to live in Marcellus. Already the little girl's thoughts of God and eternity
had made her tremble. "She was always of a serious make,
of few words, timorous and much given to melancholy,"

according to a resident of Marcellus who knew her well. Her life was quite like that of other children of the region, which was composed of bonus farms occupied by veterans of the Revolution, until she was seventeen. Then, one late November night in 1811, while she nodded in her chair, she began to sigh and groan as if she were in great agony, and to speak like one somewhat deranged. She said that she had little time left to live and she would soon be going down to hell. Her parents, according to a contemporary account, "were at first apprehensive that she was making her exit . . . however, their fears began to abate soon after she commenced talking."

For almost two months Rachel Baker suffered from such melancholy seizures as soon as sleep came to her. They reached their culmination on the evening of January 27, 1812. Her parents stated that on this occasion her horrors exceeded description. The Reverend David Rathbone of Scipio, New York, to whom they related the events of the night, reported: "Awful terrors seem to have taken possession of her; her affrighted imagination seemed haunted with dreadful spectres; she said that one of the infernal fiends was grasping her, and would drag her down to the bottomless pit! a fathomless abyss! a dread eternity were full in view! her cries were enough to shock anyone who reflected at all, that it is a fearful thing to fall a sinner into the hands of the living God!"

Suddenly, however, the tone of her discourse changed. She later said that at the moment of her greatest despair she heard the voice of God saying, "Daughter, be of good cheer, thy sins are forgiven thee." She became serene and calm, and her religious utterances assumed a happier tone.

For two years thereafter, save for a slight interim caused

by an attack of measles, Rachel Baker spoke almost nightly while she slept, urging those who heard her to repent their sins and worship God. Naturally, since her parents made no effort to keep her strange condition a secret, she became the object of great curiosity and dispute throughout the state. Many argued that she was a clever faker, others that God was using a humble vessel through which to speak to the world. Reputable residents of Marcellus who had known Rachel ever since her arrival in town and who knew that she had received but six weeks of schooling since that time were not very complimentary with regard to her abilities while conscious:

"She appears when awake to be far from possessing very quick perceptions, a penetrating discernment, or lively sensations; these and other mental faculties, in the opinion of all those best acquainted with her, are far from being beyond what is common to females. . . . Rachel never appeared to us to be endowed with a well-cultivated, sound understanding or sensible mind. . . . When she is awake she introduces no conversation with anyone and does not appear to be possessed of a clear mind in the scriptures, a retentive memory, nor a good judgment . . . she talks but little when she is awake and does not appear capable of communicating her views and exercises of mind to anyone."

Yet once let nine o'clock in the evening strike and sleep invade her senses, Rachel Baker became a fluent master of religious phraseology, an eloquent preacher whose sermons were logically divided into three parts—an invocation, an exhortation, a concluding supplication and thanksgiving. While still asleep, she could hear and answer the questions of learned theologians in their own manner and with authoritative orthodoxy, and she could recite whole hymns without a single error or hesitation.

In June, 1812, Rachel joined the Presbyterian church in Marcellus, but after she went to live with an aunt in Scipio, on the banks of Owasco Lake, in January, 1813, she almost immediately "underwent a religious submersion" and became a Baptist. Her reputation had preceded her and it was not long before great crowds of residents of the Finger Lakes district sought her out in order that they might see her, hear her, and benefit by her sleep-born utterances.

In a year's time most of upstate New York was in an uproar over her. On nights when visitors were admitted it was not uncommon for three or four hundred people, some of whom had traveled many miles, to present themselves at her door. A somewhat incredulous gentleman, who went to hear her on a night so filled with wind and rain that only about forty other auditors appeared, wrote of her: "She is a plump, hale, country lass of 19, rather above the middle size; of a smooth, equal, vacant tranquillity of visage, without mental vivacity or vigor." He was not at first impressed by Rachel, but as the "oracular corpse in deep deep sleep" spoke on, "intuitively prepared to meet questions, the most dark and abstruse," he lost more and more of his skepticism.

"The deep attention of the auditors, the sighs of the women, the pattern of the hall, the howling of the tempest, united with the speaking corpse, as it appeared uttering its awful warnings to mortality, offered one of those moments of retirement to the soul, when we shudder and shiver in sublimity . . . indeed I was ten times within an ace of coiling up my logic and uniting in the sympathies of the crowd."

The Famous Female Somniloquist

During all the controversy over her, Rachel Baker remained, in her waking hours, industrious, sedate, diffident. She looked upon her attacks of sleep-talking religious fervor as evidences of disease—probably because they left her in such a state of physical exhaustion at their completion. And so she must have been pleased when the Baptist minister, David Rathbone, whether out of his concern for her health or out of his desire to spread her influence as a religious force, arranged to leave the six Rathbone children in the hands of Scipio neighbors while he and his wife accompanied Rachel Baker on the 300-mile carriage journey through the October-colored hills and along the shining Hudson to New York City. Upon their arrival, the Rathbones immediately took Rachel to the home of the distinguished and pious physician Dr. John H. Douglass, at 61 Chambers Street, and the second part of her history began.

Dr. Douglass had but to listen to Rachel's evening demonstration to be convinced that here lay a mystery that required conference with the most able men of medicine in the city. His first thought was naturally of Dr. Samuel Latham Mitchill, who, with the possible exception of Thomas Jefferson, must have been the most versatile man of his time. Aside from his many contributions to American medical knowledge, Mitchill had interested himself in American zoology, horticulture, geology, politics (he had been a United States senator), literature, and chemistry. His studies on the anatomy of the egg, the dissection of the American skunk, American cuisine, Babylonian brick, the sanitary practices of soap boilers, war songs of the American Indian, and the fishes of New York had prompted

John Randolph to call him "the congressional library."
Joseph Rodman Drake had lampooned him amusingly:

> It matters not how low or high it is
> Thou knowest each hill and vale of knowledge
> Fellow of forty-nine societies . . .

and Fitz-Greene Halleck had written:

> Time was when Dr. Mitchill's word was law
> When Monkeys, Monsters, Whales and Esquimaux
> Asked but a letter from his ready hand
> To be the theme and wonder of the land.

The remark current among Mitchill's friends, "Tap the
doctor at any time and he will flow," had been given authority by such varied efforts as his attempt to prove that
the garden of Eden was really in the Onondaga Valley in
upstate New York and his attempts to amend the rhymes
of Mother Goose, which he said abounded in errors to
lead the infantile mind astray.

> When the pie was open
> The birds were songless
> Wasn't that a pretty dish
> To set before the Congress

wrote Dr. Mitchill. "I thus correct," he continued, "the
error that might be imbibed in infancy of the musical functions of cooked birds; and while I discard the King of
Great Britain, with whom we have nothing to do, I give
them some knowledge of our general government by speci-
fying our Congress."

To Dr. Mitchill, the problem of discovering the source
of Rachel Baker's apparently supernatural powers was

mightily welcome. Though, to give the investigation great thoroughness and authority, Dr. Douglass had invited to its deliberations three of the best-known medical men in the city—Drs. Joshua E. R. Birch, Archibald Bruce, Valentine Mott—it was Mitchill who appropriated the responsibility and, incidentally, the distinction of reporting to the world their findings as a committee of the College of Physicians and Surgeons. In a month's time he had made sufficient study of Rachel Baker's case to deliver a public lecture in explanation of it and of "Somnium or Dream" as a state different from both wakefulness and sleep.

It had been rather expected that the long journey to New York and the change to sea air might cure Rachel Baker of her strange affliction. She had, however, been subject to regular attacks on the journey, to the great interest of her fellow guests at the inns where she and the Rathbones stopped for lodging. And in New York City her attacks were longer.

According to Dr. Mitchill's account, as soon as she retired in New York, at early bedtime, the girl was invaded by an "uneasiness of the spasmodic kind, anxiety in respiration and hysteric choaking." In fifteen minutes after the beginning of the paroxysm she would be speaking in a distinct, sonorous voice, delivering her religious exhortation with proper emphasis, embellishing her expression with "fine metaphors, vivid descriptions, and poetical quotations." During her discourse she would lie as still as death, her eyelids closed, only her lips and tongue in motion. If asked questions during this period, she would answer them fluently and logically. When asked if she was awake, she invariably contended that she was. Toward the end of her talk her eyelids would begin to quiver and the eyeballs would be observed to roll upward. Her hands would clench tightly and the muscles of the back, arms, and legs would go rigid in a sudden spasm. At the same time she would seem to be strangling. Then her body would be racked with recurring sobs that lasted from two to fifteen minutes. After that, without waking, she would drift into quiet sleep.

In the morning she would waken as if nothing had happened and, upon being questioned as to the night before, assure her questioner that she remembered nothing of the actions that had so puzzled her auditors a few hours earlier.

In the report of the findings in the Rachel Baker case (published in 1815), which includes other matters relative to Somnium, Dr. Mitchill listed under "Idiopathio Somnium" seven different types of Somnium, the last being "Somnium (*cum religione*) with ability to pray and preach or to address the Supreme Being, and human auditors, in an instructive and eloquent manner; without any recollection of having been so employed and with utter incompetency to perform such exercises of devotion and instruction when awake." This he claimed to be the nature of the Rachel Baker case, and he indignantly denied any possibility of its subject's being a performer or an impostor with the statement that "more faith is required to suppose it a consummate and practical piece of deceit than to consider it the result of devotional Somnium . . . the story of imposture is totally contradicted by the correctness and propriety of her conduct."

To show, moreover, that such cases were not unknown to science, Dr. Mitchill made mention of several—one of amazing coincidence in that a contemporary young lady of Maryland, also named Rachel Baker, was reported as unable to sing a note when awake but capable when asleep of entrancing audiences with lovely melodies. Another pertinent case was that of Miss H—— of East Hampton, Long Island, who went to bed one evening after hearing much conversation about a large whale that had been captured in shallow water, killed, and brought to shore nearby. When Miss H—— awakened, she found herself in her nightdress on the shore road about two miles from her home. Neighbors took her into their home and, when morning came, discovered that her tracks led all the way from her house to the shore, where it was apparent that she had walked around the whale and had started on her return to her bed, which she might have reached still asleep if a dog had not barked at her.

While Dr. Mitchill busied himself with his theories on these prettily feminine and intriguing examples of Somnium (no male somniloquists of importance being reported), the New York meetings over the plump, hale, and prostrate form of the somniloquist continued. Physicians, ministers, teachers, literary men, almost all New Yorkers of consequence and curiosity, called at 61 Chambers Street to hear her and to witness the reported sudden spasms that produced rigidity "of the muscles of the back, arms, and legs." Experts in shorthand were seated at Rachel's bedside to take down every word of her nightly exhortations. The case aroused the whole city. Crowds gathered outside Dr. Douglass's door. Many scoffed at Rachel. Dr. Douglass reported:

"Some treated her name with derision, some with contempt, and others with a severity that would persecute. This was to be expected. That an ignorant girl of 19 years of age should dream in a course of enlightened theology and should at the same time express her thoughts in fervid and eloquent language with a clearness, an order, and a force far beyond any attainment of her waking efforts . . . was too much out of the common track of experience to be readily acknowledged."

As for the sermons themselves, as reported by stenographers, they are facile, wordy exercises in stilted, formal language. Upon being asked if she had something to say to a group of ministers present, Rachel replied, "I have nothing to say unto them that may, peradventure, be edifying," and then went on preaching her Calvinistic creed in a sermon filled with Biblical quotations and with warnings to sinners. When an irreverent person asked her, "Rachel, what kind of cap would you like best?" she seems to have been flustered and indignant. "What did you say, my friend? I did not understand what you said. Dost thou not incline to tell me what thou saidst? If not I will turn my attention to others, who will pay attention to what I say; for I must give up my account for what I have said and these must give in their account for every idle word before the bar of the Lord Jesus Christ."

Time and again she had to answer a question similar to that of Professor Joshua Griscom, who wished to know "why it should be thought in this enlightened age the duty of an illiterate female to give instructions on religious subjects." To such questions she invariably replied by abasing herself as an "unworthy worm," "a poor ignorant child," but declaring, "what I speak my God seemeth to reveal it unto me."

The Famous Female Somniloquist

The conclave of doctors that had been called to consider medical treatment of the case seems to have acted with more common sense than many another. Having tried bleeding the patient and then administering to her small amounts of opium, without getting a favorable result from either, they decided that, since Rachel was in excellent health, it would be better to leave well enough alone and forgo other experiments.

Upon hearing that they had reached this decision, Rachel announced that she would go home to her parents in Marcellus. On the date set for her departure, a multitude gathered. Some came on foot, some on horses, many in wagons and other vehicles. Rachel's carriage set out and the whole crowd escorted it to the city limits. There it became the center of a large caravan which moved slowly up the right bank of the Hudson to the tavern where the somniloquist and her party were to spend the first night of their journey. Here, in the evening, the followers witnessed the spectacle, "not of a waking preacher and a drowsy audience, but of a character abstract from outward things, holding forth to a wondering and staring company."

But Rachel was not to stay in Marcellus long. On January 3, 1815, Dr. Douglass wrote to Ezekiel Baker at Marcellus:

Dear Sir,
The high sense I entertain of the private and religious character of your daughter, Rachel, of her total unconsciousness of what she utters in her evening exercises, and of the salutary influence her performances have had upon the minds of many young females in this city, causes this communication and request.

The good doctor went on to state that a few benevolent persons were proposing to offer Rachel an education if she would place herself in their care, "pledging themselves that the breathings of her soul in her state of Devotional Somnium, should be exposed only to a few discreet, thinking, and pious persons . . . We think that it is due to the literary community, and to the church at large, that the whole history of this surprising case should be communicated. . . . Will it not confound the theory of those who think that the soul is matter highly organized, and the kindred opinion that the soul sleeps; but I confess my inability at present to account for the phenomenon in all its parts, and therefore must be silent."

The offer of the charitable persons was accepted immediately, and Rachel had spent only a few weeks upstate before she was returned by her father to New York and was enrolled in Mrs. Bowering's select seminary for young ladies at 71 Hudson Street. Here she exerted her salutary influence on the young females of the school with a series of sleep-sermons that were attended by many curious male scientists, including on one occasion the distinguished Drs. Romayne and McLeod, and on another a number of Quakers, to whom she preached eloquently.

During the previous November a book of Rachel's sermons, taken down in shorthand by Charles Mais, a stenographer, had been published. In it, Mr. Mais addressed himself to the group of medical investigators of the College of Physicians and Surgeons, asking them to publish their report, since he felt that it would tend to calm the excitement of the general public over the case.

In the summer of 1815, Mais's appeal was answered by

the appearance of a volume the title page of which began as follows:

"*Devotional Somnium* or, a collection of Prayers and Exhortations Uttered by Miss Rachel Baker in the City of New York, in the winter of 1815, during her abstract and unconscious state; To which pious and unprecedented exercises is prefixed an account of her life with the manner in which she became powerful in praise to God and addresses to man; together with a view of that faculty of the human mind which is intermediate between sleeping and waking, the facts attested by the most respectable divines, physicians and literary gentlemen, and the discourses correctly noted by clerical stenographers."

Dedicated to DeWitt Clinton, LL.D., president of the Literary and Philosophical Society of New York, and attributed to "Several Medical Gentlemen," the volume is obviously for the most part Dr. Mitchill's. It begins with an explanatory letter by Dr. Douglass and ends with a letter from the well-known Virginia planter, Ferdinando Fairfax, testifying that, although prejudiced against Rachel Baker at first, the writer, after seeing her three times, was completely convinced of her sincerity.

In this volume, Dr. Mitchill reports Rachel as receiving "the benefits of one of the most excellent Boarding Schools of the City, no longer subject to the visits of the curious, enjoying in retirement, the society of her pious friends."

So far as I know, those words give the last published information on her life. Since no further chronicle of her doings is to be found, it is reasonable to assume that boarding school succeeded in effecting what long journeys, sea air, bleeding, and opium had been unable to accomplish—the cessation of her pilgrimages into the unreal world of Somnium.

In Central York State (which in its early days was so full of Pennsylvanians and Yankees that in 1824 the famous gazetteer, Horatio Gates Spafford, dubbed it "The Land of Whiskey and Pumpkin Pie") there was a large hollow buttonwood tree. Elder Smith of Moscheto Point said it was so big that he once preached a sermon inside to thirty-five persons. When some doubt was expressed, he added in a firm tone:

"Had they chosen to come, it could have held fifteen more."

Mrs. Dildine was always waiting when Herm De Long opened the doors of his bookshop in the Maxwell Block. She would march right in after Herm and buy a copy of the Rochester *Democrat and Chronicle*. Then she would march right out again, carefully lay the paper down on the sidewalk and stand upon it. From this low platform she would then deliver a sermon which for knowledge of the Bible, fluency, and all-fired pious emphasis would rival the best efforts of Moody and Sankey.

One week an evangelist only a little less famous than these pitched his tent on the outskirts of town and began holding nightly services that promised to bring about the regeneration of many of Dansville's most steeped-in-sin citizens. No sooner had Mrs. Dildine heard of his enterprise, however, than she repaired to the tent and interrupted the preaching with such explosive ejaculations and with such pungent and prolonged comment that the good man feared his work was being impeded. He therefore called on the Presbyterian minister, the one-armed Dr. George K. Ward, to try to persuade his ardent parishioner to desist from taking up so much precious time.

"They tell me," said Dr. Ward to the good lady, "that you take too much time from the religious exercises with your talk."

"Don't you pay any attention to them, parson," said Mrs. Dildine. "They're always saying the same thing about you."

Ezekiel Radford, manufacturer of horse liniment, was a tall, fat man with red hair. He always wore a blue shirt with the sleeves rolled to the elbow, showing from elbow to wrist the red-flannel sleeves of his underwear. The children of the village of Weedsport, where Zeke made his liniment, used to wonder why he wore his winter flannels even in the summertime.

Ezekiel used to take care of the barn owned by the Western Transportation Company which rented horses or mules to canallers for towing their boats. Gradually, however, the boatmen found that it was cheaper to own their own stock instead of hiring the Western Transportation Company teams and the company went out of business.

By this time, however, Zeke had his liniment factory well established. His bottles were easily distinguishable because a feather was stuck into the cork of each one for use in applying the liquid. There was a song about Ezekiel and it had a great many stanzas. It went to the tune of "As I Walked Out by the Light of the Moon," and here are a couple of verses from it:

We towed into Weedsport about ten o'clock
And the first one I saw was Ezekiel on the dock
Says Ezekiel to me, "Who's drivin' this team?"
Says I to Ezekiel, "You are blowin' off steam."

Ezekiel he come out and began to bawl and shout
Saying, "Captain, are your horses galded any?
I've a liniment here to sell that will cure them
    up right well
I don't think that I have ever sold you any."

Storekeeper over at Raquette had a hammer stolen
from his store. Come the last of the month, he sent every
one of his customers a bill for it. He got a lot of com-
plaints but he got his hammer paid for.

Other side of the mountains by the St. Lawrence River
there was a fella got mad at his neighbor and give out he'd
pay five dollars to the man who shot him. The neighbor
heard about it and accused him of it.

"It's a lie," said the man. "I might-a said two dollars but
I never went over that."

"Old George lived up to Portageville," said the old man.
"He used to cut timber and float logs down the Genesee
to Rochester. Timber wasn't cut after George died till the
CCC. George used to load the family up and take 'em to
church every Sunday. Always had a hot toddy just before
he started.

"Some Sunday mornings his wife would say, 'George, I'll get the kettle hot and make you a glass of toddy.'

" 'No, no,' says George. 'Not this morning.'

"Then after the whole family was in the carriage he'd get down from the driver's seat, go in the house and keep 'em waitin' while he made his own toddy. They was late, always late, until it got-ta be sort of a expression around there, 'As late as the Wilmers.' . . .

"One day George's eldest came to him and said, 'Pa, whisky barrel's most empty.'

" 'Better get the wagon out,' says George.

" 'Tail gate's busted.'

" 'Take it to Joe and get it mended.'

"After they got the tail gate fixed, they drove to town and got the whisky barrel filled. Coming back up the plenty long, plenty steep hill near their house, just as they get to the top the barrel rolls back against the tail gate and the gate busts again and the barrel starts rolling downhill. Old George, he stands up and he hollers:

" 'Roll on! Roll on! Till your hoops turn to silver an' your staves turn to gold! Roll on till you come to the bottomless pit of hell and I'll be there to suck at your bung!' Then he turned around and said to his son, 'And as for Joe—born of pious parents, reared in a Christian community, educated under the Stars and Stripes, in the land of freedom and opportunity for all, and the damn fool can't mend a tail gate!' "

14

The Great Alchemist
at Utica

SIXTEEN MILES SOUTH OF FORT MYERS, FLORIDA, beside the Tampa-Miami highway called the Tamiami Trail, a sign reads—Estero. Beyond orange groves lining the road a gas station faces toward a spacious store on the front wall of which is painted—The Koreshan Unity.

On the last day of a winter visit to Florida in 1948, keeping a promise I had made to myself, I stopped at this place because I had heard vague report that here was the remnant of another of the inspired communistic and religious groups that, like the Shakers, Mormons, Oneida Perfectionists, and Spiritualists, had developed during the nineteenth century in the psychically fertile earth of a broad mystic highway running across central New York State.

In the big store I saw a showcase devoted to pamphlets and books published by the Guiding Star Press of the Unity and I bought a copy of each.

"Where can I learn more?" I said.

"Across the road at the gas station," said the girl clerk promptly. "Lou Staton can tell you all about it."

Lou has pure-white hair, sea-blue eyes, and a quizzical, humorous look on his sun-tanned regular features. I bought gas, then said:

"Can you tell me about this place?"

"Come out of that car," said Lou, "and come into my office."

A moment later I was seated before a world globe that was split open in the middle showing a map of the world spread on the inside.

"Life is in the kernel," Lou was saying. "It lies in the center of all natural spheres. It is the middle of the egg, the seed in the orange, the meat in the nut, the heart of the acorn. So mankind dwells in the inside of the world. This is what I call argument from analogy. More important is the fact that the Copernican Assumption has never been proved. It merely happens to provide what its believers consider adequate answers to questions about the universe. Ours is the only explanation of the world that has been actually proved by true and precise test. Now, come over to the Art Hall and see the paintings of Douglas Teed. You've probably seen his murals in the Arlington Hotel in Binghamton, New York. He was the son of Koresh."

"Koresh?" I said.

"Hebrew name for Cyrus. Dr. Cyrus Teed, born near Trout Creek, New York. He was the founder of Koresh-anity and one of the greatest men who ever lived."

We walked across the road and through a level and well-planted lawn toward the Art Hall, stopping on the way to admire a tree my companion called a "bull acacia."

"Thorns interlock like horns of fighting bulls," he said. "Thomas A. Edison admired this tree. Sometimes Henry Ford came with him and once the two of 'em brought John Burroughs. We had a joke on Mr. Edison. He brought a lot of friends to our Bamboo Tea Garden for a dinner to celebrate the fiftieth anniversary of his discovery of incandescent light. We had our own electric plant and it worked fine till a thunderstorm came up. They ate their anniversary dinner by candlelight."

We wandered about the big raftered interior of the Art Hall. The paintings of Douglas Teed were academic landscapes, mostly of Venice.

"Rich lady in Binghamton sent him abroad and paid his way for a while," said Lou Staton. "His mother brought him up in that town while Koresh was out over the state getting started. Now if you've got time I'd like to tell you the first scientific principles of Koreshanity."

"First," I said, "I'd like to know how you were converted."

"I was barbering at the Sherman Hotel in Chicago. Left my room for a walk down State Street. The nineteen-hundred elections were going on. Speakers were hollering about that on one corner and on another the Salvation Army was holding a meeting, but I wasn't paying anybody mind. I was out for a walk. Then I saw a fellow speaking beside a post that had a sign on it—same sign you see there on the wall—WE LIVE INSIDE. What he said made sense and I stopped to listen. I bought a copy of the *Flaming Sword* from a man standing beside the speaker. It was three cents but I gave him a nickel and said 'Keep the change.' I read it in bed that night. Before I went to sleep I was inside."

"That was simple."

"Just remember this," he said. "It's an easy experiment and you can do it yourself. Stand on the shore of Long Island Sound and look across to Connecticut. How far is it?"

"In one place I know," I said, "it's about ten miles."

"Have you ever seen Connecticut from there?"

"Yes, on clear days."

"All right, and you know the curve of the earth's surface runs about eight inches to the mile. If we're living on the outside of the round world you couldn't possibly see it. There'd be a bulge in between taller than you are. How come you can see it?"

"I don't know," I said weakly.

"It's because we live inside," he said triumphantly. "The curve of the earth is eight inches to the mile but it curves up instead of down. We live on a concave surface—not a convex."

We walked back through a winding path among orange trees. On the porch of a neat cottage a white-haired woman, very pleasant of face, was sewing.

"Hello, Mrs. Lewis," said Lou Staton. "This is a visitor, Mr. Cramer."

"Carmer," I said.

"Are you Carl Carmer?" she said.

"Yes."

"I've read your books about York State. Your family came from Dryden. My husband's father ran a gristmill there before he died."

"On Fall Creek," I said.

"Exactly."

I felt the warmth rising within me that comes from meeting home folks in a faraway place. I began thinking, as I nearly always do after meeting a native of my home country, that York State folks look as if they come from York State.

"Mr. Carmer was asking about Koreshanity," said Lou Staton.

"I was never a member but my mother was one of the first converts and my sister Rose is a Koreshan. She and I live here. We'll be glad to tell you what we know."

"I'm afraid I have too little time."

"Come in for a moment and I'll try to remember the important things. I can give you a letter to a man who must live fairly near you in the North who could tell you about Koreshanity better than anybody else. Then, if you want to, you can get the facts from him after you've gone home."

"Wonderful," I said.

On a late October midnight in 1869, thirty-year-old Dr. Cyrus Read Teed sat alone in his electroalchemical laboratory in the little city of Utica in central New York State. He had been thinking on his recent considerable progress in "alchemical elaborations" when suddenly he felt a relaxation at the back of his head, a buzzing tension behind his wide brow. Gradually from the center of his brain a vibration, "gentle, soft and dulciferous," spread to his physical extremities and beyond into the aura of his being, which seemed to extend for miles outside his body. Impelled to recline upon "this gently oscillating ocean of magnetic and spiritual ecstasy," he was conscious of the fading of his senses and to test his hearing spoke aloud.

Lying upon the vibratory sea of his delight, he heard from his own lips a voice he had never heard before:

"Fear not, my son," it said, "thou satisfactory offspring of my profoundest yearnings! I have nurtured thee through countless embodiments . . . in superlative attitudes of earthly glory and thence descending to the lowest depths of degradation into which the human animal can decline."

Then, as the young doctor, eyes closed in awe, knelt on the floor of his laboratory, the voice told him that through his many past incarnations the speaker had witnessed his triumphs and his defeats. She had seen him destroy his body by loathsome disease, had seen him fall before enemies whom his own ambitions and grasping ego had made. "Then," she said, "I have clothed thee in another body and watched thee therein."

Bidden to open his eyes, Cyrus Teed saw emerging from a sphere of purple and golden light the exquisite face of a woman, and the neck, shoulders, and arms "equally exquisite . . . to the very finger extremes adorned with the most delicate, matchless, consummate finger nails so framed as to challenge admiration." Her hair falling over her shoulders was long, luxuriant and golden, and she wore a robe of purple and gold whose folds fell in a long train behind her.

"I have brought thee to this birth," said the vision, "to sacrifice thee upon the altar of all human hopes, that through thy quickening of me, thy Mother and Bride, the Sons of God shall spring into visible creation . . . Thou shalt possess me henceforth . . . My Son, receive now the blessing flowing from my august Motherhood . . ."

This strange interview, much of it couched in metaphysical language, went on for some time. At its end, the physician accepted from his supernatural visitant his mission "to redeem the race."

"I shall achieve the victory over death," he said, "not for myself, but for those to whom I come as a sacrificial offering."

As the divine lady went from him she turned and pointed downward toward his material body lying on the laboratory couch and he soon waked to find he had re-entered it.

It was two-thirty in the morning when the bemused doctor ended his walk from the laboratory through Utica's deserted streets to his home. He was soon asleep in his bed, but was awakened two hours later by the high loud surging of a wind so violent that he was frightened. Abruptly it ceased and in the following dead stillness he heard a noise as of great wings beating, then—the rolling of chariot wheels. He rose and went to his bedroom window. Utica slept in the darkness before dawn. Again the wind, the wings, the chariot wheels—and again unearthly silence. A third time the sounds swelled and faded. When they did not return the listener went back to bed. As he lay upon it he felt that from the events of the night he had come to know the secret of immortal life.

The English ancestors of Cyrus Read Teed, early seventeenth-century immigrants, may have had within them a prophetic strain, for they also fathered another York State mystic, Mormon Joseph Smith. Soon after the birth of Cyrus on October 18, 1839, on the banks of Trout Creek, tributary of the Delaware River, Father Jesse Teed, moved his family to Utica on the Erie Canal, where he soon won recognition as an inventor of farm appliances, but much more for his miraculous cures of a plague called "black tongue."

Cyrus left school at eleven for a job "on the canal" and kept it until he began studying medicine in the Utica office of his uncle, Samuel Teed. By the time he was twenty-one he had married a girl from Meredith, fathered his son, Douglas, and enlisted in the Union Army Medical Corps. As soon as the war ended he completed his medical studies at the Eclectical Medical College of New York City in 1868. He had been practicing medicine in Utica about a year when the heavenly lady paid him her extraordinary visit.

This incident, which he described and later published under the title *The Illumination of Koresh* with the subtitle "*Marvelous Experience of the Great Alchemist at Utica, New York,*" had immediate and extraordinary consequences. Next day he called at the place of work of a cousin, Myron Baldwin, to walk home with him to dinner. Myron saw him standing in an aura of mystic light and recognizing its origin spoke a blessing upon him. Then he took the new-made prophet along home and there his wife told them that just before their arrival she had seen on her pair of carved wooden wall brackets, ordinarily used for displaying bric-a-brac, two winged cherubim poised as if alighted momentarily from flight.

A few months proved that with his illumination other blessings had come to the illuminated. Like his distant cousin Joseph Smith, he had received on the day of his annunciation the gift of languages, being suddenly familiar with both Hebrew and Greek. More remarkable even than this was the revelation of the demonstrable scientific facts of the Cellular Cosmogony, as he chose to call his concept of the universe. He had for some time been interested in measuring the curve of the earth's surface. Doubting the assumption of Copernicus that the earth is a part of the convex outside shell of a world which is an infinitesimal round in an infinite universe, he had come to the conclusion that human beings inhabit the inside of the shell of a decidedly finite sphere. And Cyrus Teed devoted the rest of his life to the education of men to the belief that they live on a concave surface and to his religious teachings.

Many of the towns and cities of New York State knew Dr. Teed after that. Scientific and religious heresies were not the best bedside talk for an ambitious doctor in Utica —household word for orthodoxy since President Lincoln had read to his cabinet Artemus Ward's tale of the visitor to a canalboat waxworks who had "kaved in" the sculptured head of the false apostle saying "Judas Iscariot can't show himself in Utiky with impunerty"—and the enthusiastic young radical soon found that much of the rest of his home state shared Utica's convictions. Wherever he went he told his patients of his new knowledge and immediately became to them a benighted heathen, a dangerous lunatic, or "that crazy doctor." They made life so dif-

ficult for the Teeds that his wife, nervous and ill, went to live with her sister and the doctor worked on alone. Binghamton denounced him as a crackpot. At Trout Creek, his home town, he was without honor. He found few patients in neighboring Deposit, Rockroyal, Bartlett Hollow, or Apex who could tolerate his doctoring for his doctrine.

A new start in Sandy Creek on the shores of Lake Ontario, far north of the Delaware, ended in the same way. Once the people of nearby Ruralhill, Pierrepont Manor, and Lorraine heard the newcomer proclaim the true religion and the true science they looked at him oddly and the next time they needed a doctor sent to Pulaski for one.

He turned home again. His parents were living at Moravia (where old Bill Rockefeller, peddler and rifleshot extraordinary, had unwittingly laid a foundation for a golden empire) and were eager to turn over to their unsuccessful son a small mop-making business. He grasped the idea hungrily. As plate silver and animal traps had enriched John Humphrey Noyes's Perfectionists at Oneida, as the sale of herbs and furniture had cared for the material needs of the Shakers at New Lebanon, Watervliet, Sodus and Groveland, making mops would support Koresh and the band of disciples he would organize. Three of the people who were present in Moravia when he established his first community in 1880 are still alive and living on community land—his sister Emma, now ninety-three, and the two daughters of convert Ada Welton, one of whom also became a Koreshan.

They left Moravia and the mop business two years later for the wider field of Syracuse. They forsook that unenthusiastic city for a third-floor New York flat at 135th Street near Eighth Avenue. Koresh established there the nucleus of his colony—four ladies, of whom one was his sister and one his cousin. A year later he had failed again. Then came a sudden reversal of his fortunes.

Cyrus Teed was invited to address a convention of the National Association of Mental Science at Chicago in September of 1886. He accepted and made so eloquent and persuasive a speech that he was elected president of the organization. On demand of the members he gave another lecture at which by use of his miraculous powers he so aided a fat lady who could walk only a few steps that she walked all the way home. The mystic-minded of Chicago were at his feet.

A few years later his Chicago Community numbered one hundred and twenty-six, all living in or near a rambling and highly decorated mansion they called Beth-Ophra, surrounded by spacious and well-planted grounds, in Chicago's Washington Heights. Koreshanity was spreading. San Francisco had a thriving "branch communistic" and there were eager groups of converts in Denver, Baltimore, Portland (Oregon), Lynn and Springfield (Massachusetts).

Dr. Teed's star was in the ascendant and he was a happy man. When he paid a visit to Pennsylvania, the Pittsburgh *Leader* (October 25, 1891) described his physical appearance in detail, complimented him on his modesty, quiet dress, clerical manner, mastery of language, and its delivery, and answered current criticisms by saying:

"If Dr. Teed does not practice his teachings, if he is seeking personal gain for personal ends, if he loves his subjects with a more earthly than platonic love, he is the most consummate, polished and best educated rogue the world ever produced . . ." The reporter continued: "He says as soon as his system of government prevails, which he says will be within ten years, he will build a six track railroad between the Atlantic and Pacific coasts, in one year employing a million men in its work. He will also construct a pneumatic passenger way across the continent which will carry one to San Francisco in 12 hours; the cars will run without wheels. More wonderful than all, Dr. Teed says one of his members in the Chicago office has a device whereby he can, from his desk in that office in Chicago, set the type for every newspaper in this country by wire and that an application for a patent is now on file in Washington."

Koresh now felt that the movement was strong enough to reach the goal of which he had dreamed—a holy star-shaped city where all Koreshans might unite—a radiant center from which his teachings would flow in increasing power until they had brought truth to the minds of all men. He would select a place set apart from the pursuits of the worldly, where his followers might live according to his creed and by their example show the peoples of the earth what a heaven life might be if they did likewise.

Now enters into the Koreshan story another of the mystic incidents that embroider its whole fabric. In 1883 a native of Germany, Gustav Damkohler, seeking solitude for solace of a deeply religious nature, came to the isolated village of Fort Myers in Lee County, Florida. Exploring

Estero Bay in his rowboat, he moved one sunny morning across waters dotted with palm-grove islands and found, behind a screen of darkly matted mangroves, a tiny river that was the color of light-struck coffee. With difficulty he pushed his boat up the winding stream. Tropic fish swarmed the current. Alligators slept on banks which grew steeper and higher as he advanced.

Through sturdy pines and tall slender cabbage palms bordering the water he saw savannas of palmetto, rooted in firm and fertile land. Pausing in the shadows of a scrub-oak thicket he heard a voice from an unseen speaker saying "Take and dress until the Lord comes." Believing the voice divine, Gustav Damkohler bought land along the Estero River, brought his wife and children to its banks.

While for seven years he awaited the meaning of the strange message, his wife died and five of his six children. One day he sailed across the bay to Punta Gorda to get his mail and found there a printed pamphlet of the teachings of Koresh. Then he thought he knew why he had been waiting and he wrote a letter.

When, on the first day of the new year of 1894, Cyrus Teed of Trout Creek, New York, stepped ashore from the boat that had brought him across the bay, Gustav Damkohler knelt before him, called him master, and said, "Ich habe dich lang erwartet."

Teed and his party of three women, selected from the leading Koreshans of Chicago, lived for a while with Damkohler, ate the fresh fish from the river and the palmetto honey of bees from their host's many hives. Then they knew they had found the site of their holy city and began to prepare for its building.

Within a month twenty-four eager Koreshans had come

from Chicago to rear the log house that was to shelter them. More followed and other structures rose among the water oaks, the pines and palms. Among them were Lee County's largest building, from the ground floor of which the communal dining hall and kitchen sent appetizing odors to two upper stories used as a sisters' dormitory; "The Temple," central home of the colony; the "Planetary Court" in which important officers had their dwelling. On Estero Island in the bay the Koreshans built a home they called "The Point" from logs drawn to the river by great logging carts and rafted downstream and across the bay to their new-built sawmill. Farther up the island they erected "Middle Carlos," the colony's farthest outpost.

Now came the golden age. The colony's approximately six thousand acres increased in value, converts to the Cellular Cosmogony and the other teachings of Koresh were plentiful. Estero's cycle of sunny days almost destroyed the memory of Chicago weather. Wisely, foreseeing possible future difficulties, Dr. Teed incorporated his colony under the laws of New Jersey as the Koreshan Unity, with a board of directors and the usual officers, reserving for himself the unique title of "Prime Counselor." At the same time, in the autumn of 1903, the Chicago branch moved, lock, stock, and barrel, to Estero.

In their isolated Floridian Utopia on the inside of the world about two hundred Koreshans were finding the secrets of happy and creative living under the benevolent direction of their prophet. Though Fort Myers, the nearest town, was a six- or seven-hour journey over a heavy sand trail through the woods, the businesses about which they set themselves prospered. Printers, machinists, carpenters, and boat builders were happily, noisily busy. Planters patiently worked a soil that demanded different treatment from that they had been accustomed to giving northern earth.

The Koreshan Unity was a gayer group than most of the communities that had their origin in New York State's psychic area. Koresh was a genial leader, a skilled and humorous raconteur, a strong believer in cultural pursuits. The Koreshans had their own schools and encouraged extra-curricular study of the arts. They built a floating stage at a bend where the river had made from its banks a natural amphitheater and there they played dramas by Lord Dunsany and other modern playwrights. They formed a brass band and had so many young people tootling that they built a practice house out of earshot upriver. They were very proud when the band, which gave weekly concerts at their new "Art Hall," won as first prize of an all-Florida band contest at the State Fair in Tampa a team of blooded horses. Some evenings their string and wood-wind orchestra gave programs of classical music on the stage of their raft theater and the audience, sitting under the palms beside the star-reflecting river, found life as good as they had thought it would be when they left their northern homes to follow Koresh.

One of the reasons why the prophet had chosen the west coast of Florida as the site of his community was that on the long sand levels beside the sea he could make the experiment that would prove that men live on the concave interior surface of the round world. The geodetic staff of the Koreshan Unity left Chicago in mid-December, 1896, and began actual operations on the beach at Naples, Florida, on January 2 of the new year.

The experiment was based on the running of an absolutely straight line above a considerable arc of the earth's surface. If the earth curve was convex, as most people believed and as it must be if we live on the outside of a spherical world, the straight line would run off into space at both ends as the rounded surface dropped away from it. If we live on the inside of the sphere and the earth curves concavely upward, then the line would be a chord that would meet at each of its ends the circle that is the outer limit of the world-sphere.

For the purpose of obtaining a surely straight line, one of the engineers on the project invented what he called a rectilineator, a series of three rectangular twelve-foot panels each of which contained two T-squares set end to end. If one of these panels could be leveled above the established mean-tide level at the arbitrarily chosen distance of 128 inches—and this would be possible by the erection of tall standards on which its height could be adjusted to a nicety—and another panel could be fitted to it with great exactness and bolted there, a straight line would have been started. The third panel could then be fitted to the second in the same careful fashion and the first could be moved forward. Thus the inventor would have accomplished a moving straight line by the mechanical adjustment of right angles.

When he had advanced several miles across the earth's surface, contiguous to a body of water from the level of which all measurements would be taken, he would be able to measure any deviation of the water surface from the line, either up or down. Since the water surface conforms to the earth's contour, he would then have proved the true curve of the earth. If the earth were convex, the line at the end of a given distance (four miles was decided upon) would be higher than at the beginning. If the earth were concave, the line would be lower than at the beginning. A great deal of care was taken that the first panel should be exactly level when the line was started, and work was painstaking and slow. Soon after it started it was handicapped by the death of the well-to-do Chicagoan who had financed the expedition, Mr. L. S. Boomer. This not only saddened the party but took from their midst their general manager, Mr. Boomer's son Lucius, who had been most active in the early preparations. (Young Lucius did not come back after his father's funeral but won himself fame as president of a New York hostelry, the Waldorf-Astoria.)

Five months were required to complete the four-mile survey but when the line reached Gordon's Pass, two and a half miles below Naples, the staff was cheered by discovering that it was already four feet nearer water level. At four miles it ran into the water and all hands celebrated their proving of the knowledge that had been given to Koresh on the midnight of his illumination over a quarter of a century before.

The triumphant leader was at the height of his happy career. In the community auditorium he spoke with the authority of the vindicated prophet. Through the years he had been teaching and clarifying the principles of Koreshanity and they were now accepted not only by the joyful two hundred but by many converts throughout the nation. His monthly magazine—the *Flaming Sword*—was carrying his message to a steadily increasing number of subscribers. He devoted himself to writing the volume that would establish the truths of the universe as he saw them— *The Cellular Cosmogony.*

"The mind that conceived the Copernican system arising

in the dark ages was so simple as to take an appearance for a fact," he wrote. "Koreshanity has the truth but the present humanity (steeped in tobacco, rum and sensualism) prefers to meet the truth of Koreshanity with ridicule rather than to give it candid consideration." The sun, he stated, is a revolving disk with a dark side and a bright side, producing night and day. The claim that it is 93,000,000 miles from the earth is balderdash. It is less than 4,000. The moon is not, as Copernicans say, 250,000 miles away, but only 1,000. The universe is a cell, a hollow globe, and the sun, moon, planets, and the stars are all within it. Koreshanity provides the true explanation of all phenomena.

Reincarnation is the central law of life. To become immortal in the flesh is possible but only if one ceases to propagate life. Celibacy, however, is only for the higher ranks, not for the world at large. The human race would destroy itself by fecundation without the counterbalance of celibate conservation on the part of its leaders. The communism of the Christian church, sharing of the goods of life, is the true path. Money and the competitive system should be destroyed. All great music and all great art exist in the absolute in the spiritual world. Human beings are only the media by which such communications are "let down" from that world.

In a prospectus of the Estero Colony, giving "General Information concerning Membership and its Obligations," the prophet wrote at about this time: "There is no difference between one who has placed one penny in the common treasury and one who has contributed a hundred thousand . . . We are celibate in doctrine and life; we are communistic in our possession of property . . . Many wonder why we set ourselves down in Estero, Florida, with the idea of reforming the world. We have located a central point from which to promulgate our views and propagate our system . . .

". . . When a family comes into the Koreshan Unity it comes with the understanding that there is a separation; that the children no longer belong to the parents, but to the institution and that the Unity claims the right to direct the education, industry, and care of the children exclusively . . . The male children belong . . . until they are twenty-one, and the female children until they are eighteen . . . and all children should be taught that they belong to the Unity and not to their parents."

The influx of two hundred active-minded and conscientious citizens had had a considerable effect upon the political situation in southwestern Florida. The supremacy of the Lee County Democratic machine, never before questioned, found itself opposed by a very articulate body commanding a considerable number of ballots. Flustered, the local politicians seized upon the fact that the Koreshans held private caucuses, at which they decided how their whole group would vote, as a basis for arguing that they should be disfranchised. They had mistaken the temper of these gentle-seeming people. Like angry bees the Koreshans poured from their hive in Estero to do battle. They formed a new party, which they called the Progressive Liberty Party, they established and printed in their own shop as its official organ a weekly paper called the *American Eagle*, and, brass band blaring, speakers shouting, they toured the county behind their prize horses.

Fort Myers was a rough, tough cowtown in 1906, and as elections drew near its political bosses were enraged to find that the Koreshans had won many adherents to the opposition party and that the outcome was in doubt. On October 13 of that year a Koreshan friend of mine, who lives not far from my upstate home, arrived for the first time in Fort Myers. A young member of the Unity at Estero met him and carried his suitcase for him up Main Street.

As they neared the center of town he saw a burly fellow in rough clothes and broad-brimmed Stetson hat walk up to a rather short, distinguished-looking man and speak to him. Apparently incensed by a reply, the fellow struck the smaller man viciously three times on the left side of the head, knocking him down. The newcomer, not realizing that he had witnessed an assault upon Koresh, was surprised to see his companion drop the suitcase and dash to the defense. In another moment the attacker had been struck to the street beside his victim. As my friend walked toward them then, he saw this man rise, throw back his coat to show his town marshal's silver star, and draw his gun. Then the Koreshans were forced to go to the police station, where after bitter and prolonged altercation they were released.

Koresh was more seriously hurt by the heavy blows than his companions realized. He had predicted his death fourteen years before in the *Flaming Sword* (March 26, 1892): "Dr. Teed will die; the termination of his natural career will be tragic. He will reach his death at the instigation of a people who profess the religion of Jesus the Christ of God," but none of his people believed that the prophecy would soon be fulfilled as a result of his injuries at the hands of the marshal. A nervous disorder developed, however, and caused many months of severe pain. Then, despite the inspired treatments of Koreshan Gustav Faber, an eccentric old German sailor who had been a nurse in the Spanish-American War and had invented a strange electrotherapeutic machine for the purpose of curing him, Koresh died at the Point on Estero Island, December 22, 1908.

The Koreshan Unity was shaken to its foundations by the loss of its leader. Strong differences arose. Many of the prophet's most devoted followers, remembering his teachings of immortality in the physical body, chose to disregard his prophecy of his own demise and demanded that all that was material of Cyrus Teed be permitted the opportunity of renewing itself. Convinced that as a messianic character he was capable of theocrasis (a process described by Teed as the incorruptible dissolution, without decay of the flesh, of the physical body by "electromagnetic combustion"), they insisted that no burial take place for at least three days.

The body lay in state. Christmas came and went, and some of the anxious watchers saw or hoped they saw evidences of a new body forming out of the remnant of the old one now fast decaying in a midwinter hot spell. At last, when decomposition was definitely advanced, Fort Myers's health authorities ordered interment. A sturdy rectangular concrete tomb was erected on Estero Island, the body was placed inside, and the tomb was sealed. In the center of the narrow front wall were engraved these words only:

Cyrus
Shepherd Stone of Israel

In the meantime the community began to fall apart. Gustav Faber claimed that as Koresh breathed his last he conferred upon him his spirit and the mantle of his leadership. Mrs. Annie G. Ordway, whom Koresh had looked upon as his highest ranking assistant and had designated Victoria Gratia, Pre-Eminent, also announced that she had received from the prophet the right of succession. A few followed her when she left Estero. Others still clung to their belief in the immortality of their human deity. They demanded to be allowed to prove that the prophet had dematerialized in the tomb and rematerialized outside. When they were refused they tried a surreptitious midnight raid to break open the cement sarcophagus. It came so near to success that the board of directors had a strong kerosene lamp with a mirror reflector placed high and directed on the tomb and stationed an old white-haired German, Koreshan Carl Luettich, as lamplighter and night watchman. Night after night, among the wild mangroves and the coconuts and the mango trees, Carl Luettich stared into the blackness that surrounded the circle of light in which he sat. Once, just before dawn, he fell asleep and the fanatics came again and opened a side of the tomb before sunlight frightened them away. Carl Luettich was more alert after that, but watching the tomb was not necessary much longer.

One October day a still yellow light fell on land and sea and once again, if his senses had survived as he had said they would, Cyrus Teed heard a sound "like a terrific windstorm having reached the magnitude of a hurricane." There are those who say that this noise of a great rushing was followed by that of great wings flying and then "noise as of chariot wheels." When this had ceased the tomb of Koresh had disappeared and with it had gone whatever remained of the body of the prophet. There was no questioning now among true Koreshans. Theocrasis had occurred and Koresh would come again.

I returned to Estero about a year after my first visit. The Koreshan to whom Mrs. Anna Lewis had given me a letter proved to be a member of the board of directors of the community and had become my good friend. I bore a letter from him to the president of the board, Mr. Laurence Bubbett, and, advised of my coming, he met me at Lou Staton's gas pump. He is a slender man of about sixty, his hair is white and curly, his regular features have about them a look of asceticism and a sort of noble serenity. Mr. Bubbett was brought into the Unity at the age of four, both his parents having been converts. He has not lived at Estero all his life, however. He is an expert proofreader and typographer and, while resident of New York in younger days was chief copyreader for *Life* magazine, then purposefully funny. He has now returned to the scenes of his boyhood as chief administrator of the affairs of the Koreshan corporation.

He guided me across the road and through the big store to a back office, where he introduced me to Hedwig Michel (he pronounced it Mitchell), a sturdy woman who looked to be in her mid-forties. She was seated at her desk and held in her lap a cat which differed from most cats in that she had one less tail.

When Miss Michel saw that my eyes were upon the animal her sensitive face and expressive gray-blue eyes at once abandoned the air of impersonal objectivity with which she had acknowledged the introduction.

"She is Manx. There have been many generations of Manx cats here. Some of her kittens have no tail and some take after a father with a tail."

"Miss Michel is our executive secretary," said Mr. Bubbett. "She is also the youngest resident member of the Unity."

"That is not difficult," laughed Hedwig Michel. "Twelve of the members of the Unity—six men and six women—live here. The youngest is a boy of fifty-seven. The eldest is the sister of Koresh. She is ninety-three."

"Since Miss Michel came," said Mr. Bubbett, "she has put the store on a paying basis, she has had worthless buildings torn down and has restored those worth keeping. Leaky roofs have been repaired, rickety porches mended, new plumbing installed."

"It has been worth doing," said Miss Michel.

"And how do you happen to be here?" I asked.

Her reply gave me the last of the many psychic tales that illustrate the tapestrylike quality of the Unity's history.

In the city of Frankfurt am Main twenty-five years ago Hedwig Michel, a gay young girl, chattered and danced about the big house of her German-Jewish parents, owners and administrators of a prosperous children's school. Though too active to prepare herself for the university as her parents wished, her inclination led her to apply for a position at the Frankfurt Municipal Theater, where after employment as a secretary she rose in an incredibly short time to the high rank of dramaturgist and manager and as such she helped initiate and establish the Open-Air Theater. At this time she was writing occasional articles for the *Frankfurter Zeitung* and short dramas, for one of which, a Christmas play, the distinguished composer, Paul Hindemith, wrote the incidental music. Next to the study of literature and art, botany was Hedwig Michel's major interest. On extensive trips to foreign countries she examined plant life, and specialized in cacti as the result of an expedition she made to Mexico in 1923.

Soon after the Nazis came to power they made her give up the theater work. She was allowed to found an orchestra for professional musicians who, like her, had lost their positions. This orchestra, conducted by William Steinberg, became eventually the Boris Huberman Orchestra of Palestine. Now she assumed the position of headmistress of a widely known Jewish children's school, Dr. Heinemann's Institute, which occupied her seventeen-room home. For some years then, at government order, she instructed about forty-five pupils, the youngest four, the eldest sixty-one, in the language and customs of countries to which they might emigrate.

Shortly before the beginning of World War II, having difficulty in finding a candidate for a position on her staff as teacher of mathematics and the English language, she came to America. While conferring in Philadelphia with prominent Quakers, who were aiding her, she received a letter of application from a German who had high qualifications and she decided her quest had ended and returned to Frankfurt.

Peter Bender, the new instructor, had been severely wounded when his plane had been shot down in World

War I. Incapable of hard physical labor after that, he had devoted himself to the study of mathematics. He was a slim, tall, dark-eyed, handsome man and he and his young and pretty wife were a welcome addition to Hedwig Michel's faculty. Soon after he had begun his duties he told the headmistress that his mathematical researches had some years before brought him to the conclusion that men live on the inside of a concave world and that his chance reading of Cyrus Teed's volume, *The Cellular Cosmogony*, in a Worms am Rhein library had confirmed his reckonings in every respect. He persuaded her to listen to his arguments and to read the book, and she was soon a believer in Koreshanity. As time went on, Peter Bender corresponded at length with the Koreshans at Estero and his employer noticed a change in him. His study of the cult's messianic leader had so affected him that he believed himself the reincarnation of Koresh, and he assumed that august identity with authority.

Meanwhile the Nazi pogroms had begun and no Jew was safe in Germany. Knowing that Hedwig Michel had received her American immigration visa, Peter Bender wrote to Estero asking the leaders of the Unity if they could make use of a woman of her remarkable abilities. They replied that they could and she obtained passage on the last American ship (plying the Mediterranean) that brought in Jewish refugees through regular process of entry. Peter Bender and his wife stayed on and were murdered in a Nazi prison camp.

"It is a good life," said Hedwig Michel to me, smiling her infectious smile. "I like taking care of the old people and I love this country. At first many people were suspicious of me. They could not understand why I whose great activity had been the theater would be living here in this quiet spot. But I am happy here. Now let us go and see what we shall see."

She and Laurence Bubbett took me to my room in the old Planetary Court, a spacious frame building of the Victorian cottage type. Then we went to lunch in the community dining hall. The six old ladies sat at one table, the six old men at the other, in accordance with the celibate teachings of their prophet. They welcomed me cordially and I renewed my friendship with Lou Staton—the barber of Chicago.

All the ladies were gay and kindly. Mrs. Emma Norton, sister of the late Cyrus Teed, was especially chipper for her ninety-three years but she said that she did not remember the old days as well as she used to. The men seemed to feel challenged by my interest to bring out choice incidents from the colony's history and they told them with gusto. One tale of a rattlesnake, which ascended to the eaves of a building and lay there under a loose tin roof, causing, whenever anyone approached, a great thundering to seem to come from a clear and sunlit sky, gave all present a feeling that further narratives would be anticlimactic.

"We don't have as many rattlers as we used to," said Hedwig Michel brightly from the foot of the women's table. "When the scientists from the Chicago Zoo came here last spring looking for them they couldn't catch one. And all last winter at Planetary Court we found only three."

In the days that followed I wandered with Laurence Bubbett and Hedwig Michel beside the dark waters of the narrow meandering river and we talked of communities like this one that had failed and discussed the reasons for their failure.

"With the death of the leader they lost the dynamic drive that gave them their initial success," said Mr. Bubbett. "Here while Koresh was alive we were very much alive too and we made many converts. We could have many now but they would not be sincere. Though we are spending our diminishing capital to keep going, there is still something left, mostly in landholdings, and, since all our stock is held in trust for the use and benefit of the Koreshan Unity, many shiftless people would like to join us just to live out their days in idleness. We're worried, too, by dimwits. Why, we could keep this place filled with crackpots who couldn't possibly get along together!"

At night in my airy bedroom sleep came easily while I read in the pages of Josephus and in Orson Fowler's *Introduction to Phrenology*, both of which I found in the shadowy old library. By day I heard tales of the old days when the colonists used to tow skiffs behind their steam launch *Victoria* downriver at night and with flaring pine torches so frighten the schools of fish coming in on the changing tide that they would leap into the air and descending fill the boats.

On the morning I was to leave, Laurence Bubbett and Hedwig Michel took me in the old high-bodied station wagon, over a woods road so lost that we sometimes had to get out to search for its track, to a spot where suddenly tall trees ended and there was beyond them only a broad savanna of palmettos and scrub oak as far as my eyes could see. Directly in front of me then I saw a rectangle marked out by rocks and shells and in it stood a dozen modest gravestones. I read the names—Peter Blem, John S. Sargent, Gustav Faber, and all the rest. Wind was blowing across the wild low level of green leaves. There was no other sound.

"This is where the twelve old folks will probably rest," said Mr. Bubbett. "We are planning to weed it and make it look nice and improve the road out here."

On our way back through the almost trackless waste we stopped at a sulphur spring bubbling into a liquid sphere above a pipe emerging from the ground.

"I wish I could tell you how grateful I am," I said, "and how fascinated I have been by Estero."

"It is like my old home city," said Hedwig Michel. "The slogan of the town is 'Frankfurt am Main steckt voll von Merkwuerdigkeiten.' I think it could be translated 'It is full of remarkable things.' "

"The Unity may lose in the material world," said Laurence Bubbett, "but its loss is a gain in the spiritual world. While old members may pass on, there will be a corresponding accretion in the spiritual spheres."

"Koreshanity is not of the past but for the future," said Hedwig Michel slowly. "It is a great truth and it will someday sweep across the world."

"It is our firm belief," said Laurence Bubbett, "that the Koreshan Unity will never die out. Its impetus and force will continue until truth is triumphant over falsity and the Golden Age will be ushered in and the human race will observe the divine rule: Do unto others as you would have others do unto you."

"Is there no one," I said, "who has assumed the place of Koresh as leader of the Unity?"

"No one," he said. Then he laughed. "Beyond the grave-yard about ten miles into the scrub a man and a woman are living in a tent and I understand they claim to be a divine couple upon whom the spirit of Koresh has descended."

"How do they eat?" I said.

"They fish and hunt," said Hedwig Michel, "and a rich lady who lives in a West Coast city believes in them and sends them baskets of food."

Laurence Bubbett bent over the round globe of water at the top of the pipe and drank. Then, still looking at the water, he stood erect.

"It is like gazing into a crystal ball," he said.

"Road into Raquette Lake had about four or five miles of slack in it," said the mountain man. "Used to wear down the guides that was going in there to take folks fishin'. They asked the supervisor for a straight road and he asked the governor, but nothing happened. The boys had a crow-flight road all figured but the ranger kept his eye on 'em so that they couldn't do nothing about it. The ranger was a real honest fella but he had a fine tenor voice he was mighty proud of. Pretty soon folks in the little church the guides belong to decided to give a show and asked the ranger to sing in it. On the day after the dress rehearsal, the trees in the path of that straight road looked just the same but in the afternoon they all blowed down. Somebody'd sawed 'em most of the way through and left the job of fellin' 'em to the wind. Hadn't been so much excitement in these parts since Captain Sam Patchin tried to jump Vicar Island in his iceboat.

"Mr. Osborne, he was commissioner then, he had a hard time gettin' anybody to own up to it. They was a load of pettyfogging but not much come of it."

The mountain man said, "Old Ben Barrett from near Luzern used to do some lumberjackin' over by Raquette Lake. Bet another jack he could throw him across the Hudson at Glens Falls. First time they was both in the town the fella says, 'Now's your chance.'

"Ben picked him up and dropped him in the water.

"The fella says, 'Give me my money. You can't do it.'

"Ben says, 'Mebbe not at the first try,' and started for him again but the fella seen a chance to slope and he sloped."

Part Five

People and Ghosts

"There's the graveyard," he said, pointing to a few weathered stones standing in bright sunlight in an open field overgrown with weeds, "and just for the hell of it I'm going over there."

15

Picker
Turned Yorker

York state has long been accustomed to problems created by influxes of people with black skins. When the big city at the mouth of the Hudson was small it had its "Negro plot" and resultant hysteria which brought about the "executions" of many innocents. In the days before the Civil War Gerritt Smith of Peterboro, the black heroine, Harriet Tubman of Auburn, and abolitionist associates kept a steady stream of escaped slaves moving on the "Underground Railroad" to freedom across the Canadian border. Now the state's colored population is annually augmented by industrious workers from the South. They are desperately needed by the York State farmers, who at first bewailed the disappearance of that itinerant and too often unstable character, the hired man, but now swear by their colored helpers. Most of them, they say, are the most efficient workers they ever employed. Although many of these migrant colored workers return to the South at the end of the season, each year a number remain behind, and this is the story of one of them.

Marthy Ann Jerdon was born in the country near Flor-

ala, which got its name by being where it is, right on the
border between Florida and Alabama. What schooling
Marthy Ann got she got right there, but it was precious
little, just a month before Christmas and maybe two
months after when some teacher out of work took the job
that hardly paid enough to live on. Marthy Ann grew up
helping her mother do washing for white folks until she
got married when she was sixteen and went to live with
Andrew Jackson Jerdon. She had Irma Jean a year later
and soon after that Andrew found out there was good pay
picking beans in Pahokee and Belle Glade and the other
towns on the shores of big Lake Okeechobee down in the
middle of Florida.

Marthy Ann did not like the life in those towns at first.
She got tired picking beans in the fields where a sunflower
grows by every hill and she hated leaving Irma Jean with
the other babies that were taken care of by the six-year-olds,
who were too young to pick. She got so she liked it, though,
for she and Andrew made good money and at night after
Irma Jean was asleep they would go out and visit all the
jukes and dance and get a little drunk. The jukes all had
fancy boxes with colored glass in them and lights behind
it and they played moany blues records while she and Andrew danced or drank with friendly folks and talked. Sometimes Andrew left her to sit with the other wives while he
joined a crap game. One wild night in Pahokee trouble
started and when it was over Andrew was dead, stabbed
by somebody or other in the drunken, smashing, cursing,
grunting battle.

After that Marthy Ann had only the money from her
picking in the season, for she did not have the knack of
picking up odd jobs like Andrew, who had worked on road

gangs or mowed white folks' lawns. Irma Jean was eating more and more and rent for the tumble-down shack where they lived went up.

One day in April Marthy Ann was laid off picking and trudged back to town. As she passed a corner juke, the Devil's Hot Box, she heard a couple of men playing a mouth organ and a fiddle beside the road and edged into the crowd around them. They stopped playing and one of them took off his hat and began talking.

"I reckon you can trust me," he said, " 'cause I ain' no handsome yellow nigger. I'm so ugly I ain' goin' t'die but just ugly myself away a little at a time and I'm so black the good Lord throwed away the inkpot after he made me an' said 'Ain' no use tryin' any more. I'll never git one blacker'n that!' "

The crowd laughed at that and moved closer.

"I'm a crew boss and I'm startin' north in three days," said the man. "I got a good place to go and I'm goin' there. I got a fast truck and I guarantees you pay at good wages. I rides you free, I feeds and sleeps you free on the road, and all I gits is a ten per cent cut."

"Where you going?" said a voice.

"Where it's cool beside a river an' they's a fish fry every night," said the crew boss. "Where they's a Lord's plenty o' easy pickin' an' high wages paid regular on Saturday, where a black man gits good treatment an' goes to church and to the movies with his white brother, where they's a long clean barracks they used to keep German white folks in in the big war, where the juke's got real fancy card tables in it, and once a month we give the white folks a singin' and they puts on the food fer it."

"I said where it is," said the voice.

"They calls it the Tennessee Valley."

"That ain't north. I'm ignant but God knows I ain' *that* ignant. It ain' north at all."

"The *Genesee* Valley," said the man with the fiddle under his arm, quietly. "It's in the state o' New York but tother end from New York City. Who's goin'?"

"I am," said the voice. "But the Lord hep you if it ain' like you say."

"Me too."

"An' me likewise."

"I'll go if I can take Irma Jean," said Marthy Ann Jerdon.

The truck had not been on the road a whole day before Marthy Ann was real sorry she had signed up. It was a big truck but the crew boss had loaded it with so many pickers that there was no place to sit down proper, and standing up all the time was like to wear everybody down even if they sang like the crew boss said they should do. The good food the crew boss promised turned out to be only coffee and a cruller for lunch at a dirty roadside stand and for supper at a South Carolina fishhouse a piece of river-cat fried in old grease that had turned rancid. The boss made them get back in the truck after supper and he drove almost to the North Carolina border before he stopped by some woods and said since it was such a clear warm night they could camp there and get an early start in the morning. Irma Jean was so tired she cried, although she was a right well-behaved child for a five-year-old. The boss handed out a lot of greasy blankets and sleeping was impossible if you did not use them to keep off the mosquitoes and impossible if you did use them on account of the heat.

The second night they camped in a grove beside a Virginia branch and it was so cold that Marthy Ann was glad she had Irma Jean to cuddle up to under their two blankets. Along about four in the morning a white man with a shotgun began shouting for the boss and told him to take that load of niggers the hell out of there and not to come back with them or he'd put him in the jailhouse. Marthy Ann was excited when somebody said they had crossed over into Yankee country and she tried to tell Irma Jean what that meant but cold rain began falling and everybody got the shakes from being so chilled. The crew boss kept yelling there were only a few more hours to go and the worst would be over and it was not his fault if it rained.

Sure enough about five o'clock in the afternoon the rain stopped and a cold sun peeked out from dark clouds and the truck stopped among some long low dark buildings on the shore of a river and the crew boss hollered "All out!" When they climbed down there was a quiet young black man standing there and the crew boss said, "This here now is the superintendent of this camp and he's a college man from Tuskegee and everybody does what he says."

The superintendent told them all where to get cots and blankets and to sign for them and they all stood in line and carried their stuff into one of the long buildings. It had been cut up into small square rooms and bachelors had to live four together, but some families that had as many as eight children got only one room too. Outside the rooms was a long sort of hallway and in that there was a rickety gas stove for each and every room. Marthy Ann thought she was lucky to share her room with a pair of sisters who did not have any other family with them. She set up the two cots, made the beds, and got out her fish-line. She took Irma Jean with her down to the river and cut a pole from a willow tree. By six-thirty she had caught one perch and a little fish that looked like a baby cat and somebody told her that Yankees called it a bullhead. One of the sisters had brought some pork chitlins with her and lent Marthy Ann some grease, so she and Irma Jean had a good fish dinner before they went to bed.

At first Marthy Ann liked the camp very much. In the bathhouse there were showers with hot and cold running water and as soon as she and Irma Jean learned how to work them they enjoyed them. There were flush toilets too, but these were always getting out of order because somebody who did not know any better would stuff them with things that would choke them and then there would be long lines waiting to use the bowls that were still running. The juke was one of the long low buildings that had not been cut up into rooms and there were counters along the sides where food things were sold and there was a bar at one end.

The crew boss ran the juke and his prices for food and liquor were higher than they were in town but most pickers bought there to save themselves the walk. In one corner of the juke a crap game was always going on and the crew boss got his cut from that game and all the gambling card games. Sometimes, if he thought not enough folks were playing, he would cut the price on drinks for a while until enough had got liquored up to start gambling. The crew boss came to Marthy Ann's room one night and told her he expected her to play in one of the games and when she said she did not want to he said for her to give him two dollars a week and he would see that it was played for her and she would get all the money it won. She paid the money but she never got anything back all summer.

On the second evening she was in camp the superintendent called a meeting and made a speech. He said that they were all expected to be nice and not to be mean or cross with the white folks uptown. There were now about twelve thousand colored pickers coming into York State every summer, he said, and of course there had to be some bad ones, but if colored pickers were going to get jobs and make money they would have to behave and be polite. He said this was a nice town and if you treated the people right they'd treat you right, but don't rile them and don't talk about living here all the time because all they want is pickers, not more population.

Then he asked a white preacher to say a few words and he got up and invited everybody to come to his church on Sunday morning and said we are all children of the same God.

The bean picking was a lot easier in the North than in Florida, Marthy Ann found, because the weather was cooler and the foreman did not drive the pickers so hard. You got paid for what you picked and nobody said anything about it not being enough.

There was dancing every night in the juke too, and the crew boss was selling whisky outside under a tree. He said it was better to do this even if he did not have a license because Negro pickers got into fights with white folks if they did their drinking in the saloons uptown. There was a fight in the juke at least once a week and sometimes oftener. About once a week a State Policeman, a big white man in a gray uniform, would stand outside the juke with the superintendent while the dancing was going on and look in. Sometimes he would walk in and tap a dancer on the shoulder and bring him outside and ask him questions. The superintendent said the officer was looking for folks who had sneaked into the United States from Jamaica and Haiti and other foreign countries and that he could usually tell them by the slick way they danced. The superintendent said that the policeman said he hated to arrest a man just because he was a smooth dancer with a lot of fancy Spanish steps and just when he was having a good time but that was the easiest way to catch foreigners who had smuggled themselves in.

Marthy Ann dressed Irma Jean up very pretty after her bath on Sunday morning and took her to the church where the white preacher had invited them. After she got inside she felt scared and when she went to take a seat a cross-looking woman said, "This pew is reserved." Marthy Ann felt sick then and started to go out and back to camp but a nice white woman got up and stopped her and asked her to sit with her and her family. The white preacher's sermon was short and he did not whoop it up at all and nobody got to shouting and Marthy Ann was real disgusted with Yankee churches. She was glad to get back to camp and hear that the superintendent had arranged for a preaching the next Sunday by a colored Baptist from Georgia.

At first Marthy Ann did not like the people who worked in the stores of the town. They seemed cross and hard-hearted and impolite when you stood them up with white folks in stores down south. After she had been working in the fields for a month, though, she decided they had their good side. They did not act amused with black customers

like a good many southern store folks. And they tried to
get you just what you wanted instead of trying to talk you
into buying something else. What she took for uppity
manners, she decided, was really just a business way with
them. You wanted to buy something, they had it to sell.
It was a deal between the two of you and nobody was
better than anybody else. She did get that old sick feeling
when she saw a sign on a restaurant that read "No Colored People Allowed" but the white preacher went to see
the owners and told them the sign was against the law and
asked them how they would feel if "colored" meant folks
with olive-colored complexions like theirs. They took the
sign down but the few Negroes who went in said when
they came out that they never seemed to get served and
none of the pickers went there any more.

As for the farmers for whom the pickers worked, Marthy
Ann was surprised that they never said anything about
lazy pickers even in joke like some of the Florida bosses
that she liked best. She missed southern talk, though, and
the kind easy way that southern white folks had with black
folks, and the music at night on the porches of the cabins
when the moon was big and red and the air was soft and
hot.

At first she took Irma Jean to the picking fields with
her but soon a young white lady from the town started
running a place for the little ones to play that she called
a Child Care Center. Irma Jean liked playing there better
than anything she had ever done.

The summer passed so quickly that Marthy Ann did not
know it had gone until the crew boss began talking about
staying on for the apple picking. Just about that time a

nice woman uptown asked her in a store one day if she would like to stay in her house and cook for her and do her laundry. Marthy Ann was scared because she remembered what the crew boss said and she said she would let the woman know. She thought about it a long time and the thing that decided her was that the woman said she and Irma Jean could have a big nice room and Irma Jean could go to school all year. The crew boss was mad when she told him she was going to stay and said it was folks like her that were spoiling the pickers' business and that New York State was getting filled up with colored folks who were too lazy to follow the crops around. He said Marthy Ann was being cheated by the woman who hired her but Marthy Ann was satisfied. Now Irma Jean is going to school and teaching all the white six-year-olds the ring games she used to play in Florida and their mothers are saying, "Mercy, I don't know what's to become of us. Junior has begun to sing with a southern accent." Marthy Ann tells Irma Jean that some of the songs are really naughty and she should not sing them, but the white children like them all and insist on singing them and Marthy Ann does not know what to do about it.

Irma Jean's Songs

Irma Jean's Songs

Here are some of the songs that the little colored girl is
teaching her white fellow pupils in the second grade:

Walking on the green grass
Dusty, dusty, dusty—
I choose to have a lady,
So hand me down that pretty white dress
And take a walk with me.
Roses red, violets blue,
Sugar's sweet but not like me . . .
Lay there some chicken soup,
Lay there some 'nana pie
And swing your partner round.

My father was the deacon of the hotel church
Down South where I was born—
All the members of the church came runnin' out
Just to see my father shout—
Hold up your hands
Step back, Gal
Two steps farther
Won't you bother, Jack?

My mamma told me
Six years ago
Not to marry no lazy man.
Oh, shake it in the diggety da!
Oh, shake it in the diggety da!
(Repeat)

Dark Trees to the Wind

I'm going down South
Gonna buy me a rocking chair—
Last one squat
Gonna tell that fella's name.
Ring round rosie
Squat for the Toesy
Every afternoon
A-boom!

Shake, shake, shake
I am a funny little duster
As funny as funny can be
With all them boys around my heart
Singing them songs to me
My fella's name is Sambo
He came from the bridge in Congo
With a big, fat nose
And hickory nut toes
Singing he, hi, he, hi, ho.
Sambo was a good ol' man.
He tried to go to heaven in a airaplane.
Airaplane went zoop de zoop
And Uncle Sambo zooped de zoop.
My mamma told me if I be good
That she would buy me a rubber dolly.
A lady told her
I kissed a soldier
And now I'm married and got two children—
One name Mary
One name Ola
I never forget that rubber dolly no more.

Dark Trees to the Wind

Oh, green field
Tell me who you love—
Oh, Miss (Irma Jean) your name is called
Come take a seat right side de wall
Kiss her once and let her go
'Cause you may not get that chance no mo'
Oh, green field, rocky low
Tell me who you love—
Rocky low.

Bluebird, bluebird through my window
Bluebird, bluebird through my window
Oh, Johnny, I'm tired
Oh, Johnny, I'm tired.
Pick a little bluebird, pat him on the shoulder
Pick a little bluebird, pat him on the shoulder
Oh, Johnny, I'm tired
Oh, Johnny, I'm tired.

And here's Aunt Dinah
Aunt Dinah's dead.
How did she die?
Oh, she died like this
Oh, she died like this.
Aunt Dinah's living.
Where does she live?
Oh, she lives in de country an' she's comin' to
    town—
She's gonna shimmy, shimmy, shimmy, till the
    sun goes down.

16

The Lavender
Evening Dress

A FEW YEARS AGO THE POSTMASTER IN A VILLAGE
that lies beside the lonely waters of the Ramapo River,
dappled by light and leaf shadow in the morning and darkened by hill shadows in the afternoon, talked often about
a lithe tawny girl with hyacinth eyes and wheat-yellow hair.
He was a sophisticated gentleman, traveled and urbane, a
member of a distinguished family in those parts. To atone
for his sins, he said, he taught a boys' class in a Sunday
school that was in session on the first day of each week
after the preaching in a tiny, weathered church back in the
Ramapo hills.

From the summits of those hills, on a clear day washed
by recent rain, the slim gray towers on Manhattan Island
seem to advance into sight and hang, like figures long ago
worked into the tapestry on the old blue sky wall. None of
the boys in the Sunday school had ever entered the city
on the horizon and only a few of them had been to Hill-
burn or Sloatsburg in York State or any of the New Jersey
towns to the west. They were a shy lot but wild as woods
animals are wild, and they found the simple lessons in
Christian ethics the postmaster was trying to teach difficult
at best and impossible at those times when that girl was
around.

The Lavender Evening Dress

She went through his class, the postmaster said, like a slow pestilence. A boy would be gone for a month, sometimes two months, and then he would come back on a Sunday, glowering and sheepish, and one of his schoolmates would be absent for a while. The Sunday-school teacher would sometimes see him and the girl picking wild blackberries on a hillside or, on a Saturday night, walking the road shoes in hand to a country dance.

There was much talk about the girl among the hill-folk gossips and the postmaster, whose job gave him speaking acquaintance with most of these, gathered from what they said that she was gay and hot tempered and amoral—feeling that the general admiration gave her the privilege of disobeying the somewhat eccentric conventions of her own community. The only time he had a good look at her was during a Wednesday night prayer meeting at which, according to an announcement the previous Sunday, the contents of three barrels of old clothes from the members of a New York City church would be distributed. The girl came in after the service and just as the preacher beat in the head of the first barrel. She was barefoot and it was obvious that she wore only a stained and patched calico-check dress much too small for her. She sat in the back pew and paid no attention as the usual pathetic garments that are contained in such shipments were displayed and granted to those who could argue the greatest need.

There was a gasp when the preacher pulled from the middle of the second barrel a lavender evening dress covered with sequins that glinted like tiny amethysts. It was cut low off the shoulders and as soon as the preacher saw that he rolled it up into a shapeless bundle holding it helpless and waiting for someone to speak for it. No one did but the girl stood up and padded swiftly down the aisle. Without saying a word she grabbed the dress from the good man's hands and raced out of the church.

From that time on, the postmaster said, no one ever saw the girl in other costume. Rain or shine, day or night, she was a brush stroke of lavender against the brown of dirt roads, the green of hill slopes, the khaki-colored shirts and pants of whatever boy strode beside her.

Frost came early that year and leaves dropped. The air was clear and the New York towers came nearer and stayed longer. The hill people were all talking about a letter that had come to the girl from cousins in Jersey City. The postmaster had told one of his Sunday-school boys that the letter had come and the next day she had stood before his window and quietly asked for it, the sequins glinting purple in the shadowy room. People who dropped in the next day said her cousins had invited her to visit them and they had sent the money for her bus fare. A week later, a witness regaled the postmaster with a description of the expressions on the faces of the bus passengers down on the asphalt highway twelve miles away when the girl climbed aboard, holding her long skirt about her waist.

In mid-December came a cold snap and the thermometer outside showed eighteen degrees below zero when the postmaster opened his window for business. The people in the line of waiters-for-mail were more eager to give him the news than to receive their letters. The body of the girl in the lavender dress had been found frozen and stiff on the road a few miles above the bus stop. Returning from Jersey City, she had left the bus and begun the long walk home, but the evening dress proved too flimsy wear for such a night.

The Lavender Evening Dress

The postmaster said that after this tragedy all the students in his class came regularly to Sunday school, and that was the end of the story of the girl.

The girl froze to death about 1939 and for a decade nothing reflected doubt on the postmaster's conclusion. But now a growing number of people feel that his narrative, the truth of which is easily provable by many witnesses, has had an inexplicable consequence, overtones that have transcended his matter-of-fact realism. For a strange report recently began its rounds of upstate towns and, particularly, colleges. It had many variants, as such tales do, but in none of them was it in any way connected with the account of the girl, her dress, and her death, a factual record known only in the vicinity of her Ramapo home, and the suggestion of such a connection is made here possibly for the first time.

As I heard it, two Hamilton College juniors motoring to a dance at Tuxedo Park after sunset of a warm Indian summer Saturday on the road that runs through the valley of the little Ramapo River saw a girl waiting. She was wearing a party dress the color of the mist rising above the dark water of the stream and her hair was the color of ripe wheat. The boys stopped their car and asked the girl if they could take her in the direction she was going. She eagerly seated herself between them and asked if they were going to the square dance at Sterling Furnace. The thin, tanned face with high cheekbones, the yellow hair, the flashing smile, the quicksilver quality of her gestures, enchanted the boys and it was soon a matter of amused debate whether they would go along with her to Sterling Furnace or she would accompany them to the dance at Tuxedo. The majority won and the boys were soon presenting their new friend to the young couple who were their hosts at the Park. "Call me 'Lavender,'" she said to them. "It's my nickname because I always wear that color."

After an evening in which the girl, quiet and smiling, made a most favorable impression by her dancing, drifting dreamily through the waltzes in a sparkling cloud of lavender sequins, stepping more adeptly than any of the other dancers through the complications of revived square dances—Money Musk—Hull's Victory—Nellie Gray—the boys took her out to their car for the ride home. She said that she was cold and one of them doffed his tweed topcoat and helped her into it. They were both shocked into clichés of courtesy when, after gaily directing the driver through dusty woodland roads she finally bade him stop before a shack so dilapidated that it would have seemed deserted had it not been for a ragged lace curtain over the small window in the door. After promising to see them again soon, she waved good night, standing beside the road until they had turned around and rolled away. They were almost in Tuxedo before the chill air made the coatless one realize that he had forgotten to reclaim his property and they decided to return for it on their way back to college the next day.

The afternoon was clear and sunny when, after considerable difficulty in finding the shack, the boys knocked on the door with the ragged lace curtain over its window. A decrepit white-haired woman answered the door and peered at them out of piercing blue eyes when they asked for Lavender.

"Old friends of hers?" she asked, and the boys, fearing to get the girl into the bad graces of her family by telling the truth about their adventure of the day before, said yes they were old friends.

"Then ye couldn't a-heerd she's dead," said the woman. "Been in the graveyard down the road fer near ten years."

Horrified the boys protested that this was not the girl they meant—that they were trying to find someone they had seen the previous evening.

"Nobody else o' that name ever lived round here," said the woman. " 'Twan't her real name anyway. Her paw named her Lily when she was born. Some folks used to call her Lavender on account o' the pretty dress she wore all the time. She was buried in it."

The boys once more turned about and started for the paved highway. A hundred yards down the road the driver jammed on the brakes.

"There's the graveyard," he said, pointing to a few weath-ered stones standing in bright sunlight in an open field overgrown with weeds, "and just for the hell of it I'm going over there."

They found the stone—a little one marked "Lily"—and on the curving mound in front of it, neatly folded, the tweed topcoat.

17

Three Crops

THOUGH WILL CHRISTMAN WAS FOR ABOUT FIVE-sixths of his long life a typical, not very successful York State farmer on a rocky hill farm (he was in a good company, and a big one, as many a Yorker family can testify), he turned out to be worth his salt after all because he spent his last decade writing true and beautiful things about the sixty years of living that had gone before it. Many farmers with about the same experience have sat out their last weary days damning the fickle soil and the more fickle weather that brought them so little return in this world's goods. This world had other "goods" for Will, and he spent ten years listing them and discussing them. Other farmers have shared and still share his point of view but as a rule they have not had Will's knack for communicating it or they have taken it out in talk instead of setting it down on paper as Will did.

Will Christman wrote poems when he saw life coming to its eventual and inevitable close. Only a few lines of them can be repeated here as "come-on" samples. The rest can be found in libraries. They were fine poems but that is not the point. The point is that Will was an honest-to-God upstate farmer and, when the time came when he could do it, he did some thinking on what he and his like had been through. Then he told what he had been thinking in language as simple as his work, and his work, take it by and large all his life through, was to make things grow—food plants, children, poems—three crops.

Drive west from Albany twenty miles and the Helderhills will be rising and falling about you in lyric rhythms. In summer long rectangles of snowy buckwheat will tilt toward you, and the dwellings of the bees, like architect's models of modernist houses, will gleam white from the deep-green shade of apple trees. Find the old Schoharie Turnpike and follow it over a roller-coaster trail to William's Hollow. A square weathered farmhouse fronts the road, and behind its honest façade older graying timbers tell a story of plodding generations.

The legend on the mailbox reads "W. W. Christman" and, though Will Christman died in 1937, Lansing Christman has preferred to leave his father's name there. The farm does not need those letters to distinguish it but they are symbols, a summing up of the identity of a unit of acres.

Lansing works at a radio station in Schenectady but he and Lucille, his South Carolina wife, have planted enough of a vegetable garden to tell the truth about this farm as a farm. If the pebble-spattered soil does not give immediate answer, look beyond the dark stone fence behind the house and see the Bozenkill—the Drunkard Creek—tipsily careening down a flight of stone steps longer and higher than the stairway of the Albany Capitol building. "Untillable Hills" Will called these slopes, and he knew them as such from the day he began helping his father at the plow and harrow.

Will was born in the midsection of what is now the barn of the William's Hollow farm. Like many of the families that lived on the Schoharie Turnpike, the Christmans had been Palatine German in the old country. They came to the Hudson Valley in the early eighteenth century, then moved west along the Mohawk and south toward the clovered flats that line Schoharie Creek. One of them aimed his musket at the British at Oriskany and another a generation later came safe home from the fight at Sackets Harbor.

Will's father was an uneducated, quiet farmer who worked hard and hated weeds. His son helped him with the chores, building wall, plowing, harvesting. The boy inherited from him a love of soil, even of the rock-bound recalcitrant ground that defied the work a man put into it. Will knew as soon as he knew anything that he would be a farmer all his days and he knew there was nothing better.

Three winters in a one-room "academy" was the best schooling the Helderhill country offered. Will took it, and never forgave its shortcomings. Thanks to a grandmother with a love of words, the boy had read all of Shakespeare by the time he was twelve and he was reading everything else he could get his hands on—especially poetry.

If his formal education was scanty, there was learning to be had from stony acres and the struggle of living things to grow there. Wildflowers blossomed in the wild valley, bird song threaded the air above it. The seasons repeated his lessons to him until they became a part of him.

"When I was about twelve years old I heard a bird singing in a swamp near a field where my father was sowing oats while I followed with the team and harrow covering the seeds . . . I knew the bird then only as a thrush.

"About two years later . . . I read John Burroughs' description of the song of the hermit. I recognized the bird more readily from Burroughs' interpretation of its song than I would from an ornithologist's description of its color and size."

Burroughs and Walt Whitman followed after Shakespeare. Will Christman rejoiced in the lucid prose of the naturalist who lived only a few miles away and described natural images no different from those visible in the valley of the Bozenkill. He found ecstasy in the verses of big, bearded Walt praising companionship and freedom. "Stick to Whitman," Burroughs wrote back to young farmer Christman, who had dared to write him a letter both admiring and confiding. "He can do you good."

Men's voices lifted old songs as the pickers set out along the turnpike for the hop fields beside the Schoharie and Will's tenor was one of them. From the mows of big red barns bouncing rhythm of fiddles rained on dancers below. Floors shook to their stomping, rafters echoed. "Swing her, swing her!" Skirts whirled upward, and screams wove into laughter. Girls were willing beside Schoharie water under the hop pickers' moon.

There was a girl at home—Catherine Bradt—an old Palatine surname that her grandfather two generations before had given to a Mohawk woman. Will was a wild blade but something told him she would give him as much of peace as a woman can give a passionate and moody man. Her family lived on the next farm, he had drawn her to school on his sled, she had come to William's Hollow when she was seventeen to help his mother at her work. Night after night she and Will spent reading aloud the poetry of Byron, Tennyson, Shakespeare, the prose of Thoreau and Burroughs. The girl must have had many heartaches then, for the son of the house was again and again in love but even as many times he returned to her and to the interests

that bound them together—verses, wildflowers, birds, the shy animals of the Bozenkill valley.

They were married when Will was twenty-two and she was twenty and the banks of the Bozenkill were blazing with October yellows and crimsons. They lived on in the Christman house while father and son kept on working the family's unfertile soil. For forty years, while the nine children—seven sons and two daughters—were being born and growing up to help in the battle with the land, Will was a dirt farmer on a York State rocky farm. He burned stumps and pulled them, plowed, hoed, and harrowed. He hitched up the long market wagon, filled it with beets and beans, peas and potatoes, and drove to the surrounding towns to sell—Quaker Street and Delanson and Duanesburg. On days of the Schoharie Fair he filled the wagon box with his children—three each to the three spring seats they kept in the front parlor—and made triumphant laughing entry to the fairgrounds: "Special Rates for Large Families."

While the children were young he fought for better schooling for them and for all children in the state—denouncing in strongly phrased letters to the Albany and New York papers the inefficiencies and inadequacies of the one-room schoolhouse.

"I grieve a little every year when the 5,000 or 6,000 one-room schools in the Empire State re-open to receive their quota of two, three or four or more unfortunate pupils; too few for a game unless it is solitaire, and too few to stir impressionable youth to friendly rivalry.

"I visualize the cheap bare buildings toeing the road just as they did 60 years ago . . . many without a playground or even a tree on which the forlorn and discouraged teacher may hang herself."

One day he did some figuring and sent out a letter for publication. His children, he said, had traveled a total of 129,460 miles for their education, 92,820 by train to high school and 36,640 by foot to a "typical meagerly equipped rural school." Railroad fares had cost him over a thousand dollars. "No consolidation, no centralization, no union free schools." Before his plain farmer's common sense the arguments of the sentimentalist advocates of the "little red schoolhouse" wilted like uprooted weeds.

Will Christman was nearly sixty when the children had got their schooling, married, found homes. "My farm stood on edge and I tilled both sides," he said. From then on he decided to till only one side and write poetry. He cut down to about twenty-five the number of acres he worked. "I'm not doing any more farming than I have to these days. I sort of like weeds and I let 'em grow in a good many places where I used to help my father dig them up and burn them. And I'm planting pines on the slopes I helped him clear. He'd be shocked if he knew." He alternated planting pines and writing verses.

His poems found an immediate market in the York State journals he sent them to—the *American Agriculturist*, the Syracuse *Post-Standard*, the Albany *Knickerbocker Press*, the Altamont *Enterprise*, the Cobleskill *Index*. They were like their author—simple, direct, observant, wise. Farmers who read them recognized their own daily doings. This was York State farming put into words, rhythmic words that reminded knowing readers of Whitman and Housman, and Hodgson, that reminded knowing farmers of birds and flowers, and plants that were around them as they worked. He wrote about his creek and his plowing, his family and his harvest, the wings and songs that flitted through his woods, his neighbors, his dogs, the wild flowers his wife had collected and transplanted to a patch beside the farm-house door, and his memories—memories of old friends, and especially of old loves, yearnings

> To hear the love drum of the grouse throbbing
> like thunder in the wild valley . . .
> To think of love without regret.

After Will Christman's death the woman he loved best and longest, "First Reader, Critic and Wife," wrote with objective tenderness: "Will was very fond of the girls and he had many love affairs which helped to make material for many of his poems." One of these was his first love—the petal-smooth Belle Williamson who lived across the hill, drawing his long steps thither on many a windy, moony night in the old wild times long before her death:

> The dear glad ways are over that were ours;
> She is a shade, past age and discontent,
> And this her clay beneath the wreaths and
> flowers;
> This is a cup from which the wine is spilled,
> An empty cup that cannot be refilled.

Three Crops

One girl was Margaret and one Elizabeth and others were
Seraphine and Gladys and Helena and the hop-field girls
of Blenheim.

> Hop fields are in clover,
> > Corn, and pasture grass;
> Dancing days are over
> > For each youth and lass.
> But one that was in denim
> > Wishes he were still
> Picking hops in Blenheim
> > By Schoharie Kill.

Will Christman did not write really great poetry. It was
remarkable poetry for a York State farmer because this
kind of man is not usually so simply expressive as Will.
If the average York State farmer could sit down and become by quick and strange magic poetically articulate, Will
Christman's poetry would be the kind he would write. It
would have the compressed dry humor of men who are
used to getting little cider from their apples, as in Will's
remarks about his neighbors, Mrs. Jeremiah Saddlemire for
instance:

> When Mrs. S. from worship came
> > The good old man would say:
> "Be keerful, little children,
> > Run out o'doors and play,—
> Your mother's been to church ag'in,
> She's full of hell today."

Or his poem about the Quaker wife whose husband asked
her where he would find a rope to hang himself:

"Thee'll find it on a nail out in the shed;
Thee'd better double it," his good wife said.

Or his report on "The Cider Hound," an alcoholic relative (by marriage), perhaps a victim of the ancestral Mohawk yearning for firewater:

Poor Will would stop and drop a hint to me:
"I'm dry," he'd say, "as a woodpecker's hole!"
Or digging ginseng, cutting a bee tree:
"A drink of cider would restore my soul."
"Wine is for boys," he said; "or ale, or Bock,
Hard cider is the draft that men demand."
Will's jug was like the shadow of the rock
That saved the Psalmist in a weary land.
Full of old Ira's cider, home he'd come
Like a sandpiper teetering up the creek;
"I'll draw my load," he'd say, "though I'm
    rum-dumb;
My soul is willing but my legs are weak."
So with his burden quite content, poor Will,
Down on all fours, would draw it up the hill.

"I raise pigs so I can live near hummingbirds," said Will
Christman, and he sat down at sixty and wrote four books
of poems: *Songs of the Helderhills, Songs of the Western
Gateway, Wild Pasture Pine,* and *The Untillable Hills.* He
wrote about the white-throated sparrow, the hermit thrush,
the nuthatch, flicker, snow bunting, mourning dove, gold-
finch, shrike, and rosy-breasted grosbeak. He helped Wife
Catherine collect her wildflower garden and he wrote about
the jack-in-the-pulpit, wild clematis, the lady-slipper, the
pinxter, bloodroot. He planted trees and wrote about wild

apple, basswood, oak, hemlock and elm, and most of all
about his pines. "I'm like an old tree," he said. "My roots
have grown so deeply in this hill-land soil, it would be hard
to transplant me now," but in the last decade of his life,
the "and ten" of his allotment, he began to think of the
inevitable transplanting:

> I leave my harvest and good will
> To red poll, siskin and cross-bill;
> To every singing soul good cheer:
> Some walker of the snow may hear
> The ringing carol of the shrike
> Where the first shafts of sunrise strike.
>
> I give, bequeath, devote, devise
> Shelter to every bird that flies;
> Harbor to all that walk or creep;
> To the red fox a bed for sleep;
> Table and roof for every guest
> And place for dove and thrush to nest.
>
> Years hence, some boy driving tranquil,
> Slow cattle up the pasture hill,
> In a spring morning dewy and sweet
> When field sparrows stay his loitering feet
> Shall see my pine spires tipped with sun
> And hear the thrushes carillon.

Men of letters, many of them distinguished and famous,
came to see him at his farm and he made them welcome
with no fuss and feathers, striding in from the barn in his
khaki wool shirt and wrinkled pants held up by galluses.
He was awarded the John Burroughs Medal for nature

writing in 1934. It had gone to professional writers and scholarly naturalists before—never to a working farmer. His living friends remember him sitting at the head of a long table, lined with children and guests (there were always extra places set for droppers-in), a pencil in his hand, a sheet of paper below it, jotting down lines of verse while good talk and laughter flowed about him. There were dances at the house sometimes and the fiddlers sat on chairs on top of the long dining-room table and the gnarled face of the farmer-poet was joyful at the swing of their rhythms and the sight of dancing boys and girls.

When the last allotted decade had passed he walked, in the May morning before his seventy-first birthday, twenty miles to Albany to see his son Henry Esmond. "I get tired behind a harrow," he said, "and this is the way I rest—I walk."

Will Christman's heart stopped beating in late February of the next year—1937. He had prayed "to die in silence like a tree" and his petition had been granted. In wordless grief the family went mechanically about the task in which his talk and his verses had long instructed them. The ashes of the strong-sinewed body that had planted the pines were strewn at their roots. Far below their pointed tops a slanting brook tumbles past a granite boulder toward the Bozenkill. A bronze plaque on the boulder tells his name and the dates of his birth and death. Two days before he died he had sent to his publisher a poem for inclusion in a new volume. Its beginning read:

> The gift of rest be with you where you lie
> Under the weeds and grass and the wild rose
> Or where steep acres run to meet the sky.

The family had its ending engraved on the plaque:

> when you went
> We grieved, we felt the bitterness, the lack,
> Then softly fell the evening of content—
> The world had changed, we would not wish you back.

To the memorial services beside the stone on the late May birthday that would have been his seventy-second came a man from the State Education Department in Albany, "speaking for the boys and girls on the farms and in the villages and hamlets of rural New York," to say that "he lives in buildings, in courses of study, in better educational opportunity which he helped to create for rural children." Came a poet to say: "Those who come here in later times will find in the spot he loved something of the man himself and remember him as he would like to be remembered."

The later visitors of whom he spoke now know he told the truth. As soon as they arrive and see the slanting acres of the old farm they remember Will's words about them:

> My hill land is so cold and lean
> It is the last to put on green
> In winter first to put on snow
> In spring the last to let it go.

Dark Trees to the Wind

It would be difficult to see his son Lansing getting the
earth of the garden behind the house ready for planting
without recalling:

> Here I labored, here I delved,
> Swung the ax-blade, hickory-helved;
> Here I drove the walking plow,
> Sweated here and wiped my brow;
> Where my father earned his bread,
> Planted, sowed and harvested.
>
> On these hills, the God I saw
> Laid the tables of His Law;
> I, like the philosophers,
> Viewed His glory in the stars;
> Found no footprints save His own
> Stamped in earth's foundation stone;
> Heard the Voice that Moses heard
> Uttering a final word
> On the cloudy mountain-head;
> "I am all that is!" it said.

The other children, all but William, the eldest, who
died young, drop in on the Lansing Christmans whenever
they feel like it—they all live within not too many miles
of the homestead. That was a good crop. Nancy and Emily
are busy, successful housewives and mothers and they bring
their children by to see the old place where their fathers
used to come courting the Christman girls. Tall, lean, earnest Philip—mail carrier and fisherman and father and
deacon—comes often with his two children. Less frequently
comes Spencer—plumber, trapper, best shot at a moving
target in the Helderhills. Neighbors say Spencer knows the

wild animals of the Helderhills so well that when he sits by a foxhole the little ones come out and play fearlessly about him. Duane drives over from Schenectady. He inherited an interest in civic improvement and last election he made the best run against a long-entrenched Republican opponent machine ever yet made. Tell him so and he laughs ruefully and says his father used to tell of the time when folks said, "In Schoharie County everybody is a Democrat or a horse thief." "Times have changed," he says. Each of the remaining three, 50 per cent of the lot, is making part of his living from writing. Walden (named for Thoreau's pond) is a patient, sure automobile mechanic, a good gardener, a rattling good columnist for the Altamont *Enterprise*. Henry Esmond, distinguished historian, author of *Tin Horns and Calico*, definitive and charmingly written history of the York State Rent Wars, loves every inch of this land and talks of building a house on the hill someday if Lansing and Lucille will let him.

Finally, there is Lansing. He talks about his father a good deal and of the many younger poets who used to come to see Will Christman and were influenced by him. There are at least five who have published volumes of verse or achieved a considerable amount of published work in magazines and anthologies. Sometimes, he says, they call themselves jokingly "The Helderberg School." Three are from Esperance, a few miles away, and one is a Massachusetts Yankee who spends his summers in Duanesburg. The fifth, he admits shyly, is himself. Though the old farm produces less vegetables from its rocky soil than it used to, the verse crop is still abundant. Bring up that subject and Lansing laughs and says that his verses help out more than you'd think in a lean season, total receipts from his sales of poems have passed the thousand-dollar mark.

The farm has kept on saying things to the man in the house. Lansing has listened to many that his father did not hear. His verses tell of "Sorting Apples," "Fixing Fence in August," "Going after Wintergreens," "Picking Wild Blackberries." They report purple finches singing in the rain, song sparrows feeding in his snow-covered garden, the first hepatica, shadbush blooms which "all in a day scatter their pyramids of white over the wild side hills," buttercups and marigolds blowing beside his roadside spring:

> Rain sings on the roof, and the horses,
> Temples throbbing, munch on the new mown hay.

He rarely writes on subjects that Will Christman chose, but, though he drives to Schenectady to work in a radio studio, he shares his father's distaste for the city. Will wrote in his "Spring Thoughts in Town":

> Here's dust and roar and men in throngs
> But never roses or bird songs
> I must go back to the wild rose
> And pasture where the black haw blows . . .

and Lansing speaks his pity of the metropolis in his "They Too Were Meadows":

> The boulders will press themselves firmly
> Into the smugness and the warmth of grass,
> In the peacefulness of the old meadow
> Worlds away from the acres of steel and smoke.
> They too were meadows once, with grass,
> And lichened stones, and wild deer loping.

Three Crops

Three crops grew on the William's Hollow farm that Will Christman's father chose for a home because a splashing creek raced from the hills there. The first was soil-born green things, the second was men, the third was songs. A stony section of York State did better than you might expect with all of them, and there are many Yorker farmers who feel that these are not unusual or not-to-be-expected products. They say if centuries hence a farmer digging in long-uncultivated ground should find a moldy, musty volume of Will Christman's verse he would discover much that would tell him how things were with us. He would find in them our stony acres, the birds and streams and winds that sang to us, the things we felt when we were plowing. That distant fellow down the future years would understand, they say, because after all, as Lansing says his brother Henry tells him, "You have to be something of a poet to be a farmer and like it."

A chant for the birds and trees,
For the flowers and fragrance of youth,
For the rooftree over the weather-stained house
And for its topmost twig where the robin swung
    to the rhythm of his evening carol,
For dark, hill pines that almost touched the stars,
From *The Basswood*, by W. W. Christman

. . . There was a picture of an old blocked quilt:
The white of the open fields; the woods, dark.

From *Snow on an October Night*, by Lansing Christman

18

The Whooper Swan
of Olivebridge

COLLECTORS OF REGIONAL LORE SELDOM WITNESS the beginning of a folk legend. No matter how sure their skill in recognizing the materials from which communal fancy builds, they will not often come upon an incident likely to stir the general imagination without discovering that those tireless coauthors, the people, have already begun their work of creative elaboration.

Because the origin of this narrative was observed by me when an occasional visitor to the community from which it emerged, and because the two main characters were my friends, here is a report of a story which the folk of a lonely mountain town have made, as most such tales are made, out of provable fact and their own fancying. . . .

From the west bank of a northern reach of the Hudson the Catskills roll back until they break around a circular plateau. There the flat highland becomes the bottom of a giant cup, its steep sides rising to a nicked rim against the sky.

In the center of the cup, haphazard as the mountain rocks, stand the houses of Olivebridge. The spire of the Methodist church is a neat white needle above the roofs of

The Whooper Swan of Olivebridge

Boyce's General Store, the post office, and a few other business buildings. One dark and rutted road meets another in the huddle below and each runs on through cleared meadow for some rods before it disappears into deep woods.

I used to turn left at an intersection in the meadowland after braking my car halfway down from the valley's rim. When my speedometer had measured six and six-tenths miles there would be a right turn into the rough and narrow approach to the low house where I would find Pierre Malakov.

I met Malakov first about 1940. My friend, the late Nikander Strelsky, professor of Russian at Vassar College, took me to Olivebridge to see him. As we drove north along the Hudson, Nik told me, in his shorthand, article-less English, the man's story.

Pierre, he said, was a younger son in a highly regarded Russian family. Soon after his graduation from the School of Imperial Theater he became a favored player of the royal court and married the lovely ballerina Nina Oginska. A captain in World War I, he was chosen to participate in the defense of Verdun when the French asked for Russian aid. His right shinbone had been shattered by a bullet during the siege and an ingenious surgeon had fitted into its place a metal substitute which served well though he still limped slightly.

When the war ended Malakov stayed on in France, knowing that he would be executed by the Bolshevik revolutionaries if he went home. He had a hard time at first but the arrival in Paris of the company of the famous Russian revue *Chauvre-Souris*, directed by the genial dialectician Baliev, improved his circumstances temporarily. Malakov was soon appearing nightly as the expressionless drummer in the show's most memorable act—"The March of the Wooden Soldiers." His quest of escape from memory of his early stage successes led him to drink, however, and the exacting Baliev, fearing profanation of the robot-perfection of his manikins, discharged him.

Without rancor and with high hopes of better things Malakov then set out for the United States of America. He wrote Nik of his coming and said that Nina, then dancing in Constantinople, would soon join him. Perhaps he and she would found a school of the theater arts in New York and be rich and fashionable again.

"He will tell you about Nina," said Nik. "She is ideal of his dreams. He will say she was greatest ballerina. And when she dance 'Dying Swan' "—he waved a hand—"she was making Pavlova novice."

"Was?" I said. "Has she stopped dancing?"

"Yes," said Nik, "under wheels of Paris metro last year."

We had made our left turn in Olivebridge and Nik excitedly counted off the decimals of the miles as they clicked into sight on the instrument panel.

"Why is he way out here?" I said.

"He is caretaker of summer shack," said Nik, "only no longer summer shack. I have good friends who ask him to live here. They think he will not drink so much here. Ha! He drinks more but he has made shack into fine Russian house. You will see."

We made the second turn, crossed a dilapidated bridge, and stopped at the edge of a black-amber pond. Dark water was pouring over a dam and beside it stood the weathered ruin of a mill. We heard a door close and looked across the pond, where, on a rising bank, stood a long, one-story house. Pierre Malakov limped toward us. He was of medium height, slim and erect. His features were strong and regular, and his deep-set eyes were a clear blue.

Nik introduced me and Malakov was politely formal. He led us to the house and became more cordial as I exclaimed over it. It had been little more than a boxlike hunting shack, he said, but he had enlarged it and built a fieldstone chimney at each end. He had artist friends among the White Russian refugees in New York. One was a mural painter, another a woodcarver, and so it went. Each had chosen to leave behind a sample of his skill.

We spent the late afternoon drinking vodka and eating black bread. Nik was a fascinating talker and he was in good form. I listened but Pierre seemed restless. He drank steadily and I was not surprised when he rose from the floor where he had been sitting cross-legged near the fireplace and walked to the center of the wide room. There he began to speak in Russian and the only word I could understand was "Nina," which seemed the emphatic end of every sentence.

"Now he tells how she danced 'Dying Swan,' " said Nik suddenly, and was glared at for interrupting. Pierre did not exactly imitate the ballet but his gestures were so full of meaning that he somehow conjured up for each of us in his separate mind's eye the sighing of the music, the pool of light, and the piteous ever-weakening flutters of a slim white creature sinking into stillness.

Then he said in English. "Man dances this dance—and never ceases. The swan is spirit. It dies each hour—each hour until—" He wavered and abruptly but not without grace slid to the floor, then stretched out with his forehead down upon the arc of his arms.

"Let us leave him," said Nik. "We must go back now to Poughkeepsie." He grinned at me. "He is very Russian."

In the next two years I saw Pierre occasionally, both at Nik's in Poughkeepsie and at Olivebridge. In the latter place he was already becoming a kind of legend. Perhaps because of his previous prowess with vodka, applejack had no terrors for him. He loved it and the hillmen who lived round about and sold him the distilled liquor without benefit of revenue stamps, circulated tales of his ability to down incredible amounts and still stay conscious and "a gentleman." The hillwomen knew him to be the latter and learned to accept his bowing over their hands and his heel-clicking compliments without self-consciousness. Nik, gay and friendly, was happy to be accepted among the mountaineers as Pierre's best friend.

There were ducks on the pond the last time Nik and I went to see him and Pierre cared for them with affection. "I love ducks," he said, "but I wish swan. They will not give me swan."

Nik explained patiently that swans were expensive, that they did not like ducks, that they were quarrelsome and sometimes dangerous. The owners of the place, he said, were entirely justified in refusing to buy a swan.

Then Pierre grew morose and said that it was just as well that there was to be no swan, for he had little time left in which to enjoy it. Nik and I laughed and reminded him of his boasts of the longevity of the Malakovs but he remained gloomy and said that he would soon be dead. He began again on his memories of Nina and her dancing and he said again, "Swan is spirit." Then he quoted a short poem by Rainer Rilke. The German words and rhythms were beautiful and I gathered that the poet was saying that life is heavy and ungainly—like the awkward walking of a swan, death is like the swan's fearful leaving of the element of earth, where he fares badly, to be borne on the unfamiliar element of water, and what comes after is the contentment and majestic serenity of the swan as he moves at last and ever more happily on the liquid surface.

That was in April, early spring in those parts, of the year 1942. On the night of May 11 the Russian house blazed fiercely in the mountain dark. Neighbors telephoned for aid but when it came only smoldering embers remained. The heat had been so intense that the windows were blobs of molten glass, the stones of the two great fireplaces had been blunted, the silverware with which Pierre had eaten his supper had been melted. Pierre's body lay among the ashes of his bed. It was recognizable only by the metal shinbone, which heat had rendered shapeless.

Standing together, the mountain people who came to Pierre's funeral whispered that he might have been murdered. There had been rough strangers in town, they said, and Pierre had quarreled with two of them in a roadside barroom. The gossipers stared curiously at the people who had come to the Catskills to attend the service—the grieving owners of the place, Vassar professors, a distinguished Russian scientist, a once-famous military officer who had a job as a uniformed doorman in New York. As the Reverend Mr. William Barringer, pastor of the little church, said what needed to be said, the motorcycles of the State Police were roaring up and down the hill roads but no evidence that Pierre died from criminal violence has been found.

After the benediction, the owners made arrangements for Mr. Barringer to feed the ducks, look after the old mill, and keep the lawn mowed. Then we all went home.

A few weeks later the owners received a letter from the Olivebridge preacher. He wrote that he had seen a white bird "of enormous size" fly in from the south on a clear afternoon and settle on the pond. He had walked over to see it. It was a swan. The bird had immediately made friends with the ducks, though they were nesting, and it had not left the pond since its arrival.

When this news got about among Pierre's friends, a few of them went to Olivebridge. Mr. Barringer had been feeding the swan white bread and corn, the customary food of the ducks. One of the women of the party, remembering Pierre's love of Russian black bread, had brought a loaf of it. The ducks would not touch it when it was offered them but the swan had no sooner taken some into its scarlet bill than it refused white bread altogether and would eat none but the black. The group were nervous and annoyed when they saw that the swan limped as if its right leg were injured. "That's a little too much," said one of the men angrily.

The hill people had heard about the swan too, and they came to look.

"Remember how he went on about swans?" they said.

The Whooper Swan of Olivebridge

"It's him, all right. Never seen a bird like that in these parts—and I reckon nobody'll see another."

A scientist who had been fond of Pierre wrote an inquiry to the State Conservation Commission at Albany and soon an ornithologist came to Olivebridge. He said the bird belonged to the genus known as whooper, whistling, or wild swan (*cygnus musicas*), native of Iceland, eastern Lapland, and northern Russia. He added that it was a very rare species of the genus, identifiable by its scarlet beak. He would not venture even a guess as to how it happened to be circling the millpond in the woods outside Olivebridge. A migratory wild bird with a song sometimes compared to the tootling of a flageolet, it was accustomed in autumn to fly from the northern arctic, at a great height and far out at sea, to distant southern waters. Why it had come out of the south to this spot, he did not know. It would fly back again in the fall.

But the swan did not leave. On fall mornings when a thin ice cover made passage for the ducks impossible it broke way for its quacking companions to the little rock island where they had built their nest. When winter came, ducks and swan lived amicably in Mr. Barringer's barnyard. The preacher insisted to his congregation that the coming of the big bird had been a strange but not inexplicable coincidence. But the hill people, even some of his own congregation, said that they knew better and there was no denying to them that, by some supernatural process, something of Pierre had its identity in the swan. Their simple belief was less disturbing to them than were puzzlement and doubt to Pierre's close friends who, in the next four years, made many trips to the Barringer farm, took snapshots, and talked much.

In the spring of 1946, Nik Strelsky died. In their grief over losing him, his friends forgot for some time his fascinated interest in the swan, his many visits to it, his poetic surmises about it. But last fall I made one more pilgrimage to Olivebridge. Mr. Barringer had moved away, neighbors reported, and the swan had stayed on for a while after his departure. A friendly man who keeps a small summer hotel nearby said, "The swan used to drop into my little lake here sometimes, but he always went back to his own water. Last time I saw him, though, was—let me see—spring of 'forty-six—little over a year ago."

"So you've been up to the old millpond," said an old lady who stopped to chat. "I don't go there no more. Them burned-black stone chimneys look sad standin' there. Cold too. It's lonesome since they left."

"Who?"

Her candid blue eyes were suddenly wary.

"You know."

She shrugged her bent shoulders and walked away.

This conversation led me to pay a visit to an elderly man who lives alone in a shack near the headwaters of Jake Dubois's Creek. Braced by a pull or two on a flask filled with genuine Catskill applejack, we made a slow and friendly approach to the story. At length he said:

"I ain't sayin' that another swan showed up but I ain't sayin' he didn't. Course, word got around that Pierre's friend had died. Then we begun to hear things. Some folks who don't lie much said they seen the two of 'em. There's a kind of noise the first one used to make when he wasn't whoopin'. Reverend Barringer used to say it sounded like laffin'. Well, the two of 'em was makin' that noise—accordin' to the tell of these folks. Then one day they was gone."

"And that's the story that's going around in these hills?"

"Rickashayin'," he said, "sort of rickashayin'."

That Dutch stone house, the college president said, is a real old one—so old that the Colonial Dames decided perhaps through psychic powers that a general in the French and Indian Wars had lived in it. So the Society bought it for their headquarters and put a bronze plaque on it.

One thing the aristocratic first-family ladies didn't know about this ancient landmark was that around the turn of the century it had been the most notorious disorderly house in this neck of the woods. The chairman of their Board of Regents said the other day something that proved this regrettable ignorance and at the same time made understandable an incident that seemed most mysterious to her and her associates.

She said, "The Board of Regents was meeting in the front room the other night when someone used the brass pre-Revolutionary knocker on the front door. I opened it and saw standing there a slim, erect, elderly gentleman, perhaps seventy years old. He bowed quite low, taking off his straw hat and sweeping it out to the side, and he said:

" 'Good evening, madam.'

"I said, 'Good evening. Is there something you wish?'

" 'Why, I wish to come in,' he said and there was a

strange light in his eye but, since all the members of the board were inside, I was not alarmed.

" 'You wish to see the old house?' I said. 'Well, it's after hours but since you seem so interested you may.'

"I led him first into the front room where the members of the Board of Regents of the Society of Colonial Dames were sitting, and he stood in the middle of the room for a moment, scratching his head with the same hand that held his hat. Then he said—I know you'll pardon the expression—

" 'God-a-mighty, madam, there *must* be some mistake!' and before I knew it he was gone."

19

Green Valley Grange 881

SOMETIMES TWO THINGS WITH NO CONNECTION anybody can see will happen at about the same time and in such a way that the result that comes along seems to have been just bound to be. For example, there was the time Green Valley Grange 881 won first in the state and second in the nation in the contest Sears, Roebuck set up to reward the granges that did the most for their communities in the year 1948. If Ola Scudder had not developed a heart condition and if Amos Avery had not walked into the cemetery on a snowy day to see how the men digging his mother's grave were coming along, the whole thing might never have happened and Halcott Center would not be so happy a town as it is today.

Halcott Center is a neat village that lies back in the Catskills about twelve miles from the big resort town of Fleischmanns. Its grange, Green Valley 881, is small—only a hundred and thirty-six enrolled—but it includes many of the national bloodstreams that have made this country what it is. There are the Hansons—once German refugees; the Pavlos family from Greece; the Van Valkenburgs—old Dutch; and a good many more including samples of Italian, Polish, Finnish stocks.

Ola Scudder had been chairman of the committee on community improvement for many years when the doctor told her about her heart condition—but how much can you do for civic betterment when you are running a summer boardinghouse and have to feed twenty to thirty hungry guests three meals a day through the vacation months and write letters to prospects, help with the cows, and do your share in the Ladies' Aid when the snow is deep on the roads? So in a way, Ola says, that tired heart was a godsend because she and Bruce, her husband, cut out taking boarders and she had time to work on her committee.

Ola Scudder was born in Finland and she came to this country when she was four. Her father's place was on Seely Hill near West Danby, New York, near Candor. His name is Lektonen and he is one of those Finns that settled over there—hard-working farmers who built bathhouses in the backyards where a man could throw water on the heated rocks and get a real old-country steaming. Ola went to Ithaca one winter to take a short course in Home Economics at Cornell and she met Bruce Scudder, who was taking a short course in Agriculture.

After their wedding the young people went to live in Halcott Center on the Scudder place that had been in the family for generations. Bruce's grandfather had said when he went off to the Civil War that when he came back he was going to build a new house and pay for it out of the $1,500 he got for going as a substitute for somebody else, but—once a farmer always a farmer—when he came back he built a barn. Bruce promised Ola a new home when he was courting her in Ithaca thirty-odd years ago but now the three children have all grown up and their parents are still in the same old spot and their son will be the fourth-generation Scudder to live there and run the farm.

For twenty-two years Ola made Sunshine Valley Farm a good place to spend vacations. Someone asked her recently if she took in both Jews and Gentiles and she said, no, she had had all Jews except for one Roman Catholic. "I admit I discriminated," she said, "first against people with special diets and then, when we had a waiting list, against folks I just didn't like."

At the end of those years came Ola's heart condition, and Bruce told her she could have no more guests for a while. So she immediately thought now she could do something about being chairman of the community-improvement committee.

Amos Avery is a solid man, pink cheeked and blue eyed. Light wispy hair thatches his round face, which does not change expression often though there is much feeling behind it. The Averys, like the Scudders, are old-timers in Halcott Center. They have a fine farm and Mrs. Avery takes good care of her husband and his tall grizzled father and manages to get in a good deal of grange work and church work too. It was midwinter when Amos's mother died and at the first meeting of the grange after her funeral there was Ola Scudder saying that, now she had a heart condition and had stopped taking boarders, she could put in more time on her committee and she wanted members to tell the things they thought the community needed so that the committee could go to work on them.

Amos Avery got up then and made a speech and the grange will never forget it. He told them they knew how people would be going about their everyday business and not realizing what a town needed until the need was brought home to them in a personal way. Take him, for example. He had never thought much about what happened when somebody died in the coldest months of winter until he lost his mother. When he went into the cemetery next day to see about things the snow was so high you could just see the tops of the headstones and the two fellows he knew who were going to dig her grave had shoveled a path through to the spot. They were digging there and nobody ever saw soil give up so hard. Took all they had to claw that little hole out of frozen ground. A spade would come up out of there and there would be just a hard clot rattling on top of the others in the pile like it was stone. As he stood looking, Amos Avery said, he got to thinking—this is just like digging a hole to put some dumb animal away in. It isn't the way to treat humans that belong to you—and he made up his mind right then that what this town needed was a vault where folks that died in winter could be kept until spring when the ground wasn't frozen any more.

That speech had everybody feeling so bad by the time Amos Avery stopped speaking that the grange was stirred up to go and do something not only about the vault but about the rest of the things the town needed. They then figured out seven projects and there was a committee for each one. Amos Avery was chairman of the Vault Committee, of course, and there was a committee to make the old creamery down by Vly Creek into a good Grange Hall with a kitchen in it, and a committee to make fire ponds on the farms so that there would be water in case a house caught fire, and committees on cow testing, and making a Juvenile Grange, and organizing a basketball team to play in the league over at Margaretville, and on sending books and clothes to hospitals and food to starving folks abroad.

Then they started in. Ola Scudder says they never even had time to take their coats off. They had not done any thinking about the contest the *National Grange Monthly* said Sears, Roebuck was running, but when they remembered it they decided, since they were going to do this thing anyway, that they might as well be in on it and signed up.

The biggest job was fixing over the old creamery into a community hall. Since farmers have no extra daylight time, the first thing was to set some electric floodlights high up where they would illuminate the whole working area. Then the building committee sent out a series of invitations.

Here is a sample: "You are invited to a bee Wednesday night to take down the West Wall of the Grange Hall. Everybody meet at the Hall after supper. Hamburgers and Watermelon! Bring shovels, picks, and ambition."

Sometimes as many as fifty came. They were not all grangers. They came from all around—Fleischmanns, Kelly Corners, Margaretville, even from as far north as Stamford. They all knew the job had to be finished before the next morning or the work schedule could not be kept up, and so they stayed right at it until they were through.

People cannot work that hard without being fed, so Ola Scudder went to Fleischmanns and told the storekeepers what the grange was trying to do. The Jewish butchers over there chopped up their sirloins into hamburger and loaded her down with it and absolutely refused to take payment. She asked a fruit man about watermelons. "Here," he said. "Think nine'll be enough?" she said, "Three's all we need," but he gave her the lot. The grange wives made the coffee and the ice cream right on the grounds and somebody was always contributing ginger ale or Coca-Colas for the young people. Since the grange stand on alcoholic beverages is strictly disapproving, anything of that nature was brought by the volunteers themselves. One worker will be remembered because he had got all his liquid refreshment somewhere else before he arrived—been getting it there for years. He worked steadily with a pick for three hours and his shirt got so wet you could have wrung it out and his hair was plastered down but he finally left happier and soberer than anybody had seen him in some time. And one morning, after a lot of out-of-towners had put in their licks the night before, Ola Scudder picked up forty-eight empty beer bottles, ran them over to Fleischmanns, and turned them in to get the deposit the purchasers had paid on them. She bought paint with the money.

Since Halcott Center is a small place, the committee wrote letters to the merchants they traded with in the bigger towns around. They wrote to the undertaker at Margaretville—he has done a lot of business in Halcott Center and probably counts on more—and he sent them window shades, really good ones. The Margaretville Theater, where Green Valley Grange members go to the motion pictures sometimes, was being remodeled and the owner sent in a hundred of his old seats. They were built for an inclined floor but the boys who are taking a government school course for ex-GIs got short of something to do and fixed every one of those seats so that it will set level on the Grange Hall floor. A letter to a plumber at Fleischmanns brought in return an invitation to visit his dump. There the committee found a lot of perfectly satisfactory plumbing fixtures that some of the fancy hotels had discarded. A new plumber just come into the county wanted to do something to let people know he was open and ready for business, and so the committee said, "The drain pipe needs laying," and he laid it. There was an auction nearby at the former country house of Galli-Curci, the opera singer, and the committee bid in the stove, a good one to cook for a lot of people, and Ola Scudder got the dining-room curtains there for only fifty cents a pair. And about that time the Halcott Center Methodist Church gave the grangers a hundred dollars for their expenses and Tom Taylor, the preacher, said that was certainly putting the cart in front of the horse as the fellow says because it was the first time he had heard of the church not being on the receiving end.

Of course, all these things took time and so did the work the other committees were doing. When summer wore on and the harvesting finally took almost all hands away from their unfinished undertakings the prospects were gloomy. A whispering began—"They'll never finish"— and the committee chairmen became cross and testy because they were afraid in their hearts that the whisperers were right. There was an occasional humorous moment as when one of a group of sleepy men telephoned Ola Scudder very early one morning and said, "Ola, the cement mixer is busted and we're all wasting time down here. What had we better do?" and Ola said, "Get the nearest mechanic to fix it." But these were the dog days and depression had become a disease, almost an epidemic. Nevertheless, the committees kept on working.

When they heard that the judges were coming, all the workers—grangers, townspeople, and out-of-towners—got together for one last big effort. The judges were picked by the National Grange and they were really important men. One of them was president of the Quaker Oats Company and one was an officer of Pillsbury Flour and another was master of the Minnesota State Grange. They had been flying around the country in an airplane—a big DC-3 with Sears, Roebuck painted on the side—and they had been on Nantucket Island the day before they landed at Kingston and were brought by automobile into the hills to Halcott Center. They were taken to the new Grange Hall and there in the just finished community dining hall the grangers fed them baked ham, green peas, hot rolls, coffee, and strawberry shortcake; and they ate as if they were hungry.

After dinner the committees told what they had done. The judges were right in the Grange Hall and had just been given a sample of what the community kitchen and the dining room had to offer. They could see on the bulletin board how important that building already was to the community. There were the square dances, for example. Even before the walls were up Amos Avery and his wife were running square dances there and they cleared nearly $150 for the grange in about ten dances. The Fish and Game Club was meeting regularly in the Hall, and the Ladies' Aid and the Juvenile Grange, and the GI school movies were being shown there.

Amos Avery told the judges about the vault. He had raised the money for that and he had had good advice from the Margaretville undertaker. Now it was built and it was wired and a thermostat inside was keeping the temperature at forty degrees all the time.

As for the fire ponds, Bob Johnson, who is the twenty-three-year-old master of the grange, was chairman of that committee and he told how they now had seven ponds and were not going to stop work until they had a pond on every one of the thirty-five farms of Halcott Center.

The Junior Grange, jolly bustling Mildred Kelly told them, was meeting every two weeks and every child who wanted to come was invited. The children were learning their parts and speaking the rituals well and they were taking on projects like cleaning up the town and decorating it with flowering shrubs and they loved the work.

Others reported that the basketball team had won a league game in Margaretville, and the committee on sending things to people who needed them said they had shipped a hundred and eighty books to the Marine Hospital in New York, four scrapbooks to the Margaretville Hospital, and eight boxes of clothes and food to the needy in Finland. The Cow-testing Association proudly told how it got started and how Earl Johnson, cousin of the grange master, went to Cornell University to take the cow-tester's course so that now they were knowing which cows were doing their job and which ought to be killed for beef.

The judges listened and went away and the result of it all was that Green Valley Grange 881 was not only first in New York State but second in the United States. As Amos Avery said, "When you think of all the granges there are in the country—it's pretty good." Green Valley had won two $100 bonds and $1,500 worth of equipment. The members were proud of that but they say they were prouder of the fact that 80 per cent of them did voluntary work on the contest projects and they figure they got about eight thousand value and spent only about three thousand.

They say they suppose they will never be satisfied now. They want a new and shorter road to Kingston, for one thing, and they want to fix up the terrace on the Vly Creek side of Community Hall, finish off the fire-prevention pond job, get everybody checked for health with chest X rays and blood typing and have every child's teeth given the new fluorine treatment.

Ola Scudder says, "I've got one more job I want to supervise. When a stranger comes to town he sees a road-sign that says on it 'Halcott Center.' We're going to re-paint it and under the name of the town we're going to put 'Home of Green Valley Grange 881.'"

Afterwords

The Averys were giving a large cocktail party one afternoon in their sumptuous, begabled cottage on the high bluff above the waters of a Finger Lake.

"Here comes Cap'n Tom's sightseeing boat," said Ed Avery, "with Cap'n Tom himself at the megaphone. Very salty and pungent fellow, Tom, never says the same thing twice. Be still and listen to him."

From down below came a cracked, nasal bellow.

"Estate o' old Ed Avery," shouted Cap'n Tom. "Married rich an' ain't done a lick since."

Cap'n Tom's sightseeing launch used to make him a pretty good living but in slack times when tourists were scarce he would take out fishermen or sailing parties. On one of the latter occasions he had no sooner tacked to the middle of Finger Lake than he was becalmed. For an hour he and his two customers sat in a broiling sun while not a breath of air stirred the bright waters.

"All we need with this boat," said Tom hopefully, "is two cents' worth of wind."

Still the air was moveless, the lake was calm. Fearing his companions' dissatisfaction with their bargain, Tom took two pennies from the pocket of his greasy pants and tossed them overboard.

"Now, God damn ye," he said, "give us two cents' worth of a wind."

Thirty seconds later a line squall appeared from nowhere and before Tom could lower sail the boat had heeled over and its occupants were in the water.

Patiently Tom helped the two others to clamber out and sit on the upturned bottom, then took his place beside them.

"If I'd known 'twas goin' to blow so," he said mildly, "I wouldn't-a bought so much."

"About that hog stealin'," said the lawyer, "I know the judge and I'll tell him it's hard to get our witnesses over here from back in the hills. He'll continue the case and that's the best we can do."

Three years later, a brisk new judge announced no more continuances.

"You'll have to show up Monday," said the lawyer. "Better throw yourself on the mercy of the court."

Monday morning everybody in the courtroom rose as the robed justice entered.

"First case," he said sharply. "Wait! What's that terrible odor? Worst stink I ever smelled."

"Reckon that's me, judge," said the hog stealer, rising. "Had to git up 'fore daylight to git to court on time and when I come through Toad Holler I jest didn't see a couple o' polecats that lives there and—"

"Case continued," roared the judge, hastily getting up and making for his chamber.

As the hillman passed the counselor on his way out of court, he said, "And *you* call yourself an attorney."

Hank Feathers is over seventy and he can still drive a

trottin' horse at the County Fair and come under the wire around 2:12. He just naturally loves speed and when he gets into his 1935 roadster with the top down he is likely to do over sixty, even though his white beard blowing behind him slows him up some.

One day he went over to Steuben County where he don't know many folks, and he was doin' close to seventy when he seen in the mirror on his windshield a State Trooper followin' him on a motorcycle. Hank knew he was in for trouble, but he speeded up to keep ahead of the officer while he thought what he was going to do. He was just comin' into Bath when he seen a funeral procession just turnin' into a cemetery. He jammed on his brakes, and got in between two of the cars in the long line, drove into the cemetery and parked his car with the rest. Then he stepped out and followed the mourners and took a stand beside the grave, holdin' his hat respectful over his heart.

He was a little surprised a minute later, when the preacher was about to begin, to see the State Trooper standing beside him with his hat off, too.

"Fine old man," says the Trooper jerkin' his head toward the coffin.

"Yep," says Hank. "Lived a long life and a good one."

"He was the mother of four of my first cousins," says the Trooper, "and now if you'll follow me to the Justice of the Peace. . . ."

"That was the woman," said the mountain man, "that the boy's pa traded with Johnny Diggs for a fiddle and a pint of rum. Johnny didn't have no woman—that's why he had to put in a pint of rum."

Ferd had been a popular member of valley society—rich as devil cake and slick as rye straw. Owing to a financial peccadillo committed during a presidential administration when similar actions were popular, however, he had been indicted and convicted, and he was sentenced by a not-unsympathetic judge to a moderate number of years in the penitentiary.

Naturally when Ferd got out his valley friends gave him a celebration and it turned out to be one of the most glad and delightful of parties. Though cocktails had not yet become the usual apéritif, the guests, excited by the unusual motive for the affair, were almost hysterically gay and more than a little self-conscious in their desire not to let Ferd sense by any word or action that they were aware of his whereabouts during the past few years. As they romped through a game there came the sudden announcement that dinner was ready in the dining room.

"Let's all march in lock step," shouted Mattie. That brought about the first silence.

At table Flo dropped her spoon, and reaching under the table, said:

"I can't find it."

"Lock the doors," screamed Liz merrily, and conversation stopped a moment.

The last pause came with the coffee when, grown sentimental with wine and good food, the men were reminiscing about the days of their happy childhood.

"The older you get," said Newt, "the more clearly you recall little unimportant incidents out of the past that have no special bearing on anything—" he laughed delightedly— "like the time Ferd and I stole old man Doty's watermelons."

On a Saturday night, filled with hard cider, Ob Hoag fell into bed beside his spouse. Soon his dreams were interrupted by a natural consequence of much drinking.

Obeying long custom he staggered out the back door to the corner of the house. A slight rain was fallin' and the drain pipe near which Ob took his stance gave out a gentle, sibilant sizzling sound which, in his befuddled state, he associated with the result of his own efforts.

Thus he stood one hand braced against the side of the house waiting for the sound to cease. Minute after minute went by without interruption, and a feeling approaching awe swept over him. He was a phenomenon! Realization of the fact was not to be coped with alone and so finally in a great voice that aroused the slumbering neighbors, he bellowed:—

"Matilda! Matilda! Wake ye! I've sprung the eternal and everlasting leak!"

The country here has the very look of the old romances that I love best. . . . In every direction narrow lonely "dirt roads" wind through far-away valleys and over remote hilltops, leaving behind them, as their perspectives diminish, that peculiar thrill that seems to come down to us from the generations. . . . It is an impression that has to do with horsemen journeying, Inn-lights beckoning, journeys' ends coming to lovers, to tramps, to hunters, to camp-followers, to adventurers, to the life-weary Dead. . . .

. . . This vague sense of old-world romance . . . can only appear under particular conditions in the history of any landscape and it requires a particular kind of landscape for it to reveal itself at all. These conditions are precisely fulfilled in the hilly regions of "up-state" New York. . . .

. . . The presence of both stone walls and hedges gives this landscape, combined with the bare grassy uplands between the wooded hills, a look sometimes, especially in the winter, that stirs up in me feelings that must revert to far-away impressions of my Salopian ancestors of the Welsh Marches.

John Cowper Powys: *Autobiography*

Apple Pickers
(Orleans County)

They are walking lonesome up the south road,
Their leathery faces turned to the low, wide trees,
And the farmer calls them into the reddening orchard,
Every last one he sees.

They lift the ladders to their certain pointing—
Two fingers each to the mist-encircled sun;
They beat the barrelheads to syncopation
Till the day's whole stint is done.

Only at noon comes stillness for an hour
To spread across the fields in shimmering waves.
Then apples roll again from swollen pick bags,
Dull thundering on the staves.

On Saturday they load the truck with barrels,
Ride gay astride them all the way to town,
But girls wave from the porches by the depot
And they shyly shinny down.

Afterwords

When the late button clicks, puts out the street lights,
And front doors close on shadows down the walk,
Folks snug in bed hear pickers hollering homeward,
And it's no sort of talk.

The night freight, screaming, couples their piled loadings,
Grinds past the crossing, car by groaning car,
While sudden plumps from full, high-hanging branches
A windfall star.

By Carl Carmer,
published in *The New Yorker*

Acknowledgments

HOMETOWN REVISITED

Charles C. D'Amico, Principal of Albion High School, Albion, N. Y.

Joseph B. Achilles, Orleans County Historian, Albion, N. Y.

William Beckwith Hart, New York, N. Y.

Eloise Hazard, New York, N. Y.

THE NEXT HAPPIEST MAN IN THE WORLD

Robert A. Pinkerton, President, Pinkerton's National Detective Agency, New York, N. Y.

Edward J. Pennington, Jr., University of Minnesota, Minneapolis, Minn.

William L. Nunn, Director of University Relations, University of Minnesota, Minneapolis, Minn.

Pierre Ward, Geneseo, N. Y.

Willis Carmer Bailey, Geneseo, N. Y.

Mrs. Guy A. Bailey, Geneseo, N. Y.

Miss Hazle H. Smith, Geneseo, N. Y.

Justice Edward T. Fairchild, Supreme Court of the State of Wisconsin, Madison, Wis.

Miss Jacqueline Parsons, New York, N. Y.

Mrs. Muriel Tyson Parsons, New York, N. Y.

Wilfred E. Rauber, Dansville, N. Y.

Everett Kent Van Allen, Rochester, N. Y.

Hugh McNair Kahler, New York, N. Y.

Louis C. Jones, Director, New York State Historical Society, Cooperstown, N. Y.

Acknowledgments

Warren I. Lee, New York, N. Y.
John Proctor's Ride—Ridge Road Revere
Joseph B. Achilles, Orleans County Historian, Albion, N. Y.

"I AM A CAYUGA"

Aloys Derso, New York, N. Y.
Miss Hazle H. Smith, Geneseo, N. Y.
Melvin M. Johnson, Grand Secretary, Indian Defense League of America, Niagara Falls, N. Y.
Reverend Glenn B. Coykendall, Angola, N. Y.
Arthur Parker, former President of New York State Historical Association, Cooperstown, N. Y.
Ray Fadden (Aren Akweks), Secretary, Akwesasne Mohawk Counselor Organization, St. Regis Mohawk Reservation, Hogansburg, N. Y.

TISRI, 5586

Mrs. Muriel Tyson Parsons, New York, N. Y.

THE IRISH WONDER AND THE SWEDISH NIGHTINGALE

Miss Lucy Gilhooly, Alexander, N. Y.
Miss Hazle H. Smith, Geneseo, N. Y.
Miss Jacqueline Parsons, New York, N. Y.
The late Joseph Burke, Alexander, N. Y.

THE BIG EAT-ALL DINNER

Miss Jacqueline Parsons, New York, N. Y.
Reverend Alexander M. Stewart, Rochester, N. Y.

"CREATURE OF A HIGH WROUGHT FANCY"

William Kaye Lamb, Dominion Archivist, Public Archives of Canada, Ottawa, Canada
Norman Fee, Assistant Dominion Archivist, Public Archives of Canada, Ottawa, Canada
Mr. and Mrs. Alex Skelton, Ottawa, Canada
R. N. Beattie, Toronto, Canada

Acknowledgments

Professor D. G. Creighton, University of Toronto, Toronto, Canada

H. Pearson Gundy, Librarian, Queen's University, Kingston, Ontario, Canada

Professor R. G. Trotter, Queen's University, Kingston, Ontario, Canada

Miss Barbara Pentland, Toronto, Canada

Marshall Emm of Syracuse University Graduate School, Syracuse, N. Y.

Miss Jacqueline Parsons, New York, N. Y.

Mrs. Muriel Tyson Parsons, New York, N. Y.

Holger Lundbergh, New York, N. Y.

Professor W. Freeman Galpin of Syracuse University, Syracuse, N. Y.

Albert B. Corey, State Historian, Director, Division of Archives and History, University of the State of New York, Albany, N.Y.

Charles D. Abbott, Librarian, University of Buffalo, Buffalo, N. Y.

Louis C. Jones, Director, New York State Historical Association, Cooperstown, N. Y.

J. F. Cahill, Executive Secretary, American Irish Historical Society, New York, N. Y.

Professor Harold Thompson of Cornell University, Ithaca, N. Y.

THE GREAT ALCHEMIST AT UTICA

Claude J. Rahn, Verona, N. J.

Louis Staton, Estero, Fla.

Miss Hedwig Michel, Estero, Fla.

L. W. Bubbett, Estero, Fla.

Mrs. Frank Lewis, Estero, Fla.

John Hinternhoff, Suffern, N. Y.

PICKER TURNED YORKER

Henry Van Blake, Geneseo, N. Y.

Miss Hazle H. Smith, Geneseo, N. Y.

Mrs. Victor Okkerse, Geneseo, N. Y.

Acknowledgments

THE LAVENDER EVENING DRESS

Mrs. Wheeler H. Peckham, Sloatsburg, N. Y.
Dudley Carleton, Ringwood, N. Y.
Louis C. Jones, Director, New York State Historical
Society, Cooperstown, N. Y.
Starr Nelson, New York, N. Y.

THREE CROPS

Henry Esmond Christman, New York, N. Y.
Lansing Christman, Delanson, N. Y.
Philip Christman, Delanson, N. Y.
Spencer Christman, Delanson, N. Y.
Duane Christman, Delanson, N. Y.
Walter Christman, Delanson, N. Y.

THE WHOOPER SWAN OF OLIVEBRIDGE

Mrs. Katherine Anderson Strelsky, now of Florence, Italy
Henry Esmond Christman, New York, N. Y.

GREEN VALLEY GRANGE 881

Mr. and Mrs. Bruce A. Scudder, Halcott Center, N. Y.
Harry L. Graham, Director, New York State Grange,
Expansion Department, Ithaca, N. Y.
Fred Bouton, Halcott Center, N. Y.
Mr. and Mrs. Amos Avery, Halcott Center, N. Y.
Mr. and Mrs. William Gratwick, Geneseo, N. Y.
Robert Johnson, Halcott Center, N. Y.

MISCELLANEOUS ACKNOWLEDGMENTS

Frederic E. Kast, New York, N. Y.
Mr. and Mrs. William Gratwick, Geneseo, N. Y.
Arthur Parker, former President of New York State
Historical Association, Cooperstown, N. Y.
Hugh McNair Kahler, New York, N. Y.
Jay Kieffer, Mahwah, N. J.
Duane Featherstonhaugh, Duanesburg, N. Y.
Mrs. Marie Noll Cormack, Schenectady, N. Y.

Acknowledgments

Mr. and Mrs. Charles Tibbits, North River, N. Y.

Mr. and Mrs. Charles S. Kenwell, Wevertown, N. Y.

E. R. Eastman, Editor, *The Agriculturist*, Ithaca, N. Y.

Mrs. H. Irving Fiester, Elmira, N. Y.

Free Burley, North River, N. Y.

Mrs. Margia W. Proctor, Buffalo, N. Y.

Sylvester L. Vigilante, Head of the American History Room, N. Y. Public Library, New York, N. Y.

Sources Consulted

THE NEXT HAPPIEST MAN IN THE WORLD

Archives of Pinkerton's National Detective Agency, New York.
Asbury, Herbert. "Jim, the Penman," New York: *American Mercury*, Sept., 1915.
Dougherty, George S. "Whiteman the Master Swindler," *True Confessions*, Dec., 1923.

"I AM A CAYUGA"

Decker, George P. *Must the Peaceful Iroquois Go?* Rochester: Lewis H. Morgan Chapter, N. Y. State Archeological Assoc., 1923.
Chief Deskaheh. *The New Story of the Iroquois*, Rochester: broadcast over Station WHAM, March 10, 1925.

TISRI, 5586

Cone, G. Herbert. *New Matter Relating to Mordecai M. Noah*: American Jewish Historical Society.
Friedman, Lee M. *Jewish Proverbs and Patriots*, Philadelphia: Jewish Publications Society of America, 1942.
Noah, Mordecai M. *Founding of the City of Ararat on Grand Island*: read before Buffalo Historical Society, March 5, 1866 by Hon. Lewis F. Allen: Buffalo Historical Society, Vol. I.

THE FOWLERS, PRACTICAL PHRENOLOGISTS

Fowler, Orson. *A Home for All*, New York: Fowler & Wells, 1856.

Sources Consulted

THE IRISH WONDER AND THE SWEDISH NIGHTINGALE

Anonymous. "A Memoir of Jenny Lind in Buffalo," Buffalo: *Buffalo Arts Journal*, Dec., 1926.

Anonymous. "Song Bird—The Love Story of a Great Prima Donna," New York: *True Romances*, Beautiful Womanhood Publishing Co., Oct., 1931.

Haswell, Charles H. *Reminiscences of New York by an Octogenarian*, New York: Harper & Brothers, 1896.

Hone, Philip. *The Diary of Philip Hone, 1828-1851*, edited by Allan Nevins, New York: Dodd, Mead & Co., 1936.

Ireland, Joseph N. *Records of the New York Stage*, New York: T. H. Morrell, 1866.

Maude, M. C. *The Life of Jenny Lind*, London: Cassell & Co., Ltd., 1926.

Obituary, "Jenny Lind (Madame Lind-Goldschmidt)," London: *The Illustrated London News*, Nov. 12, 1887.

Odell. *Annals of the New York Stage*, New York: Columbia University Press, 1928.

Two Continental Playbills in N. Y. Public Library.

THE BIG EAT-ALL DINNER

Colby. *Canadian Types of the Old Regime*.

Charlevoix, Pierre François Xavier de. *Histoire et description générale de la Nouvelle France*, 1744.

Garreau (S. J.), F. X. *L'Historie du Canada*, translated by Andrew Bell, 1862.

Hawley, Charles. *Early Chapters of Cayuga History, 1646-1684*, 1879.

Holland, Hjalmar R. "Radisson's Two Western Journeys," *Minnesota History Quarterly*, June, 1934.

Première Supérieure des Ursulines de Québec en Canada—Letter from Quebec. "Choix des Lettres Historiques de la Vénérable Mère Marie de L'Incarnation," Oct. 4, 1650.

Prud'homme, Louis. *Notes Historiques sur la vie de P. É. de Raddison*, 1892.

Radisson, Peter. *Voyages of Peter Esprit Radisson*, transcribed from original manuscripts in the Bodleian Library and the British Museum by Gideon D. Scull, Boston: Prince Society, 1885.

Sources Consulted

Shea, John Gilmary. *Catholic Missions among the Indian Tribes of the United States*, 1854.

Stewart, Alexander McGinn. *Rene Menard, 1605-1661,* Rochester: Alexander M. Stewart, 1934.

Thwaites, Reuben Gold (ed.). *The Jesuit Relations and Allied Documents,* Cleveland: Burrows Brothers Company.

"Groseilliers and Radisson, the First White Men in Minnesota,"—a complete Radisson bibliography of 107 titles is attached thereto, Minnesota Historical Collection, Vol. 10, 449-594.

"CREATURE OF A HIGH WROUGHT FANCY"

Cleivine, Charles. *The Empress of the Isles or the Lake Bravo,* Cincinnati: 1853.

Corey, Albert B. *The Crisis of 1830-1842 in Canadian-American Relations,* New Haven: Yale University Press, 1941.

Dent, J. C. *Story of the Upper Canadian Rebellion,* 2 vols., Toronto: C. Blackett Robinson, 1885.

Guillet, Edwin C. *The Lives and Times of the Patriots,* Toronto: Thomas Nelson & Son, 1938.

Haddock, J. A. *History of Jefferson County.*

———. *Souvenir of the Thousand Islands,* 1895.

Heustis, Daniel. *Narrative of the Suffering of Daniel Heustis,* Boston: Bedding & Co., 1947.

Lindsey, Charles. *The Life and Times of William Lyon Mackenzie,* Vol. I, Toronto: P. R. Randall, 1862.

Lindsey, E. G. *A History of the Navy Island Campaign,* 2 vols.

Lizars, Robina & Kathleen M. *In the Days of the Canada Company.*

Miller, L. W. *Notes of an Exile to Van Dieman's Land,* 1846.

Read, D. B. *The Canadian Rebellion of 1837,* Toronto: C. Blackett Robinson, 1896.

Smith, H. Perry. *History of the City of Buffalo,* Syracuse, Mason, Vol. 1, 1884.

Struthers, Irving E. "The Trial of Nils von Schoultz. A myth of history explained," *The Canadian Magazine,* XLVIII, No. 4, Feb., 1917.

Theller, E. A. *Canada in 1837-38,* Vol. 2.

Tiffany, O. E. *The Relations of the United States to Canada,* Buffalo: Buffalo Historical Society Publications, VIII, 1905.

Wright, Stephen Smith. *Narrative and Recollections of Van*

Dieman's Land during Three Years' Captivity, New York: J. Winchester, 1844.

Geschichte der Deutscher in Syracuse und Onondaga County, Syracuse: Deutsche Verein, 1897.

"The New Yorker," H. Greeley & Co., Vol. VI, No. 14, Dec. 22, 1938.

THE GREAT ALCHEMIST AT UTICA

Chester, Lord. *The Great Red Dragon*, Estero: The Guiding Star Publishing House, 1916.

Cyrus. *Emanuel Swedenborg, His Mission*, Chicago: The Guiding Star Publishing House, 1889.

Hinds, William Alfred. *American Communities*, Chicago: Charles H. Kerr & Co., 1902.

Koresh. *Cellular Cosmogony*, Estero: The Guiding Star Publishing House, 1922.

———. *Fundamentals of Koreshan Universology*, Estero: The Guiding Star Publishing House, 1927.

———. *Joseph, A Dramatization from Biblical History in Seven Acts Act the Second*, Estero. The Guiding Star Publishing House, 1904.

———. *The Illumination of Koresh*, Estero: The Guiding Star Publishing House.

———. *Interpretation of the Book of Revelation*, Estero: The Guiding Star Publishing House, 1925.

———. *Koreshan Science*, Chicago: The Guiding Star Publishing House, 1896.

———. *The Mystery of the Gentiles*, Estero: The Guiding Star Publishing House, 1926.

———. *Reincarnation*, Estero: The Guiding Star Publishing House, 1919.

Rahn, Claude J. "Brief Outline of the Life of Dr. Cyrus R. Teed (Koresh) and of the Koreshan Unity," Unpublished notebook, Nov., 1940.

Articles from *The American Eagle and Horticultural Review*, Estero: Koreshan Unity, Nov. 28, 1946; Dec. 5, 1946; Jan. 23, 1947; Aug. 7, 1947; Aug. 14, 1947; Oct. 9, 1947; Oct. 16, 1947; Oct. 23, 1947; Nov. 20, 1947; Nov. 27, 1947; Dec. 4, 1947; Dec. 11, 1947.

Articles from *The Flaming Sword*, Estero: The Guiding Star Publishing House, 1945; 1946; 1947; 1948.

Sources Consulted
THREE CROPS

Christman, W. W. Scrapbook.

——. *Songs of the Helderhills*, Boston: Harold Vinal, 1926.

——. *Songs of the Western Gateway*, New York: Lewis Copeland Co., Inc., 1930.

——. *The Untillable Hills*, Montpelier: The Driftwind Press, 1927.

——. *Wild Pasture Pine*, Albany: The Argus Press, 1933.

MISCELLANEOUS

Anonymous. *The Book of the Roycrofters*, East Aurora: Roycrofters, 1928.

Barber, John W. and Howe, Henry. *Historical Collections of the State of N. Y.*, New York: S. Tuttle, 1842.

Bunnell, A. O. (ed.). *Dansville, 1789-1902*, Dansville: Instructor Publishing Co.

Coonley, John Stuart (copyright by). *Chronicles of an American Home*, New York: Privately printed by J. J. Little & Ives Co., 1930.

De Veaux, S. *The Travellers' Own Book to Saratoga Springs, Niagara Falls and Canada*, Buffalo: Faxon and Read, 1842.

Devens, R. M. *Our First Century*, Springfield: C. A. Nichols & Co., 1876.

Fox, Dixon Ryan. *The Decline of Aristocracy in the Politics of New York*, New York: Columbia University Press, 1919.

French, J. H. *Gazetteer of the State of New York*, 10th Edition, Syracuse: R. P. Smith, 1860.

Goodrich, C. A. *The Family Tourist*, Hartford: Case, Tiffany & Co., 1848.

Gunther, John. *Inside U.S.A.*, New York: Harper & Brothers, 1947.

Hubbard, Alice (ed.). *An American Bible*, East Aurora: Roycrofters, 1918.

Moscow, Warren. *Politics in the Empire State*, New York: Alfred A. Knopf, 1948.

Nordhoff, Charles. *The Communistic Societies of the United States*, New York: Harper & Brothers, 1875.

Shambaugh, Bertha M. H. *Amana That Was and Amana That Is*, Iowa City: State Historical Society of Iowa, 1932.

Shay, Felix. *Elbert Hubbard of East Aurora*, New York: Wm. H. Wise & Co., Inc., 1926.

Sources Consulted

Toynbee, Arnold J. *A Study of History* (Abridgement by D. C. Somervell of Vols. I-VI), New York and London: Oxford University Press, 1947.

The Coming of Jesus & Elijah, Rochester: The Megiddo Mission Band.

History of the Megiddo Mission, Rochester: The Megiddo Mission Band.

Life and Work of the Rev. L. T. Nichols, Founder of the Megiddo Mission, Rochester: Megiddo Mission (as part of centennial exercises on 100th anniversary of birth of Rev. L. T. Nichols), Oct. 1, 1944.

The Spiritual Creation, Rochester: The Megiddo Mission Band.